DON'T BET ON THE PRINCE

For Carol
With Hope for a Better Future

DON'T BET ON THE PRINCE

CONTEMPORARY FEMINIST FAIRY TALES IN NORTH AMERICA AND ENGLAND

Jack Zipes

ROUTLEDGE

NEW YORK

Published in 1987 by Methuen, Inc., and
Gower Publishing Co., Ltd.
Reprinted in 1989 by
Routledge, an imprint of
Routledge, Chapman and Hall, Inc.
29 West 35th Street
New York, NY 10001

Printed in the United States of America
© Jack Zipes, 1986

Library of Congress in Publication Data
Main entry under title:

Don't bet on the prince.
  Bibliography: p.
  Includes index.
  1. Feminism—Fiction.   2. Women—Fiction.
  3. Short stories, American.   4. Short stories, English.
  5. Fairy tales.   6. Fairy tales—History and criticism—
  Addresses, essays, lectures.   7. Feminist literary
  criticism—Addresses, essays, lectures.   8. Women in
  literature—Addresses, essays lectures.   I. Zipes,
  Jack David.
  PS648. F4D66   1986   813'.01'08352042   85—29794
  ISBN 0-416-01371-6
  ISBN 0-415-90263-0 (pbk.)

Further copyright © details are given on the
acknowledgements page.

Contents

III FEMINIST LITERARY CRITICISM

Acknowledgements

The plans for this book were initiated by David Hill, Caroline Lane and Lynne Jarché, who helped me develop my ideas in fruitful discussions. As the book began to take shape, I benefited from the suggestions of Jessica Benjamin, Lois Kuznets, Anita Moss, Wolfgang Mieder and, in particular, Janice Price, who provided needful prodding. In more ways than one, Ken Silverman served as a provocative muse, and I am grateful for his support as critic and friend. In the final stages of my work, I was fortunate to have the advice and help of John Irwin and the editorial staff of Gower. Throughout all the stages my wife Carol Dines made valuable recommendations and helped me redefine many of my notions. I can only express my gratitude for her encouragement by dedicating this book to her.

The cover illustration is *The Little Girl Who Did Not Believe in Fairies*; Eleanor Fortescue-Brickdale R.W.S. (1872–1945). Copyright © F. Fortescue-Brickdale esq. Reproduced with the kind permission of F. Fortescue Brickdale esq. and by courtesy of Chris Beetles Watercolours Ltd. A greetings card reproducing this painting under the title *Fairyland* has been published by the Bucentaur Gallery Ltd.

'The Princess Who Stood On Her Own Two feet' in *Stories for Free Children*, Ed. Letty Pogrebin (New York: McGraw Hill, 1982). Copyright © 1982 by Jeanne Desy. Reprinted by permission of Floricanto Press, Oakland CA. This story will be published in 1986 in a bilingual (Spanish/English) picture book edition by Floricanto Press, 604 William Street, Oakland, California 94612, USA. (ISBN 0-915745-05-4).

'Prince Amilec' in *Princess Hynchatti and Some Other Surprises* by Tanith Lee. Copyright © 1972 by Tanith Lee. Reprinted by permission of Macmillan, London and Basingstoke and Farrar, Straus and Giroux, Inc., New York.

© 1984, Michael de Larrabeiti. Reprinted by kind permission of the author.

'Bluebeard's Egg' by Margaret Atwood (Toronto: McClelland and Stewart, 1983). Copyright © 1983. Margaret Atwood. Reprinted by permission of Phoebe Larmore, Venice, CA.

' "Some Day My Prince Will Come": Female Acculturation through the Fairy Tale' by Marcia Leiberman in College English, **34** (1972) pp. 383 – 95. Copyright © Marcia R. Leiberman, 1972. Reprinted with the permission of the National Council of Teachers of English, Urbana, Illinois, USA.

'The Queen's Looking Glass' in *The Mad Woman in the Attic. The Woman Writer and the Nineteenth-Century Imagination.* (New Haven: Yale University Press, 1979). Copyright © 1979, Sandra M. Gilbert and Susan Gubar. Reprinted by permission of Yale University Press.

'Feminism and Fairy Tales' in *Women's Studies.* **6** (1979) pp. 237 – 57. Copyright © 1979 Karen E. Rowe. Reprinted by kind permission of the author.

Preface

It is obviously difficult to define *the* feminist fairy tale. Part of the difficulty is due to the fact that some feminist fairy tales are written by authors who would not necessarily define themselves as feminists. Despite this fact, their tales, and the others in this collection, are imbued with a particular vision of the world which I would call feminist. Not only do the authors challenge conventional views of gender, socialisation, and sex roles, but they also map out an alternative aesthetic terrain for the fairy tale as genre to open up new horizons for readers and writers alike.

Created out of dissatisfaction with the dominant male discourse of traditional fairy tales and with those social values and institutions which have provided the framework for sexist prescriptions, the feminist fairy tale conceives a different view of the world and speaks in a voice that has been customarily silenced. It draws attention to the illusions of the traditional fairy tales by demonstrating that they have been structured according to the subordination of women, and in speaking out for women the feminist fairy tale also speaks out for other oppressed groups and for an *other* world, which may have appeared Utopian at one time but is now already within the grasp of those people seeking to bring about more equality in social and work relations. Thus the aesthetics of the feminist fairy tale demands an open-ended discourse which calls for the readers to complete the liberating expectations of the narrative in terms of their own experience and their social context.

Although one can find feminist fairy tales throughout the world, the most innovative ones in the West are being written in England and America. Such experimentation is largely an outcome of the women's movement, which, in my opinion, has been strongest in these two countries. Ever since the late 1960s there has been a growing tendency on the part of women in England and America – and not only women – to express a non-sexist view of the world through fairy tales or through criticism about fairy tales. The political purpose and design of most of the tales are clear: the narratives are symbolical representations of the authors' critique of the patriarchal status quo and of their desire to change the current socialisation process.

The primary intended audience of feminist fairy tales consists of children and women, but this does not mean that men are excluded. By reconstructing fairy-tale worlds along non-sexist lines, the writers of feminist fairy tales address society at large, question recurrent patterns of values and the stable expectations about roles and relations. They do not naïvely believe that one can change gender arrangements and social behaviour by simply reformulating the traditional fairy tales. On the other hand, it has been demonstrated by psychologists and educators time and again that stories and fairy tales do influence the manner in which children conceive the world and their places in it even before they begin to read. Arthur Applebee has shown conclusively how story characters become part of a child's 'real world' and form part of their cultural heritage. Thus, tales play an important role in early socialisation. For instance, upon hearing a fairy tale, children of four and five will 'assimilate the story to their past experience of similar tales, providing themselves with expectations about such things as types of characters, patterns of behaviour, and suitable endings. On the other hand, their understanding of "fairy tales" will be somewhat altered and expanded by the new characters and actions which they meet in the particular tale'.[1] As a key agent of socialisation, the fairy tale enables the child to discover his or her place in the world and to test hypotheses about the world. For years the classical literary tales were mainly articulations and representations of a male viewpoint.[2] Even when women wrote and told the tales, they submerged their voices to serve a patriarchal social order or to disguise their discontent with it. The fact now that male and female writers have explicitly altered the aesthetic constructs and social contents of the tales to present a feminist viewpoint is an indication that there have been major changes in the socialisation and education of children in England and America since the 1960s. That is, the feminist tales themselves have emerged from the struggles of the women's movement and are being used to elaborate social choices and alternatives for both females and males. As indicators of social, psychological, and political change, they are also agents of a new socialisation.

What is also new is that many feminist tales and criticism have been written by males, some who would refer to themselves as socialist feminists and others who are just generally dissatisfied with male domination and privilege in English and American society. Moreover, numerous male educators and psychologists have drawn connections between gender arrangements and the miseducation and abuse of children in England and America. They have found that it is impossible to assume a critical stance of society as a male without adopting some of the criteria elaborated by feminists and, of course, by other under-privileged groups. Or, to put it more succinctly, I would claim that it is impossible today to be a critic without being a feminist. Such an assertion is not intended to be doctrinaire. Rather it emanates from my experience and work as teacher, writer, and storyteller. The rigid principles of fairness by which I governed my life were principles which I dictated to women and which restricted my own experience. Most men suffer from male myopia, and our vision can only be corrected by adjusting our lenses to include a feminist viewpoint. There is a moral imperative behind such an adjustment just as there is a moral view to all art and especially to feminist fairy tales and feminist criticism. Neither male morality nor female morality in American and English society is superior to the other. Yet, we have governed our lives and continue to govern our lives according to male 'norms' as though they were normal and superior. Such recent studies as Carol Gilligan's *In a Different Voice* and R.C. Lewontin, Steven Rose, and Leon J. Kamin's *Not In Our Genes* have shown that forms of gender behaviour have been produced culturally through social interaction and ontogenetic development. The gender specific upbringing in England and America has led to *different* sets of moral ideologies which need better integration and *not* the rationalisation of the male view for domination which most men prefer. Gilligan has studied the ways in which men are reared to cultivate an ethic of justice based on abstract and rational principles and the ways in which women are reared to value an ethic of care based on nurturing and personal responsibilities.

> In the representation of maturity, both perspectives converge in the realization that just as inequality adversely affects both parties in an unequal relationship, so too violence is destructive for everyone involved. This dialogue between fairness and care not only provides a better understanding of relations between the sexes but also gives rise to a more comprehensive portrayal of adult work and family relationships.[3]

In the history of the literary fairy tale one can trace the development of a debate and possible dialogue about sex roles and domination which corresponds to the actual practice of child rearing and value systems which have come to be established in England and America. Obviously the different fairy tales contain many different concerns other than gender formation and politics. Yet, the social essence of the fairy tale in particular as well as the manner in which we continually return to it and reformulate it to conceive new worlds, or to reinforce our belief in the present one, indicates that we attribute great moral and ideological power to it in the process of socialising and educating our children.

In documenting the rise of the contemporary feminist fairy tale and the feminist critique, my aim has been to bring together material which will enable us to understand the vitality of the fairy tale and the significance of the transformations which have taken place in the last 15 years. The make-believe of the feminist fairy tales will perhaps make believers out of many children, and as adults, these children will undoubtedly conceive other tales which speak to the tensions and struggles of their lives. For the time being, however, the feminist fairy tales are here to stay, and, if the tales and criticism in the present collection are any indication, then they will continue to provide us with intriguing choices to chart our lives for years to come.

Notes

1 *The Child's Concept of Story* (Chicago: University of Chicago Press, 1978), pp. 3–4.
2 See my book, *Fairy Tales and the Art of Subversion: The Classical Genre for Children and the Process of Civilization* (London: Heinemann and New York: Wildman, 1983).
3 *In a Different Voice* (Cambridge: Harvard University Press, 1982), p. 174.

Introduction

Jack Zipes

For centuries now theologians, educators, literary critics, psychologists, and librarians have debated the pros and cons of reading fairy tales to children. The basic question they continually ask is whether children should be exposed to the cruelty, violence, and superstition of make-believe worlds. This debate began practically the very moment the tales were written down and established a genre with children in mind – children as targets. From the late seventeenth century to the present, serious talk has centred on the moral aspect and related psychological effect of the *literary* tales. Yet, the pedantic posture of moralism has always been suspect, for its rigidity has prevented us from focusing on the real problem, if there is such a thing as the 'real problem' *with* fairy tales. Instead of examining social relations and psychological behaviour first – the very stuff which constitutes the subject matter of the tales – *both* the proponents and opponents of fairy tales have based and continue to base their criticism on the harsh scenes and sexual connotations of the tales, supposedly suitable or unsuitable for children. Take your pick: 'Away with smut and violence!' vs. 'Let our children open their eyes to sex and resolve their oedipal problems'. The code words of the debate change, but there is, in fact, a 'real problem' which remains: the moral attack against fairy tales (censorship) and the rational defence of the tales (liberal civil rights) emanate from a *mutual repression* of what is actually happening in society.

Recent feminist criticism and feminist fairy tales in America and England have sought to confront the 'real problem' which lies *beyond* and *around* fairy tales. At the very least, feminists endeavour to alter our gaze and challenge our perspective with regard to literature and society. And they accomplish this change by forcing us to look at and take our everyday occurrences more seriously than we do. As we know, the everyday for a woman often consists of menial tasks at home or at work where her rights and needs are denied in various ways and her rewards are unequal. The lack of good, inexpensive daycare centres, the meagre salaries in comparison to men's wages, the danger simply in walking out alone on a street, the male protocol in social, political, and business affairs, the emphasis on sport as national pastimes that celebrate male power and make women into fringe adornments – these are just some of the factors which contribute to the exhaustion, reification, and exploitation of women. Moreover, the increase in wife battering and child abuse by men is also a sign of how hazardous the normal home routine, invisible to the public eye, has become. It would be foolish to exaggerate the 'desperate' situation of women in American and British societies today or to maintain that men are not suffering from many of the same social and political conditions such as technological rationalisation, unemployment, and discrimination that create great frustration and anger. In fact, one could even argue that some of the difficulties experienced by women today are due to the great gains they have made toward their liberation, and that they have qualitatively easier lives than ever before. Still, the liberation and ease have brought with them more subtle forms of oppression, and the daily life of a woman is fraught with harassment and obstacles that men rarely experience. Or, to put it another way, a woman's life is far from that of a fairy tale, and feminist fairy tales depict the struggles women undergo to define their lives in opposition to the daily lives they experience.

To talk about fairy tales today, especially feminist fairy tales, one must, in my opinion, talk about power, violence, alienation, social conditions, child-rearing and sex roles. It is no longer possible to ignore the connection between the aesthetic components of the fairy tales, whether they be old or new, and their historical function within a socialisation process which forms taste, mores, values, and habits. And it is too simple or simplistic to maintain that children need fairy tales more than any other form of literature to work through psychic disturbances as many pseudo-Freudians like Bruno Bettelheim[1] have done without challenging the premise of the oedipal paradigm. It is also too ethereal and idealistic to argue that the fairy tales contain archetypal patterns which point the way to happiness as many Jungians[2] have done without questioning the historical validity of the archetypes.[3] What is needed is a socio-psychological theory based on the recent findings of feminist investigations and critical reinterpretations of Freud that will help us grasp how fairy tales function historically in a mediatory role within the American and British socialisation processes.

Since the late 1960s feminist criticism has been moving in this direction. Such writers as Simone de Beauvoir, Kate Millet, Shulamith Firestone, Elizabeth Janeway, Adrienne Rich, Robin Morgan, Sheila Rowbotham, Betty Friedan, and Juliet Mitchell among others have provided the basis for a radical analysis of patriarchal practices in western industrial societies.[4] As Hester Eisenstein has demonstrated,[5] the development of feminist thought can be divided into three phases: (1) During the early 1970s socially constructed differences between the sexes were judged to be the chief source of female oppression, and it was argued that social control of women could be reduced by diminishing gender polarisation and moving toward some form of androgyny. (2) From the mid-1970s to the beginning of the 1980s androgyny was largely rejected in favour of a woman-centred perspective. The polarisation between masculine and feminine was to be maintained, and women were urged to 'isolate and to define those aspects of female experience that were potential sources of strength and power for women, and, more broadly, of a new blueprint for social change'.[6] (3) Since 1980 the woman-centred perspective has led some writers such as Mary Daly and Susan Griffin to argue for the intrinsic superiority of women due to physiological causes, the renunciation of rationality as masculine, and an undifferentiated view of women as powerless victims of male violence. Eisenstein believes that feminism has reached an impasse because there has been a 'divorce from Marxism and the political left; a consistent emphasis on psychology at the expense of economic factors; and a false universalism that addresses itself to all women, with insufficient regard for differences of race, class, and culture'.[7]

Bearing Eisenstein's analysis of feminist thought in mind, I want to suggest that one of the major contributions of the feminist critique still pertains to the power relations of domination in capitalist societies and their reinforcement by a specific arrangement within child-rearing and the family and the sexual division of labour.[8] Children are conditioned to assume and accept arbitrary sex roles. These socially conditioned roles prepare females to become passive, self-denying, obedient, and self-sacrificial (to name some of the negative qualities) as well as nurturing, caring, and responsible in personal situations (the more positive qualities). They prepare males to become competitive, authoritarian, and power-hungry as well as rational, abstract, and principled. The result of the symbiotic child-rearing process in which underprivileged women assume the major responsibility for the children and the household is a type of reinforcement of the capitalist socio-economic system in which it has become second nature for men to compete against one another for material rewards in the name of progress, to dominate their own nature and the natural surroundings without regard for the consequences. Thus, social relations have become so reified and instrumentalised that we are *almost* unaware of how alienated we are from one another and how close we are to self-destruction. At least this is the warning sounded by Dorothy Dinnerstein in her book *The Mermaid and the Minotaur:*

> It is senseless, I shall argue, to describe our prevailing male-female arrangements as 'natural.' They are of course a part of nature, but if they should contribute to the extinction of our species, that fact would be part of nature too. Our impulse to change these arrangements is as natural as they are, and more compatible with our survival on earth. To change them, however, we need to understand not only the societal mechanisms by which they are supported, but also the central psychological 'adjustment' of which they are an expression. What makes it essential for us to understand this 'adjustment' is that its existence rests on our failure to understand it: it is a massive communal self-deception, designed to allay the immediate discomfort and in the long run – a run whose end we are now approaching – suicidal.[9]

Though it is difficult to summarise feminist literary criticism as a whole, it is possible to argue that it generally adheres to the impulse behind Dinnerstein's work. In particular, the criticism which deals with fairy tales has stressed the positive notion of change. That is, the criticism underscores our deep desire to change the present male – female arrangements and endeavours to demonstrate that we can raise our awareness of how fairy tales function to maintain the present arrangements, how they might be rearranged or reutilised to counter the destructive tendencies of male-dominant values. To understand the vast undertaking of both feminist literary criticism and feminist fairy tales, I want to present a brief survey of the criticism, then discuss major features of the tales themselves, and finally draw some socio-psychological conclusions about the Utopian function of the fairy tales.

I

The feminist discussion about the social and cultural effect of fairy tales began in the early 1970s. In her article ' "Some Day My Prince Will Come": Female Acculturation Through the Fairy Tale' (1972), Marcia Lieberman took issue with two essays printed in the *New York Review of Books* by Alison Lurie, who had recommended certain tales in Andrew Lang's nineteenth – century collections as feminist.[10] Lieberman did a close textual study of the tales and found that they were indeed very much sexist: most of the heroines were passive, helpless, and submissive, and in the course of each narrative they functioned largely as a prize for a daring prince. Lieberman questioned whether the acculturation of such normative values conveyed by the tales could foster female emancipation. Since it has never been proven that there is such a thing as a biologically determined role for women, she argued that fairy tales which disseminate notions of rigid roles for male and female characters are detrimental to the autonomous development of young people.

Most feminist critics tend to agree with Lieberman that the traditional fairy tales spread false notions about sex roles. For example, Andrea Dworkin speaks about the nefarious effect of these tales in the first two chapters of her book *Woman Hating:*

> The point is that we have not formed that ancient world—it has formed us. We ingested it as children whole, had its values and consciousness imprinted on our minds as cultural absolutes long before we were in fact men and women. We have taken the fairy tales of childhood with us into maturity, chewed but still lying in the stomach, as real identity. Between Snow White and her heroic prince, our two great fictions, we never did have much of a chance. At some point the Great Divide took place: they (the boys) dreamed of mounting the Great Steed and buying Snow White from the dwarfs: we (the girls) aspired to become that object of every necrophiliac's lust—the innocent, *victimized* Sleeping Beauty, beauteous lump of ultimate, sleeping good. Despite ourselves, sometimes knowing, unwilling, unable to do otherwise, we act out the roles we were taught.[11]

Dworkin examines such traditional role models as the evil stepmother, the passive virgin, the active prince, and the powerful king to show how fairy tales manipulate our notions about sex roles. Unfortunately her arguments are too reductionist, and she fails to make careful distinctions about the possible positive effects of the tales. Implicit in her analysis is the assumption that the tales are automatically received in fixed ways and that all fairy tales contain the same messages. Certainly it is difficult to see how women-hating stems from her analysis of fairy tales, and, if women-hating was the motive behind the writing and production of fairy tales, she does not document this. Her contribution to feminist criticism about the complex reception of fairy tales remains limited because she stereotypes the tales in much the same manner as she perceives the fairy tales to be conveyors of stereotypes for children.

This limitation is also a glaring defect in Robert Moore's political essay, 'From Rags to Witches: Stereotypes, Distortion and Antihumanism in Fairy Tales' (1975), [12] which, to his credit, incorporates an anti-racist critique with feminism. Moore maintains that the classical fairy tales represent the cultural values and prejudices of white people from Europe and that they uphold male privileges. Consequently, they must be carefully scrutinised and criticised for the manner in which they spread anti-humanist stereotypes. Like Dworkin he emphasises primarily the negative features of the tales: (1) Females are poor girls or beautiful princesses who will only be rewarded if they demonstrate passivity, obedience, and submissiveness. (2) Stepmothers are always evil. (3) The best woman is the housewife. (4) Beauty is the highest value for women. (5) Males should be aggressive and shrewd. (6) Money and property are the most desirable goals in life. (7) Magic and miracles are the means by which social problems are resolved. (8) Fairy tales are implicitly racist because they often equate beauty and virtue with the colour white and ugliness with the colour black. In sum, there is very little in the classical fairy tales which Moore would consider positive and worthwhile in the interest of a humanist education. Fortunately, he does not argue that these tales should be eliminated. Rather, he stresses that educators and parents should pay more attention to the dark side of the tales.

Undoubtedly there is a dark side to the tales, and both Moore and Dworkin are empirically correct in demonstrating the sexist and racist aspects of many traditional fairy tales. However, they deal only with a small selection of the tales and with surface features. If one were to take the complete Grimms' fairy tales, for instance, one could point to tales which focus on the solidarity of old people *(The Bremen Town Musicians)*, the compassion and heroism of a sister who saves her brothers *(The Seven Swans, Brother and Sister)*, the common soldier who uses his wits to revenge himself on a king *(How Six Travelled through the World)*, the shrewd behaviour of a cook who outwits her master *(Clever Gretchen)*. Even in such a 'sexist' tale as *Cinderella*, there are matriarchal remnants of a folk tale which still play an important role in the outcome of the tale, for it is the dead mother who enables her daughter to attain her goal. [13] Though Dworkin and Moore raise important questions about classical fairy tales, they also neglect to deal with their Utopian allure and historical evolution. One of the important tasks of feminist criticism is to discover how and why certain changes were made in the tales during the course of centuries so that women can regain a sense of their own history and possibly alter contemporary socio-political arrangements. This is obviously the point of Kay Stone's essay 'Things Walt Disney Never Told Us' (1975). [14] She compares the original Grimms' fairy tales with the British and

American translations of the past two centuries as well as with the Disney versions of the twentieth century, and the results of her study reveal that the products of the modern culture industry specify that a woman can only be considered a heroine if she is patient, industrious, calm, beautiful and passive. Or, in other words, mass-marketed fairy tales of the twentieth century have undergone a sanitisation process according to the sexual preferences of males and the conservative norms of the dominant classes in America and England. In contrast, Stone points to another folk tradition in America and England which portrays women in folklore as aggressive, active, clever, and adventurous. Unfortunately, these tales have been suppressed in literature and the mass media. Stone interviewed 40 women between the ages of seven and sixty-one in North America to discover whether they were aware of this 'other tradition'. The majority of the women were mainly familiar with the Disney and sanitised versions and were surprised to learn that there were tales about independent women to which they could relate in a more satisfying manner.

The historical re-examination and rediscovery of matriarchal features in folk and fairy tales constitute some of the most important work being conducted in the field.[15] For instance, Heather Lyons investigates a variety of tales with feminist implications in her interesting essay 'Some Second Thoughts on Sexism in Fairy Tales' (1978),[16] and she also discusses ways in which traditional tales can be altered. Similarly, Jane Yolen, a gifted fairy-tale writer in her own right, has presented a convincing demonstration of how an active and strong heroine was transformed into a docile and submissive girl in 'America's Cinderella' (1977)[17] She studied different European folk versions of *Cinderella* and established that the original heroine had never been 'catatonic', but rather she had always fought actively for justice and truth. It was only toward the end of the seventeenth century that Perrault began to transform the Cinderella protagonist into a passive and obedient young woman. His adaptation paved the way for the Grimms and numerous American authors who produced dainty and prudish Cinderellas *en masse* in the nineteenth century. The final result of this mass-market development was the Walt Disney film of 1949, which presented Cinderella in her most 'perverted' form – the patient, submissive, defenceless young woman, whose happiness depends on a man who actually defines her life. It is evident that Yolen wrote her critical essay to rectify history and suggest alternatives to our common picture of Cinderella so that women could use cultural material to realise their own essence through art and literature. This purpose also underlies her own remarkable version of the tale entitled

The Moon Ribbon, in which a young woman is guided and protected by her dead mother until she achieves her own independence.

The movement toward autonomy – women should govern their own destiny and write their own history – has been a dominant tendency in feminist literary criticism, and it provided the basis for the first complete study of fairy tales and everyday occurrences by Madonna Kolbenschlag. Her book, *Kiss Sleeping Beauty Good-Bye: Breaking the Spell of Feminine Myths and Models,*[18] endeavours to grasp and overcome the negative features in the role models of Sleeping Beauty, Snow White, Cinderella, Goldilocks, and Beauty. Kolbenschlag is not interested in the literature *per se,* but in the habitual manner in which women are forced and influenced to adopt particular roles and identities. There are two major arguments which are developed on a sociological and philosophical level. First, she believes that most women are conditioned to internalise rigid spiritual notions about life. Many women are religious, pious, and ascetic not because they have independently chosen their own religion or spirituality but because the teachings of the church itself have conceived normative patterns for women which hinder them from realizing their own spiritual and sensual unity. Secondly, she maintains that the contemporary crises between men and women are symptomatic of the feminine need for ethical autonomy that is prevented by men and institutions. Thus she calls for the destruction of the traditional feminine identity in Kant's sense of a categorical imperative. What is a given for men – the capacity for self-realisation which is reinforced by the socialisation process and cultural education – should be a given for women as well, but for the most part they must seek, grasp and appropriate this capacity in ways that are often painful and traumatic.

The goal of Kolbenschlag's book is to provoke both men and women to think about alternatives to the commonly accepted role models in our lives. The fairy tales themselves are not responsible for the creation of these roles. Rather they are the symbolical forms which reinforce self-destructive social and psychological patterns of behaviour in our daily lives. This is also the major idea in Colette Dowling's 1981 best-seller *The Cinderella Complex: Women's Hidden Fear of Independence.*[19] Again it is not the fairy tale that is responsible for the dependency of women. The fairy tale is only important in so far as it reflects how women are oppressed and *allow* themselves to be oppressed. Dowling is of the opinion that:

> personal, psychological dependency – the deep wish to be taken care of by others – is the chief force holding women down today. I call this 'The

Cinderella Complex' – a network of largely repressed attitudes and fears that keeps women in a kind of half-light, retreating from the full use of their minds and creativity. Like Cinderella, women today are still waiting for something external to 'transform their lives'.[20]

On the basis of personal experience and empirical studies Dowling demonstrates how women themselves psychologically invent various traps and tricks to play the role of Cinderella. The significance of her book is not so much in her analysis of the social and psychological situation of American women because she remains too impressionistic, but she does draw remarkable connections between fairy-tale images and wish-fulfilment that shed light on the contemporary dilemma of many women.

It is not by coincidence that numerous feminist critics, women *and* men, feel that the fairy tales of their childhood stamp their present actions and behaviour in reality. There are certain fairy-tale patterns, motifs, and models which constantly arise in our life and in literature which appear to have been preserved because they reinforce male hegemony in the civilisation process. And the exploration of the mediations between society and fairy tales seems to be breaking new ground in feminist literary criticism. In their significant study *The Madwoman in the Attic*[21] Sandra M. Gilbert and Susan Gubar rely upon fairy-tale motifs to examine the socio-psychological situation of women writers inscribed in the dominant male discourse of the nineteenth century. In particular *Snow White* serves them as the paradigmatic dramatisation of a male-manipulated conflict between two types of females, the witch and the angel, who are played off one against the other. In their view the stepmother/witch wants to kill Snow White because the witch has become an artist who also wants to lead an active life with stealth, and the submissive, innocent and passive stepdaughter is a threat because she has not been entrapped by the masculine mirror, and she naïvely accepts the world as it is. In contrast, the stepmother, who has learned to practise the art of black magic in a world dominated by men, has no longer any chance to attain independence. This is why she is jealous of Snow White and attempts to kill her. However, *she* must die so that Snow White can continue her role.

Gilbert and Gubar outline Snow White's future and comment on the significance of her destiny:

> Surely, fairest of them all, Snow White has exchanged one glass coffin for another, delivered from the prison where the Queen put her only to be imprisoned in the looking glass from which the King's voice speaks

daily. There is, after all, no female model for her in this tale except this 'good' (dead) mother and her living avatar the 'bad' mother. And if Snow White escaped the first glass coffin by her goodness, her passivity and docility, her only escape from her second glass coffin, the imprisoning mirror, must evidently be through 'badness,' through plots and stories, duplicitous schemes, wild dreams, fierce fictions, mad impersonations. The cycle of her fate seems inexorable. Renouncing 'contemplative purity' she must now embark on that life of 'significant action' which, for a woman, is defined as a witch's life because it is so monstrous, so unnatural. [22]

Gilbert and Gubar analyse how this basic cultural pattern in *Snow White* is linked to other images of women and the portrayal of conflicts between women in the English literature of the nineteenth century, and they draw parallels with other fairy tales, which ostensibly had an effect on women writers, for it is not by chance that particular fairy-tale motifs continually appeared in their writings. For instance, Karen Rowe has demonstrated that Charlotte Brontë's *Jane Eyre*

begins with an echo of *Cinderella* and then transforms into a variant of *Beauty and the Beast,* one modified however by Gothic shadows and psychological depths permitted to nineteenth-century novelists. From its opening *Jane Eyre* plays upon a collective, folkloric unconscious, engaging readers to transfer youthful romantic expectations from their own psyches into the fiction and to judge its success by the fidelity to fantasy paradigms. [23]

Rowe's subtle analysis makes it clear how Brontë felt compelled to confront stereotypical fairy tale roles to try to define her own needs. And, indeed, Brontë was not alone in her endeavours. [24] Numerous women writers up to the present have felt compelled to confront the stereotypical fairy tale roles in some form or another to establish a sense of their own identities and voices.

In a lecture on 'The Beast, the Mermaid and the Happy Ending' delivered at the 1980 MLA Meeting in San Francisco, the novelist Carolyn See expanded the discussion begun by Gilbert, Gubar, and Rowe. [25] She examined the function of the 'Beauty and Beast' motif in contemporary literature. For instance, Alix Kate Shulman's *Memoirs of an Ex-Prom Queen,* Sylvia Plath's *The Bell Jar,* and Alison Lurie's *The War Between the Tates* depict 'beautiful' women who fall in love with 'beast-like' men only to learn that the men do not turn into princes when they, the women, sacrifice their lives for them. The women break their relations with these men either to take destiny in their hands or to succumb to a bitter fate. In this way, according to See, the novels reveal

the patriarchal lie of the happy end in the classical fairy tale. Underlying See's interpretation of the fairy tale patterns in certain contemporary novels is Karen Rowe's thesis from her essay 'Feminism and
Fairy Tales' (1979) that

> romantic tales exert an awesome imaginative power over the female
> psyche – a power intensified by formal structures which we perhaps take
> too much for granted. The pattern of enchantment and disenchantment,
> the formulaic closing with nuptial rites, and the plot's comic structure
> seem so conventional that we do not question the implications. Yet,
> traditional patterns, no less than fantasy characterizations and actions,
> contribute to the fairy tale's potency as a purveyor of romantic
> archetypes and, thereby, of cultural precepts for young women.[26]

If most feminist critics argue like Rowe and See that the traditional
fairy tales are unacceptable today because of their atavistic notions of
sex roles and their ideology of male domination, we must now ask what
the alternatives are. Or, how have feminist-oriented writers tried to
reformulate sexual arrangements and aesthetics to suggest that we have
choices as individuals with regard to the development of gender
qualities and characteristics, social values, and norms?

II

In her essay 'The Tale Retold: Feminist Fairy Tales' (1982) Ruth
MacDonald suggests that there are three solutions to the dearth of folk
tales acceptable to modern feminists:

> One may present the tales, unaltered, with their traditional endings, and
> the devil take the consequences of the possible damage to a young girl's
> career expectations; one may rewrite the tales, deemphasizing physical
> beauty and marriage, but thereby violating the objectivity of the folklore
> collector by imposing one's own language and bias on the narrative; or
> one may write new tales, using folklore motifs with less conventional
> endings.[27]

As examples of the new tales, MacDonald discusses *The Practical
Princess and other Liberating Tales* by Jay Williams and *The Five
Wives of Silverbeard* by Adela Turin, Francesca Cantarelli and Nella
Bosnia, and she finds them lacking because the male characters are
presented as one-dimensional and inadequate in comparison to the
females. With regard to the rewritten folk tales, she examines the two
collections by Ethel Johnstone Phelps, *Tatterhood and Other Tales*
(1978) and *The Maid of the North: Feminist Folk Tales Around the*

World (1981), and here she questions the right of an editor, 'who is not a teller but rather a feminist and scholar',[28] to make changes which comply with her bias. Finally, she praises the unaltered folk tales in Rosemary Minard's *Women Folk and Fairy Tales* (1975) because the editor refrains from tampering with them (as if they had not already been changed!). She concludes her essay by asserting that 'to subvert the ending [of a tale] by altering the reward structure or to de-emphasize the essential values of goodness in a fairy tale — beauty, wealth, potency against evil, or even marriage — is inherently unsatisfying. To reconstruct the fairy tale world in the image of modernity may be possible, but success at this point in history seems illusive'.[29]

Perhaps it may be illusive for MacDonald, but the fact of the matter is that she is barely in a position to make such judgements when she considers such a minute selection of new and retold fairy tales. More-over, she appears to believe that there are eternal and essential values in fairy tales which are 'inherent', as if the literature were organic and as if values were natural and universal. As most feminists argue, it is this notion of biologically determined traits and values with regard to sexuality and society which needs questioning, and their experimental literature of the last 20 years reveals a fascinating transformational tendency within the fairy tale genre that is linked to key social changes in the civilisation process itself.

As I have already suggested, MacDonald has failed to indicate the great breadth and quality of experimental feminist fairy tales which seek to provoke the reader to re-examine his or her notion of sexual arrangements and the power politics of those arrangements. For instance, she should have at least mentioned if not discussed in more detail the following works published before her article appeared: *The Donkey Prince* (1970) by Angela Carter, *Princess Hynchatti and Some Other Surprises* (1973) by Tanith Lee, *The Forest Princess* (1974) and *The Return of the Forest Princess* (1975) by Harriet Herman, *The Girl Who Cried Flowers* (1974), *The Hundredth Dove* (1977), *Dream Weaver* (1979), and *Sleeping Ugly* (1981) by Jane Yolen, *The Clever Princess* (1977) by Ann Tompert, *All the King's Horses* (1976) by Michael Foreman, *Little Red Riding Hood* (1978) and *Snow White* (1978) by the Merseyside Fairy Tale Collective, *Kittatinny* (1978) by Joanna Russ, *Clever Gretchen and Other Forgotten Folktales* (1980) edited by Alison Lurie, *The Skull in the Snow and other Folk Tales* by Toni McCarty, *Stories for Free Children* (1982) edited by Letty Cottin Pogrebin, all designed largely for young readers, and *Transformations* (1971) by Anne Sexton, *The Green Woman* (1973) by Meghan Collins,

In the Suicide Mountains (1977) by John Gardner, *Beginning with O* (1977) by Olga Broumas, *Beauty* (1978) and *The Door in the Hedge* (1981) by Robin McKinley, and *The Bloody Chamber* (1979) by Angela Carter for adult readers. What is interesting about the experimental 'tampering' with traditional fairy tales is that the authors cut across ages, social classes, race and gender and write their tales as socially symbolic acts to pursue alternatives to the destructive and also self-destructive processes in American and British child rearing and socialisation.

As I have already noted, there are numerous experiments with the traditional fairy-tale repertoire that could be called feminist. Such experiments did not appear out of thin air. Aside from a long tradition of matriarchal tales that were printed and continue to be printed in folklore collections of various lands, there were feminist precedents set in the literary fairy-tale tradition by the end of the nineteeth century. Such Victorian writers as Mary De Morgan, Mrs Molesworth, and Evelyn Scharp (who incidentally played a major role in the British suffragette movement) conceived tales with strong heroines who rebel against convention-ridden societies. At the beginning of the twentieth century E. Nesbit wrote, among other significant tales, *The Last of the Dragons* and *The Nine Whirlpools,* which are remarkable for their critique of tyrannical patriarchs and their depiction of resourceful women, who work with men to form humane societies. It was exactly during this time, too, that L. Frank Baum wrote his Oz books, which portray a Utopian society governed by nurturing women. Later in the century, Catherine Storr wrote *Clever Polly and the Stupid Wolf* (1955), which reverses the motif of the traditional Red Riding Hood tale by having a smart and intrepid girl continually outwitting a bumbling wolf. Thus, the contemporary feminist fairy tales have drawn upon a rich tradition of feminist tales or tales with strong women which may not be widely known but have nevertheless provided models and the impetus (along with the feminist movement itself) to challenge the dominant male discourse. In reviewing the contemporary feminist experiments, I want to focus on those tales that reveal the manifold ways in which present-day writers have rearranged familiar motifs and characters and reversed plot lines to provoke readers to rethink conservative views of gender and power. The aesthetics of these tales are ideological, for the structural reformation depends upon a non-sexist (and non-racist, I might add) world view that calls for a dramatic change in social practice. This point has been made convincingly in Ellen Cronan Rose's essay 'Through the Looking Glass: When Women Tell Fairy Tales' (1983), in which she discusses the works of Sexton, Broumas, and Carter.[30] My discussion of feminist fairy tales will be broader and cover narratives written for young and old. Obviously, the aesthetic complexity of those tales written for older readers does prevent younger readers from grasping or even following the plot. However, *all* the tales emanate from a basic impulse for change within society, and though the writers have reacted to this impulse on different levels, they share the same purpose of questioning socialisation, have influenced one another to some degree, and have been stimulated by feminist criticism to rethink both fairy tales as aesthetic compositions and the role they play in conditioning themselves and children. As a cultural phenomenon, the new feminist fairy tales seek to break boundaries and speak in the name of future generations which may not need a feminist literature of this kind in the future. This is the basic irony of feminist fairy tales: they aim ultimately at discarding the adjective feminist and at conceiving worlds in which the contradictions are not concerned with sexism and domination.

In the fairy tales for younger readers the most noticeable change in the narratives concerns the heroine who actively seeks to define herself, and her self-definition determines the plot. As she moves to complete this task, traditional fairy-tale topoi and motifs are transformed to indicate the necessity for gender rearrangement and the use of power for achieving equality. For instance, in *The Forest Princess*[31] Harriet Herman reverses the Rapunzel tale by having a princess, who has grown up alone in a forest tower, rescue a prince. After she returns with him to his father's kingdom and is treated in a patronising way by the king, she demonstrates that she is equal to all the males at the court and rejects the sexist society by departing for her home in the forest. Herman's tale is illustrated with pictures that emphasise the key scenes of self-discovery, joy, and disappointment. The initiation ritual of this tale is totally different from that in *Rapunzel*. Absent is the female witch who imprisons Rapunzel and punishes her lover. Here the princess grows up 'sexless' so to speak, and she gradually discovers that there are arbitrary sexual distinctions made in society, largely by men. She is unwilling to be socialised by such a court and rebels as an example to the other children, both in the narrative as characters and as implied readers of the narrative. Herman does not belabour her point. Neither the king nor the prince is villainous. Rather they are stuck in a tradition which they have never questioned, and the princess as outsider can more readily challenge the authoritarian structure of the court, which incidentally begins to break down and become more egalitarian in the sequel *The Return of the Forest Princess*.

Herman's tale obviously seeks to overcome the atavistic nature of numerous classical fairy and folk tales which are sexist. This is also the case in Jeanne Desy's *The Princess Who Stood on Her Own Two Feet.* [32] Here Desy takes issue with such tales as *King Thrushbeard* and Shakespeare's misogynist rendition of the tale in *The Taming of the Shrew,* which poke fun at and humiliate women likened to witches and shrews. Clearly the definition of 'shrew' has depended on masculine images of women, and Desy is most concerned with what lies underneath the definition and images. Her tale is about a tall, young princess, bright as a sunflower, who has mastered everything she has undertaken. However, she is unhappy because she cannot find somebody to love and to love her. The court wizard, a sensitive and droll figure, provides her with a miraculous talking Afghan hound as companion, but a dog is nothing but a dog, so the princess thinks, despite his sage counselling and compassion for her. Therefore, she falls in love with a prince who cannot tolerate the fact that she is taller and more talented than he is. After he humiliates her numerous times and finally causes her talking hound to die out of love for her, she rejects the prince and finds someone who accepts her for what she is. By portraying the prince as a pompous, insensitive person, Desy shows how absurd and unfair his sexist actions are. Moreover, she employs humorous figures such as the good-hearted wizard and his clever cat and comic reversals to parody the patriarchal notion of achievement and the male quest for power.

There are a number of unusually funny feminist fairy tales whose main purpose is to show the farcical side of sexist expectations in classical fairy tales. For example, *Cinderella* is treated to various satirical interpretations in the hands of Tanith Lee, John Gardner, Richard Gardner, Roald Dahl, and Judith Viorst. In Lee's *Princess Dahli,* [33] the underprivileged princess rebels against her rich relatives and finds a poor prince of her own choosing. In John Gardner's *Gudgekin the Thistle Girl,* [34] the poor girl refuses to be humiliated by a prince, who must learn to respect her integrity. In Richard Gardner's *Cinderelma,* [35] a young woman succeeds in attending the royal ball through her own initiative and reaches a mutual decision with the prince that they are not suited for each other. In Roald Dahl's verse rendition of *Cinderella,* [36] the prince turns out to be a sadistic head-chopper, who is ultimately rejected by Cinderella, and the ironic rejection of an ugly prince is also the theme in Judith Viorst's short poem. [37] Each one of these writers relies largely on humour to poke fun at outworn sexist notions in tales which are still cherished today as delightful reading for children. Going against the grain of sexist classical fairy tales, the above writers have also written other parodies mocking *Little Red Riding Hood, Snow White, The Three Pigs, Rapunzel, Sleeping Beauty, The Little Mermaid,* and *The Frog Prince.* In addition to the comic reversals of classical tales, there have been some remarkable adaptations of folk tales and motifs from a feminist point of view. For instance, Dorothy Van Woerkom has adapted a German folk tale in *The Queen Who Couldn't Bake Gingerbread* (1975).[38] Here King Mulligatawny learns to bake his own gingerbread and to respect his wife's other talents. In Marcia Sewall's newly illustrated book containing P.C. Asbjornsen's literary version of a Norwegian folk tale, *The Squire's Bride,*[39] a farmer's daughter outwits a rich old squire, who wants to marry her, by dressing up an old mare to be his bride. In Anita Lobel's *The Straw Maid,*[40] which has elements of central European folk tales, a peasant girl tricks the robbers who capture her and makes off with some of their treasure to help her poor parents.

In all three of these tales, the women rely on their wits which enable them to overcome oppressive conditions. In many other feminist fairy tales it is magic, symbolising the latent potential of women, which helps them grasp and subdue inimical forces which might keep them in a submissive position. Whereas the heroes of traditional folk and fairy tales often pursue power to dominate and rule others, the heroines of the new feminist tales use power to rearrange society according to a more nurturing moral concept and to attain independence for women and mutual respect. For instance, there are several remarkable fairy tales which revolve around the question of sexual domination and relations of power in society, and they reveal how changes must be made in the private and public sphere if a young woman is to come into her own. Michael Foreman's *All The King's Horses*[41] suggests that a strong woman will not settle in a sexist society so long as the rules are set by domineering men. In Ann Tompert's *The Clever Princess*[42] Lorna solves three riddles with the help of magic that she has learned from a sage woman named Old Krone, and thus she becomes a wise and independent queen who rules by allowing the people to rule themselves. In Betty Miles's *Atalanta*[43] another young princess decides her fate by standing up to her father and winning a race. In the process she finds a young man who respects her courage and individualism, and together they symbolise the possibility for a new type of relationship between the sexes. In none of these tales is marriage a necessity or a goal for young women, rather it is a possibility which may or may not enter their plans. The important narrative shift which takes place during the course of the story is one from a male-centred to a woman-centred world. In addition, the lives and the careers of the young women are not telologically shaped by marriage.

When marriage does become a question, as in Jay Williams's *Petronella,*[44] it assumes a different function. In this tale it is part of the recognition and fulfilment which the princess achieves at the end of her own personal quest. In the process the male figures play a peripheral role in the action of the story. Though it may be argued, as MacDonald has done in her essay, that the females in Williams's collection of liberating tales are much more interesting that the males, Williams does not degrade the male characters. Some are talented and adept like the magician, whom Petronella chooses to become her husband, while others are bungling power-seekers. As a male writing to question present gender arrangements, Williams, like Foreman, Richard Gardner, and others, is more concerned about generating respect for women, learning from them, and exposing male foibles. Like the feminists, his goal, too, is the rearrangement of gender and social roles so that power is not used to gain advantage but to resolve contradictions.

Another tale which ends in marriage but suggests that gender roles are not biologically determined and that power can be used for the liberation of both sexes is Angela Carter's *The Donkey Prince.*[45] Daisy, a young working girl, who knows a trick or two, enables Bruno, the enchanted donkey prince, to recover a magic apple in the Savage Mountains. Due to her courage, cleverness, and skills, she helps Hlajki the wild man and Bruno to survive a dangerous mission, and in the end she marries Bruno, who is transformed into a human due to her compassion and deeds. The entire quest in Carter's tale is a humanising one: the beast becomes human and humane in more ways than one, and the hard work of a working girl is recognised and duly rewarded in a way that she appreciates. Ironically, what happened long ago in another country becomes a Utopian model which Carter projects in her fairy-tale construct as a goal for which we should strive.

In most feminist fairy tales the use of power raises moral questions which have political ramifications in society. For instance, Charlotte Pomerantz's *The Princess and the Admiral*[46] is based on an incident from the thirteenth century involving Vietnam and the Imperial Navy of the Kubla Khan, and a clear parallel is drawn to the American invasion of Vietnam during the 1960s and 1970s. In addition, the general question of colonisation and imperialism is posed. Here the ruler of Tiny Kingdom is a lean, dark-eyed princess named Mat Mat, who uses wisdom to defeat a vain admiral and his fleet in a non-violent way when they seek to attack and conquer her country. A similar perspective, which makes the personal into the political, underlies Claus Stamm's translation of the Japanese folk tale *Three Strong Women.*[47] The huge wrestler Forever-Mountain, who is on his way to the imperial wrestling marches, learns humility from a young woman named Maru-me, who easily subdues him when he tries to tease her in a patronising way. To his surprise, Forever-Mountain comes to enjoy the company of Maru-me, her mother, and grandmother on their farm rather than to participate in the imperial wrestling matches.

In the fairy tales by Pomerantz and Stamm, power is used to bring about peace and understanding, not domination. Both Mat Mat and Maru-me want *re-cognition,* or, in other words, the two powerful male figures, the Admiral and Forever-Mountain, are obliged to undergo a different cognitive process based on their new experiences with women which will hopefully alter their behaviour in general. Neither Mat Mat nor Maru-me seek revenge when attacked. They are self-confident and want to develop the talents which they possess without imposing their will on anyone. All this is in contrast to numerous traditional folk and fairy tales which depict males rising to power by killing, destroying, or outwitting competitors. Often the protagonist fights for a woman as property or defines the woman's destiny through his heroic act which feminist writers now declare is more degrading that uplifting for women.

Perhaps one of the most radical reactions to the manner in which women are 'heroically' treated in fairy tales can be found in Joanna Russ's fantasy novel *Kittatinny.*[48] At one point her heroine Kit, who is lost in a forest while undergoing an initiation ritual, discovers a story entitled *Russalka or The Seacoast of Bohemia,* which is a critical adaptation of Hans Christian Andersen's *The Little Mermaid.* Whereas Andersen affirmed the tortuous self-sacrifice desired by a mermaid, who is eventually rewarded for such denigration by God, Russ deplores the actions of Russalka, a mer-woman, who begins to read land books and catch the human disease, which involves self-deception and self-betrayal. Russ demonstrates in a poignant manner how a man's love can kill a woman, especially when there is no basis for understanding. Of course, it is Russalka, who is at fault for denying her true essence in this tale — as is the mermaid in Andersen's. But there is a difference: Andersen was petrified of women and wanted to keep them under control, and he rewarded the submissive, pliant women in his tales with God's love. Russ is angry at women who sell themselves for a 'romantic' vision of love. Her tale of self-betrayal and self-denial ends on a tragic note because it is intended to serve as a warning to her fictitious heroine Kit in her novel and to her readers as well. In a man's world love can be poison, and the walls of life can feel like a prison.

Though less pessimistic, Jane Yolen also explores the mermaid theme in an original and provocative mannner in her book *The Hundredth Dove*. [49] Two tales, *The White Sea Maid* and *The Lady and the Mermaid,* have women return to the sea rather than live in male-governed worlds. Crucial in all of Yolen's many fairy tales is a reaffirmation of female cultural life. This can be seen clearly in her revision of *Cinderella* entitled *The Moon Ribbon*. [50] When the continuity and development of female culture is disrupted, Yolen points to the tragic aspects in such tales as *The Girl Who Cried Flowers* [51] and *Brother Hart*. [52] For the most part, Yolen emphasises the caring and nurturing of women as constitutive of moral integrity. Though she rarely assumes an outright, radical feminist position in her tales, her sensitive rearrangement of traditional stories does lead to a contradiction of the patriarchal view of the world. Certainly this notion is at the centre of the tales written by the Merseyside Fairy Story Collective. [53] For instance, in the Merseyside version of *Red Riding Hood,* a timid girl and her great-grandmother confront and overcome a wolf without the help of a male hunter. In *Snow White* the young princess becomes the leader of a group of insurgents who defeat a power-hungry queen. In each tale the parallels to actual social conflicts in British society are apparent, and the endings point to new beginnings in which underprivileged groups take destiny in their own hands with a new *political* consciousness.

In most feminist fairy tales for older readers the patterns and themes are also designed to stress liberation and transformation. But there is a more guarded position or sober attitude with regard to the possibilities for gender rearrangement. In some cases the writers are outright pessimistic, or pessimistic in a provocative manner that makes the reader desire change. For instance, Anne Sexton, one of the first writers to use fairy tales as a vehicle to comment on the plight of women in a male-dominated society, portrays her 'heroines' as prisoners or commodities. In her book *Transformations* (1971) she adapted 17 of the Grimms' fairy tales in verse form to demonstrate the multifarious ways in which women are circumscribed by language and custom in daily life so that the possibility for them to attain self-expression and free movement is curtailed. In general, Sexton begins each one of her poems with a first-person exposition that elaborates her 'transformed' position regarding the original Grimm tale. In *The Frog Prince* she comments that:

Frog has no nerves.
Frog is as old as a cockroach.
Frog is my father's genitals.
Frog is a malformed doorknob.
Frog is a soft bag of green. [54]

This male frog has immense power over Sexton the poetess because he wants to envelop her in his world.

Mr. Poison
is at my bed.
He wants my sausage.
He wants my bread. [55]

After examining the phallic threat posed by the frog, Sexton then retells the Grimms' story line in the third person to illustrate the situation of women in general. Her bias is clear: she is constantly concerned with the manner in which women are *obliged* to internalise conventional norms and values not of their own making which prevent them from pursuing their own desires. After all, she asks,

Why
should a certain
quite adorable princess
be walking in her garden
at such a time
and toss her golden ball
up like a bubble
and drop it into the well?
It was ordained.
Just as the fates deal out
the plague with a tarot card.
Just as the Supreme Being drills
holes in our skulls to let
the Boston Symphony through. [56]

Sexton describes each step the princess takes as part of a destiny planned for her by others. Though she wants to rebel against this destiny, there is literally nothing she can do to save herself. The frog is indeed a type of poison which takes on various shapes.

Like a genie coming out of a samovar
a handsome prince arose in the
corner of her royal bedroom.
He had kind eyes and hands

and was a friend of sorrow.
Thus they were married.
After all he had compromised her.
He hired a night watchman
so that no one could enter the chamber
and he had the well
boarded over so that
never again would she lose her ball,
that moon, that Krishna hair,
that blind poppy, that innocent globe,
that madonna womb. [57]

Each one of Sexton's transformed fairy tales is a foreboding of that fate which awaits the young woman as she matures. Actually, there is no maturation but total enclosure by male and market dictates. Such pessimism is best summed up by the ending of her *Sleeping Beauty*:

There was a theft.
That much I am told.
I was abandoned.
That much I know.
I was forced backward.
I was forced forward.
I was passed hand to hand like a bowl of fruit.
Each night I am nailed into place
and I forget who I am.
Daddy?
That's another kind of prison.
It's not the prince at all,
but my father
drunkenly bent over my bed
circling the abyss like a shark,
my father thick upon me
like some sleeping jelly fish.
What voyage this, little girl?
This coming out of prison?
God help—
this life after death? [58]

Sexton, who never considered herself a feminist, does not pose the possibility of sexual rearrangement, but she does nevertheless question the present arrangement in such a radical way that the reader of her poems must ask why sex roles must be so destructive. There is an urgency in the rhythm and tone of Sexton's poems which give rise to an increased awareness about the alienation and reification of women, about the need to transform the socialised human condition before it is too late.

One poetess who has heard Sexton's voicce and definitely heeded her warning is Olga Broumas. Perhaps because she is younger and has benefited from the women's movement, Broumas is more optimistic and is convinced that there are ways for women to determine their own lives. She, too, has transformed fairy tales into verse in her book *Beginning with O,* [59] and in two poems which use quotes from Sexton as points of departure she suggests another style of life. For instance, in her *Cinderella,* she begins with Sexton's statement

> ... the joy that isn't shared
> I heard, dies young. [60]

Here Broumas depicts the successful career woman who has broken the male royal code, and, after being accepted at the male court, so to speak, she realises how she has betrayed her sisters and resolves to change:

> ... A woman co-opted by promises: the lure
> of a job, the ruse of a choice, a woman forced
> to bear witness, falsely
> against my kind, as each
> other sister was judged inadequate, bitchy, incompetent,
> jealous, too thin, too fat. I know what I know.
> What sweet bread I make
> for myself in this prosperous house
> is dirty, what good soup I boil turns
> in my mouth to mud. Give
> me my ashes. A cold stove, a cinder-block pillow, wet
> canvas shoes in my sisters', my sisters' hut. [61]

The answer to Sexton is sisterhood. That is, Sexton talks about this in her poetry, but she never envisages it as a real possibility. She glimpses the possibility in such statements as 'a woman / who loves a woman / is forever young'. [62] However, it is Broumas who then develops this notion fully in *Rapunzel.* Here the antagonism between the old witch and the young woman is transformed into a love relationship which is celebrated. Since numerous fairy tales, as Gilbert and Gubar have suggested in *The Madwoman in the Attic,* often pit old women against the young, Broumas goes against the grain and prefers to depict the tender concern and passion of two women as in *Little Red Riding Hood.* Time again she reflects upon the need for sisterhood in her fairy-tale poems, the need to find adequate means for self-expression. In *Rumpelstiltskin* she poses the question:

How to describe
what we didn't know
exists: a mutant organ, its function to feel
intensely, to heal by immersion, a fluid
element, crucial
as amnion, sweet milk
in the suckling months.
Approximations,
The words we need are extinct.
Or if not extinct
badly damaged: the proud Columbia
stubbing
her bound up feet on her damned
up bed. Helpless with excrement. Daily
by accident, against
what has become our will through years
of deprivation, we spawn the fluid
that cradles us, grown
as we are, and at a loss
for words. Against all currents, upstream
we spawn
in each others's blood.[63]

Poetry appears to be especially suitable for women who want to speak their mind and in their own voice about fairy tales. Aside from Sexton and Broumas, Sara Henderson Hay, Helen Chasin, Judith Rechter, and Kathleen Spivack have experimented with fairy-tale motifs in unusual poems which ask questions about oppressive gender expectations in the socialisation process.[64] Most of the poems are filled with laments, bitterness, and disappointment, and heterosexuality is viewed askance. If there is hope for women, the poems project it in a woman-centred society, in which men can no longer interfere with the lives of women.

In contrast to the poets, Robin McKinley takes a more optimistic view of men and heterosexuality. She portrays self-confident, courageous young women who take the initiative in a world which they help to define with men. In her adaptation of *Beauty and the Beast* (1978)[65] and in her transformed fairy tales in the collection *The Door in the Hedge* (1981),[66] it is the woman who dares to oppose tyranny, to seek alternatives to oppression. For instance, in *The Princess and the Frog,* a princess takes the initiative in overcoming a powerful prince named Aliyander, who had turned his own brother into a frog and threatened the father of the princess. Though McKinley is often naïve and too facile in the manner in which she depicts women assuming

active roles, it is this very unquestioning attitude which is significant.
That is, for McKinley there is no reason why women cannot live the
lives they choose for themselves if they are willing to struggle and sur-
mount obstacles which apparently hinder men, too, from realising
their identities. This is also the major theme of Michael de Larrabeiti's
Malagan and the Lady of Rascas (1984), in which a noble woman
demonstrates that the beauty of her soul and her humanitarian
character can conquer black magic and despotism. It is her mag-
nanimity that liberates her husband and sets a standard for his future
actions.

One of the more unique fairy-tale depictions of the quest for identity
and transformed heterosexual arrangements is John Gardner's *In the
Suicide Mountains.*[67] He sends three characters, Chudu, a dwarf,
Armida, a blacksmith's daughter, and Christopher Sullen, a Crown
Prince, into the mountains because they cannot live up to the sexist and
racist 'norms' of their society. For instance, though he has never
harmed anyone, Chudu has been blamed for using his magic to cause
evil. Armida cannot gain acceptance on her own terms because she is so
strong and intelligent. Christopher is shunned at court because he
dislikes tournaments, fights, and politics and professes a love for
books and music. Ironically, the three of them are diverted from their
suicide plots in the mountains by a sinister, six-fingered abbot, whom
they eventually defeat by combining their talents. In the process they
gain mutual respect for each other and begin their lives anew. Such
regeneration is only possible because they find that their 'otherness' is
accepted in each other's eyes and that they do not have to lead socially
defined roles. Gardner weaves fairy-tale motifs and tales throughout
his novel around the theme that 'things are not as they seem'. Indeed,
the genuine qualities of the characters do not surface until the
appropriate conditions give rise to them, and it is at this point that the
protagonists become what they are and want to be. Ultimately it is
Gardner's aesthetic construct composed of fairy-tale reformulations
which provide such conditions and allow us as readers to glean Utopian
possibilities in the rearrangement of genders.

The form which Gardner's Utopian model assumes is most
comforting, but 'Utopian reformulations' of classical fairy tales can
also be discomforting. For instance, Angela Carter in *Bloody
Chamber*[68] and Tanith Lee in *Red as Blood*[69] have rewritten tales by
Charles Perrault, the Grimm Brothers, and other classicists to indicate
that the path to Utopia is filled with thorns. It is not by chance that
both authors project the image of blood in the title of their collections.
If women are to control their destinies, if there is to be a rearrangement

of gender in child rearing, then blood will indeed be shed and it will not be simply the blood of one sex. As Ellen Cronan Rose demonstrated,[70] most of Carter's stories disclose the machinations of male domination and depict how women discover their own sexuality and human dignity through intense struggles. Each one of Carter's revisions of traditional patriarchal schemes in *Bluebeard, Beauty and the Beast,*and *Little Red Riding Hood* prepares the way for an unusually original narrative entitled *Wolf Alice.*Here a woman as outsider learns about her uncanny powers and is able to aid another outsider, the duke as werewolf, both of whom stand in opposition to the violent hunters of so-called civilisation.

There is a haunting quality to all of Carter's tales which can also be traced in the narratives of Lee. Whereas Carter rewrote mainly French tales, Lee's focus is more on the Grimms' tales such as *Sleeping Beauty, Rapunzel, Cinderella,* and *Brother and Sister,* and the tales are intended to move chronologically toward the future where the gender arrangements become fully transformed in a science-fiction version of *Beauty and the Beast.* While each tale is poignant in its own way, the version of *Little Red Riding Hood* entitled *Wolfland* is especially significant since it picks up the thread of transformation in the figure of the wolf developed by Carter, Ursula LeGuin[71] and other writers. Here the grandmother is a werewolf called Anna the Matriarch, who initiates her granddaughter Lisel into the vicious ways of the male-dominated world by recalling the past and by showing her how she can retain power over her own life. Again, it is no coincidence that writers such as Carter and Lee insist that women seek contact with the 'wolfish' side of femininity, that is, their sensuality, to be proud of their animistic ties to nature. The celebration of the 'wolf' should not be misread as a celebration of 'brute power'. Rather it is more like the celebration of the witch in Meghan Collins's *The Green Woman*[72] and other feminist tales[73] which view the 'black magic' of witches as the true healing power of women and possibly of men. As we know, witches, werewolves, and wolves were once revered in archaic societies as the mediators between the wilderness and society. They provided contact with the *other* world, a sacred divine and forbidding world. And this contact was necessary if the civilised world were to rejuvenate itself. So, the witch, as in *The Green Woman,* lives on the outskirts of society like all witches and werewolves, on the edge of society and the wilderness, and represents the true healer of society, one who will be used and abused until 'civilised' peoples learn to live in harmony with nature again, which also means living in harmony with our own bodies. The rearrangement of bodies demands a political experiencing of a different mode of child rearing and sex roles in which exploitation of nature no longer takes place.

Just how difficult it is for many women to develop the consciousness necessary to bring about the rearrangement of sex roles in a liberating manner is the theme of Margaret Atwood's *Bluebeard's Egg* (1983). Set in contemporary Canada, Atwood's story is about a doctor's wife named Sally, who builds a mirage so that she cannot see to what extent her husband, a heart specialist, is a modern Bluebeard, someone who operates coldly on the hearts of others. Sally typifies the middle-aged, middle-class woman whose comfortable, but lonely life is filled with distractions such as university courses and part-time jobs. Most of all, she constantly deceives herself by imagining how superior she is to her supposedly dumb husband and how much she is in control of him. Her awakening at the end of the story is the possible first step toward liberation, and here Atwood cautiously leaves Sally's future open to indicate that she has a long way to go before she realises what it means to be alive as an egg, red and hot inside.

Almost all the fairy tales which I have discussed explore new possibilities for gender arrangement. The reversal of the traditional fairy-tale patterns is more than a simple formal matter. All the tales are linked to power, violence, social conditions, child rearing and sex roles. How we have arranged ourselves, our bodies and psyches, in society has been recorded and passed down through fairy tales for many centuries, and the contemporary feminist tales indicate that something radical is occurring in Western society to change our social and political relations. At this point, it is fruitless to ask whether the feminist fairy tales can have the impact they obviously seek because they have not been widely distributed, nor have they been in existence very long. What is more important to ask at this stage is why have they come into being and what do they reveal about social and psychological conditions in America and England. Here I want to draw mainly on two essays by Jessica Benjamin and Ilene Philipson [74] to make my concluding remarks.

III

Benjamin's starting point is a critique of Christopher Lasch's *The Culture of Narcissism,* in which he asserts that the Oedipus complex is no longer the prime organiser of psychic life or the prevalent cause of psychic disturbances in American society thus eroding a significant sense of the past and all forms of patriarchal authority. [75] In contrast, Benjamin questions 'whether the oedipal model, with its affirmative view of paternal authority as a *sine qua non* of autonomy, is an ideal or universal path to individuality'.[76] In fact, she perceives the oedipal paradigm as hindering the free development of gender identity.

> The oedipal father represents our peculiar form of individuality; his authority represents the only alternative to remaining undifferentiated; his freedom up till now is the only freedom. He teaches us the lesson that she who nurtures us does not free us, that he who frees us does not nuture us, but rules us. As we shall see later, this constellation is the basis for gender domination in our culture.[77]

For her purpose, Benjamin focuses on the dyadic experience of differentiation in the preoedipal phase of childhood and employs Heinz Kohut's work on narcissism and the restoration of the self to elaborate her critique of Lasch.

If the decisive years of developing gender identity and individuality occur in the preoedipal phase, then it is the responsiveness or non-responsiveness of the mother which influences the child's basic drives. The attachment to the mother and a mutual recognition of needs can encourage the independent development of a child. In the ideal constellation posited by object relations theory a child can learn to differentiate between self and other and appreciate the other's independent existence as an equivalent centre so long as the mother is independent and strong enough to respond to the child's needs in the preoedipal phase. It is this phase which is key to the future gender identity and autonomy of an individual. However, as Benjamin remarks, this phase is rarely completed in a successful way in American society because the father is internalised as an ideal of absolute autonomy, and the same can be said about English society.

> This form of false differentiation can ... be seen as institutionalized in the Oedipus complex and perpetuated in oedipal socialization. Man/father achieves absolute autonomy because woman/mother represents dependency. Individuality, then, is constituted by what is male, by the permanent assignment of man to the role of subject, through the father's assertion and insistence on complete independence. Originally it is through this denial of subjectivity to women that men lose the mirror of their subjectivity. Recognition occurs not through the love relationship but only in the competitive struggle with other men. Man's domination of woman has found expression in the oedipal relationships in which the split between male and female is reproduced in each generation.[78]

To combat false differentiation and male domination, Benjamin insists, like Dorothy Dinnerstein, Nancy Chodorow, and Meg Stacey

that the rearing of children in America and England must change, that
men must share equally in the parenting of a child, and that relations
between the sexes at the work place must become more democratic.
Here Benjamin qualifies her argument in a significant way:

> But this demand covers a far broader terrain than the rearing of children.
> It implies a challenge to the entire sexual division of labour as well as to
> the separation of domestic/personal and productive/public spheres in
> our society. And this separation has been absolutely intrinsic to the
> growth of capitalism. It is this separation that, on the societal level,
> embodies the split between activity and recognition — the former is
> depersonalized and the latter is privatized. To women as mothers is
> assigned the Promethean task of raising individuals who can har-
> moniously balance what society pulls asunder. The family must bear the
> entirety of the individual's needs for recognition, needs that our small,
> child-centered families tend to cultivate intensely. [79]

Of course, it is a well-known fact that the family has not been able
to bear this burden, but it is not due to narcissism or lack of paternal
authority. Rather, it is the bureaucratically transformed mode of
paternal control which prevents individualisation. The rise of the
narcissistic personality and narcissistic disturbances can be interpreted
as signs of revolt against the impersonalised forces of reason which
continue false differentiation and the patriarchal quest for
omnipotence. That is, if we regard the narcissistic phase in a more
positive manner, as a period of bonding with the mother and
differentiating from this bond, then the initial goals of the child are
love and self-esteem, a fundamental need for the other which can
engender self-definition if this need is requited. Since this narcissistic
need is rarely realised or fulfilled, it remains as a 'revolutionary spark',
so to speak, which can explode and engender either liberation or
destruction. Whereas Benjamin would agree with Lasch that Western
society is becoming more callous, indifferent, instrumentalised, and
commodified, she disagrees with his one-sided use of the term
narcissism to describe the pathology. The *healthy* narcissistic longing
leads in our society to a questioning of the pathology, which is the
obsession with control, possession and subordination of nature
maintained by a capitalist economy and ideology of competition and
rational domination. In this regard the crisis of the family and
authority has a healthy side to it: the challenge to the oedipal model
stems from our indomitable narcissistic longings that have given birth
to experiments with long-range goals of androgyny and parenting
based on mutuality, equality, and true differentiation.

Such goals are condemned by conservative forces in American and English society presently seeking to restore the authority of the oedipal family with a strong father in control of power. Ironically, by endeavouring to move backward, the social policies of conservatism are only aggravating the contradictions within the family and public sphere and are signing the family's death warrant. Benjamin's sober analysis of authority, autonomy and the New Narcissism points to the necessity of further loosening oedipal structures and paradoxically creating instability in the private and public spheres with the goal of creating a new form of 'stable' family life that depends on mutual recognition of parents and children and equal sharing in child rearing. Her critique is developed from another stimulating perspective by Ilene Philipson, who discusses the crisis in the family and the politics of mothering in a more historical manner. Like Benjamin, she deplores the fact that women have generally been obliged to assume the major role of child rearing, and she analyses the negative aspects of this division in the family primarily in the period following World War II to understand the contemporary crisis which consists of state intevention in the family, a soaring divorce rate, wife battering, violence against children, etc. She argues that

> the history of the post-World War II period is a history of family life in which mothers were compelled through ideological, social and economic forces to live for and through their children. Because their own needs for recognition, meaningful work, and relationship to other adults were so frequently denied, child-rearing assumed a significance in the minds and activities of women that was historically unprecedented.[80]

Like Alice Miller's[81] work in Europe, Philipson is concerned with the way mothers were and are forced to play the primary role in child rearing and unconsciously engender early narcissistic disturbances by using and misusing their children in a variety of ways. It is due to the failure to develop a consistent sense of self-worth in the preoedipal phase of a child which leads to narcissistic disturbances and social behaviour that are exploitative and parasitic. In the present framework of child rearing, the mother's faulty empathy gives rise to a false gender differentiation that in turn leads to heterosexual antagonisms.

> There are asymmetrical ways in which men and women come to deal with a particular situation experienced in early childhood that can result from women as mothers having sole responsibility for child-rearing in isolated, unstimulating and frequently emotionally barren nuclear families. In response to the erratic or faulty maternal empathy occasioned by such

socially constructed circumstances, sons are more likely to develop a need to be admired, a fear of dependence, and an exploitative stance toward relationships with women. Daughters, on the other hand, are more likely to have a profound need to identify with and/or live through other people, to have markedly deficient ego boundaries, and to be capable of feeling good about themselves (to have self-esteem) only when then are attached or 'fused' with some significant other. Both of these unconsciously based situations can make heterosexual relationships very difficult. [82]

Philipson maintains that the post-World War II family in America depended on sending women, who were already in the work force, back home into isolated and frustrating circumstances. This same development also occurred in England. And, despite some changes in the work force, this policy of keeping the woman at home has been maintained to the present. Thus, it is no wonder that the family is being torn asunder from inside and outside. 'By indirectly aiding in the production of individuals who are incapable of maintaining enduring relationships with others, the ideology and social policy that attempts to keep mothers at home through 'expert' advice or assertion, the lack of child care, and restrictive employment practices, undermines that which it explicitly tries to sustain.' [83]

Like Benjamin, Philipson argues for family ties based on emotional intimacy, reciprocity, and equality, and this demand is not to be understood as some kind of idealistic declaration of rights in behalf of children and women. The feminist critique of the family and child-rearing practices emanates from a careful examination of the mediations between psychic and social structures. The conclusions to be drawn from the critique lead to political struggles in both the private and public sphere which are still in the process of being waged as has been clearly documented in the significant books *Women's Oppression Today*[84] and *Powers of Desire*[85] concerning America and Europe. Power is at stake, and the control exercised by fathers as authority figures and mothers as their surrogate legislators will not be abandoned easily, especially when social policies do not encourage and increase the self-esteem of an individual.

The revisions, reforms, and rearrangements in family and social life proposed by feminists such as Benjamin and Philipson are rooted in the very experience of women and men who have already explored alternative life styles and family living. In some cases lesbians and homosexuals have created new forms of communal life just as single women and men with children and without children have conceived ways of going beyond the bourgeois nuclear family in opposition to traditional gender expectations. In both America and England, though it is perhaps wise not to exaggerate the profundity of the change, there has been a shift away from the male-centred society which has improved the experience of women qualitatively in their struggle to live by their own definitions — and the side effects for men have not been without their benefits, particularly those opposed to the dominant mannner in which gender is socially arranged. Such experience has been at the root of the feminist literary criticism and the feminist fairy tales which originated during the social upheavals of the late 1960s and 1970s.

If we compare the feminist literary criticism of fairy tales to the work of Benjamin, Philipson, and other psychologically oriented critics, particularly those who have been influenced by object relations theory, it becomes apparent that the literary criticism has *not* drawn sufficiently enough upon the studies of mothering and narcissism. With the exception of the work by Gilbert and Gubar, the literary critics have not explored the subtle connections between traditional tales which reveal *contradictions* of patriarchal societies and the oedipal model upon which numerous tales were based. Nor have the critics made much headway in examining the new feminist fairy tales as reflecting mass social changes since 1945 that have affected the psychic structure of individuals and the general socio-genetic development of American and English culture.

For instance, it would seem to me important to take into consideration such developments as the 'Cinderella Syndrome', in writing about the traditional tale and contemporary literary experiments. This syndrome[86] was first discussed in the *American Journal of Psychiatry* and concerns girls between the ages of nine and ten, who are living in foster homes and have been apparently neglected and maltreated by their foster parents. At least, they dress in tattered clothes and are dishevelled when the authorities find them. However, upon investigation, the authorities often discover that the girls do this purposely to attract attention to the fact that they are in danger of being mistreated and abused by their mothers, who often have the same case histories as their foster daughters. There are numerous questions which one could pose here. For example: Are the girls rejecting the Cinderella role by using it? Is the Cinderella role the only one they can use to draw attention to their miserable plight? What is at the base of conflict between the foster mother and the foster child that brings about a repetition? Why have psychologists called this syndrome the Cinderella syndrome? Are there contemporary fairy tales which have explored this syndrome to some degree?

In fact, there have been endeavours, particularly by Sexton and Broumas, to explore an aspect of the Cinderella syndrome, but the point that I want to stress here is that feminist literary criticism, though more oriented toward social conflicts than the general literary criticism of fairy tales, has failed to keep pace with the contemporary feminist fairy tales. In this regard, the significance of the feminist fairy tales lies in their Utopian function to criticise current shifts in psychic and social structures and to point the way toward new possibilities for individual development and social interaction.

If we take the feminist tales for children and adults as a whole and generalise about their aesthetic and ideological features, we can see how closely they are related to feminist demands for gender rearrangement and equality in the family and at the work place — demands central to the work of Dinnerstein, Chodorow, Benjamin, Philipson, Stacey, Barrett, and others. First of all, the structure of most of the feminist tales is based on the self-definition of a young woman. The female protagonist becomes aware of a task which she must complete in social interaction with others to define herself. Instead of pursuing power for the purpose of self-aggrandisement or omnipotence, the heroine rejects violence and seeks to establish her needs in harmony with the needs of others. Power will only be used in self-defence or to prevent violence. Though the heroine may be wronged, she will rarely seek revenge. Rather, the form of the fairy tale resembles the nurturance provided by a parent who does not project her/his wishes on a child but respects the need for the child to define her or his self. That is, the aesthetic form is derived from a sense of nurturing rather than competition. Thus, there is a reversal of the morphological structure of the traditional fairy tale based on power plays and the male protagonist's quest for power.

Though it is clear that the male characters in the feminist fairy tales have other interests than the heroines, they are not portrayed in a one-dimensional way. Generally, they are associated with false differentiation or with the oedipal phase which undermines healthy narcissistic longings. However, the male characters are also capable of learning and changing just as the traditional fairy-tale form itself reveals a capacity for transformation. The aesthetics of each individual tale depends on how each writer intends to explore the contradictions of gender antagonisms which are often linked to social problems. As we have seen, the writers who address adults as primary audience tend to focus more on the conflicts between men and women and stress solidarity among women as the necessary first step to overcome the instrumental rationality of a male word. Ultimately, self-trust and trust of other women are the prerequisites for the creation of a new society. From a heterosexual viewpoint, such a society can have its limitations because it tends to exclude or even eliminate men. On the other hand, the critique of male domination in the fairy tales is tempered by compassion and also reflects a certain degree of frustration with male intransigence. Thus, until the regulatory male norms are transformed, the sceptical attitude of feminist writers toward marriage, the family, and heterosexuality is certainly justified.

The writers who address young readers as primary audience are more optimistic about forming a new world with men just as long as mutual respect is achieved. It is only in a dialectical relationship with men that the heroine, often the symbol of a healthy narcissistic drive, defines herself and has an impact on society. Though some of the feminist fairy tales end in marriage, this is rarely the goal of these narratives. Feminist fairy tales experiment with the language, topoi, motifs, and characters of the traditional tales in pursuit of expression commensurate with alternative forms of child rearing that lead to encouraging the self-worth of an individual. To change the fairy tale for feminists is not simply an act of symbolical writing for self-gratification, but it is also a political act based on their experience with male brutality and general social violence which is the result of the legitimising interests of male control. Ultimately, to write a feminist fairy tale is to write with the hope that future generations will not adapt the atavistic forms and ideas found in traditional tales, but that they will arrange their lives in repsonse to non-sexist social conditions and the different options presented in the feminist fairy tales which are still seeking to prove their humanitarian value.

Notes

1 Cf. Bruno Bettelheim, *The Uses of Enchantment. The Meaning and Importance of Fairy Tales* (New York: Knopf, 1976).
2 Cf. Marie Luise von Franz, *Problems of the Feminine in Fairytales* (New York: Spring, 1972).
3 I have endeavoured to deal with the failings of both the Freudian and Jungian approaches in my book *Breaking the Magic Spell: Radical Theories of Folk and Fairy Tales* (London: Heinemann and New York: Methuen, 1979). in particular, see 'On the Use and Abuse of Fairy Tales with Children: Bruno Bettelheim's Moralistic Magic Wand', pp. 160–82 which is unfortunately often misconstrued as an attack on Freudianism. My point is simply that neither Freud nor Jung can be used in an uncritical manner when interpreting fairy tales.
4 I have mainly mentioned the key figures here. Since 1970 there has been a plethora of remarkable feminist studies. For a thorough account of these works, see Elizabeth Fox-Genovese, 'Placing Women's History in History', *New Left Review,*133 (May – June, 1982), pp. 5–29. See also Nannerl O. Keohane,

34   *Don't Bet on the Prince*

Michelle Z. Rosaldo, and Barbara C. Gelpi, eds.,*Feminist Theory. A Critique of Ideology,* (Chicago: University of Chicago Press, 1982) and Ann Snitow, Christine Stansell, and Sharon Thompson, *Powers of Desire. The Politics of Sexuality* (New York: Monthly Review Press, 1983).
5   *Contemporary Feminist Thought* (Boston: G.K. Hall, 1983).
6   *Ibid.,* p. xii.
7   *Ibid.,* p. xii. See also pp. 136–45.
8   See Michele Barrett, *Women's Oppression Today* (London: Verso, 1980) as well as the constructive and elaborate critique of the book by Johanna Brenner and Maria Ramas, 'Rethinking Women's Oppression,' *New Left Review,* **144** (1984), 33–71.
9   *Sexual Arrangements and Human Malaise* (New York: Harper & Row, 1977) p. 9. See also Nancy Chodorow, *The Reproduction of Mothering* (Berkeley: University of California Press, 1978).
10 *College English,*34 (1972), 383–95.
11 New York: Dutton, pp.32–3.
12 *Interracial Books for Children,*6 (1975), 1–3.
13 See Alan Dundes, ed., *Cinderella. A Casebook,* New York: Wildman Press, 1983.
14 In *Woman and Folklore,* ed. Claire R. Farrer (Austin: University of Texas Press, 1975), pp. 42–5.
15 Most of this work is being conducted outside America. See Heide Göttner-Abendroth, *Die Göttin und ihr Heros* (Munich: Frauenoffensive, 1980), Yvonne Verdier, *Facons de dire, facons de faire. La laveuse, la couturière, la cuisinière* (Paris: Gallimard, 1979), and Bernadette Bricout, 'L'aiguille et l'épingle. Oralité et écriture au XVIIème siècle', *Bibliotheque blue nel seicento o Della letteratura per il populo,* **4** (1981), 45–58. Cf. my book *The Trials and Tribulations of Little Red Riding Hood* (London: Heinemann and South Hadley: Bergin & Garvey, 1983).
16 In *Literature and Learning,* eds. Elizabeth Gugeon and Peter Walden (London: Open University Press, 1978), pp. 42–58.
17 *Children's Literature in Education,* **8** (1977), 21–9. This essay has also been reprinted in Alan Dundes, ed., *Cinderella: A Casebook* (New York: Wildman, 1983), pp. 294–306.
18 Garden City: Doubleday, 1979.
19 New York: Pocket Books, 1981.
20 *Ibid.,* p. 21.
21 *The Woman Writer and the Nineteenth-Century Imagination* (New Haven: Yale University Press, 1979).
22 *Ibid.,* p. 42.
23 ' "Fairy-born and human-bred": Jane Eyre's Education in Romance', in *The Voyage In,* eds. Elizabeth Abel, Marianne Hirsch, and Elizabeth Langland (Hanover: University Press of New England, 1983), p. 89.
24 By the end of the nineteenth century there were numerous writers such as Isabelle Anne Ritchie (Miss Thackeray), Maria Craik, Mrs Molesworth, Mary De Morgan, and Evelyn Sharp, who incorporated fairy tales in their works or wrote their own from an unusual perspective.
25 Unpublished manuscript which was held as a talk on 27 December, 1980 at the Modern Langugage Association Meeting in San Francisco.
26 *Women's Studies,* 6 (1979), 248.
27 *Children's Literature Association Quarterly,* 7 (Summer, 1982), 18.
28 *Ibid.,* p. 19.
29 *Ibid.,* p. 20.
30 In *The Voyage In: Fictions of Female Development,* eds. Elizabeth Abel, Marianne Hirsch, and Elizabeth Langland (Hanover: University Press of New England, 1983), pp. 209–27.

31 Berkeley, California; Rainbow Press, 1974. The sequel was published the following year.
32 In *Stories for Free Children,* ed. Letty Cottin Pogrebin (New York: McGraw-Hill, 1982), pp. 43–6.
33 In *Princess Hynchatti and Some Other Surprises* (New York; Farrar, Straus & Girous, 1973).
34 In *Gudgekin the Thistle Girl and Other Tales* (New York: Knopf, 1976).
35 In *Dr. Gardner's Fairy Tales for Today's Children* (Englewood Cliffs: Prentice-Hall, 1974).
36 In *Revolting Rhymes* (London: Jonathan Cape, 1982).
37 In *If I Were in Charge of the World* (New York: Atheneum, 1982).
38 New York: Knopf, 1975.
39 New York: Atheneum, 1975.
40 New York: Greenwillow Books, 1983.
41 Scarsdale, New York: Banbury, 1976.
42 Chapel Hill, North Carolina: Lollipop Power, 1977.
43 In *Free To Be ... You and Me.,* eds. Carole Hart, Letty Cottin Pogrebin, Mary Rodgers, and Marlo Thomas (New York: McGraw-Hill, 1974), pp. 128–35.
44 See *The Practical Princess and other Liberating Tales* (New York: Parents Magazine Press, 1978), pp. 63–80.
45 New York: Simon and Schuster, 1970.
46 In *Stories for Free Children,* ed. Letty Cottin Pogrebin (New York: McGraw-Hill, 1982), pp. 17–20.
47 *Ibid.,* pp. 49–52.
48 *Kittatinny: A Tale of Magic* (New York: Daughters Press, 1978), pp. 43–51.
49 New York: Crowell, 1977.
50 *The Moon Ribbon and Other Tales* (New York: Crowell, 1976).
51 In *The Girl Who Cried Flowers and Other Tales* (New York: Crowell, 1974).
52 In *Dream Weaver* (New York: Collins, 1979).
53 See *The Prince and the Swineherd* and *Red Riding Hood* (Liverpool: Fairy Story Collective, 1972) and 'Snow White' in *Spare Rib* (October 1976), 44–6.
54 *Transformations* (Boston: Houghton Mifflin, 1971), pp. 93–4.
55 *Ibid.,* p. 94.
56 *Ibid.,* p. 95.
57 *Ibid.,* p. 98.
58 *Ibid.,* p. 112.
59 New Haven: Yale University Press, 1977.
60 *Ibid.,* p. 57.
61 *Ibid.,* pp. 57–8.
62 *Ibid.,* p. 59.
63 *Ibid.,* pp. 65–6.
64 See Sara Henderson Hay, *Story Hour* (Fayetteville: University of Arkansas Press, 1982); Helen Chasin, *Coming Close and Other Poems* (New Haven: Yale University Press, 1968); Judith Rechter, 'Fay Wray to the King', in *No More Masks! An Anthology of Poems by Women,* eds. Florence House and Ellen Bass (Garden City: Doubleday, 1973), pp. 257–8; Kathleen Spivack, *Flying Inland* (Garden City: Doubleday, 1974).
65 New York: 1978.
66 New York: 1981.
67 New York: Knopf, 1977.
68 London: Gollancz, 1979.
69 *Or Tales from the Sisters Grimmer* (New York: Daw Books, 1983).
70 'Through the Looking Glass', pp. 222–7.

71 See LeGuin's 'The Wife's Story' in *Changes,* eds. Ian Watson and Michael Bishop (New York: Ace, 1983), pp. 29–34.
72 In *Fine Lines. The Best of Ms. Fiction,* ed. Ruth Sullivan (New York: Scribner, 1982), 121–39.
73 See Susan M. Shwartz, ed., *Hecate's Cauldron* (New York: Ace, 1982).
74 Benjamin, 'The Oedipal Riddle: Authority, Autonomy, and New Narcissism,' in *The Problem of Authority in America,* eds. John P. Diggins and Mark E. Kann (Philadelphia: Temple University Press, 1981), pp. 195–224; Philipson, 'Heterosexual Antagonisms and the Politics of Mothering', *Socialist Review,* 12 (November-December, 1982), 55–77.
75 See Christopher Lasch, *The Culture of Narcissism* (New York: Norton, 1979), especially the first two chapters and the last entitled 'Paternalism without Father'.
76 Benjamin, 'The Oedipal Riddle', pp. 198–9.
77 *Ibid.,* p. 202.
78 *Ibid.,* p. 208.
79 *Ibid.,* pp. 211–12.
80 Philipson, 'Heterosexual Antagonisms and the Problem of Mothering', p. 61.
81 See *The Drama of the Gifted Child* (New York: Basic Books, 1981) and *Am Anfang war Erziehung* (Frankfurt am Main: Suhrkamp, 1983).
82 Philipson, 'Heterosexual Antagonisms and the Problem of Mothering', p. 71.
83 *Ibid.,* p. 74.
84 See Michele Barrett, *Women's Oppression Today* (London: Verso, 1980).
85 See Ann Snitow, Christine Stansell, and Sharon Thompson, eds., *Powers of Desire. The Politics of Sexuality* (New York: Monthly Review Press, 1983).
86 See Jean Godwin, Catherine G. Cauthorne and Richard T. Rada, 'Cinderella Syndrome: Children Who Simulate Neglect', *American Journal of Psychiatry,* 137 (October, 1980), 1223–5.

I Feminist Fairy Tales for Young (and Old) Readers

1 The Princess Who Stood On Her Own Two Feet

Jeanne Desy

A long time ago in a kingdom by the sea there lived a Princess tall and bright as a sunflower. Whatever the royal tutors taught her, she mastered with ease. She could tally the royal treasure on her gold and silver abacus, and charm even the Wizard with her enchantments. In short, she had every gift but love, for in all the kingdom there was no suitable match for her.

So she played the zither and designed great tapestries and trained her finches to eat from her hand, for she had a way with animals.

Yet she was bored and lonely, as princesses often are, being a breed apart. Seeing her situation, the Wizard came to see her one day, a strange and elegant creature trotting along at his heels. The Princess clapped her hands in delight, for she loved anything odd.

'What is it?' she cried. The Wizard grimaced.

'Who knows?' he said. 'It's supposed to be something enchanted. I got it through the mail.' The Royal Wizard looked a little shamefaced. It was not the first time he had been taken in by mail-order promises.

'It won't turn into anything else,' he explained. 'It just is what it is.'

'But what is it?'

'They call it a dog,' the Wizard said. 'An Afghan hound.'

Since in this kingdom dogs had never been seen, the Princess was quite delighted. When she brushed the silky, golden dog, she secretly thought it looked rather like her, with its thin aristocratic features and delicate nose. Actually, the Wizard had thought so too, but you can never be sure what a Princess will take as an insult. In any case, the Princess and the dog became constant companions. It followed her on her morning rides and slept at the foot of her bed every night. When she talked, it watched her so attentively that she often thought it understood.

Still, a dog is a dog and not a Prince, and the Princess longed to marry. Often she sat at her window in the high tower, her embroidery idle in her aristocratic hands, and gazed down the road, dreaming of a handsome prince in flashing armor.

One summer day word came that the Prince of a neighboring kingdom wished to discuss an alliance. The royal maids confided that he was dashing and princely, and the Princess's heart leaped with joy. Eagerly she awaited the betrothal feast.

When the Prince entered the great banquet hall and cast his dark, romantic gaze upon her, the Princess nearly swooned in her chair. She sat shyly while everyone toasted the Prince and the golden Princess and peace forever between the two kingdoms. The dog watched quietly from its accustomed place at her feet.

After many leisurely courses, the great feast ended, and the troubadors began to play. The Prince and Princess listened to the lyrical songs honoring their love, and she let him hold her hand under the table — an act noted with triumphant approval by the King and Queen. The Princess was filled with happiness that such a man would love her.

At last the troubadors swung into a waltz, and it was time for the Prince and Princess to lead the dance. Her heart bursting with joy, the Princess rose to take his arm. But as she rose to her feet, a great shadow darkened the Prince's face, and he stared at her as if stricken.

'What is it?' she cried. But the Prince would not speak, and dashed from the hall.

For a long time the Princess studied her mirror that night, wondering what the Prince had seen.

'If you could talk,' she said to the dog, 'you could tell me, I know it,' for the animal's eyes were bright and intelligent. 'What did I do wrong?'

The dog, in fact, *could* talk; it's just that nobody had ever asked him anything before.

'You didn't do anything,' he said. 'It's your height.'

'My height?' The Princess was more astonished by what the dog said than the fact that he said it. As an amateur wizard, she had heard of talking animals.

'But I am a Princess!' she wailed. 'I'm supposed to be tall.' For in her kingdom, all the royal family was tall, and the Princess the tallest of all, and she had thought that was the way things were supposed to be.

The dog privately marveled at her naîvete, and explained that in the world outside this kingdom, men liked to be taller than their wives.

'But why?' asked the Princess.

The dog struggled to explain. 'They think if they're not, they can't . . . train falcons as well. Or something.' Now that he thought for a moment, he didn't know either.

'It's my legs,' she muttered. 'When we were sitting down, everything was fine. It's these darn long legs.' The dog cocked his head. He thought she had nice legs, and he was in a position to know. The Princess strode to the bell pull and summoned the Wizard.

'Okay,' she said when he arrived. 'I know the truth.'

'Who told you?' the Wizard asked. Somebody was in for a bit of a stay in irons.

'The dog.' The Wizard sighed. In fact, he had *known* the creature was enchanted.

'It's my height.' she continued bitterly. The Wizard nodded. 'I want you to make me shorter,' she said. 'A foot shorter, at least. Now.'

Using all his persuasive powers, which were considerable, the Wizard explained to her that he could not possibly do that. 'Fatter,' he said, 'yes. Thinner, yes. Turn you into a raven, maybe. But shorter, no. I cannot make you even an inch shorter, my dear.'

The Princess was inconsolable.

Seeing her sorrow, the King sent his emissary to the neighboring kingdom with some very attractive offers. Finally the neighboring King and Queen agreed to persuade the Prince to give the match another chance. The Queen spoke to him grandly of chivalry and honor, and the King spoke to him privately of certain gambling debts.

In due course he arrived at the castle, where the Princess had taken to her canopied bed. They had a lovely romantic talk, with him at the bedside holding her hand, and the nobility, of course, standing respectfully at the foot of the bed, as such things are done. In truth, he found the Princess quite lovely when she was sitting or lying down.

'Come on,' he said, 'let's get some fresh air. We'll go riding.' He had in mind a certain dragon in these parts, against whom he might display his talents. And so the Prince strode and the Princess slouched to the stables.

On a horse, as in a chair, the Princess was no taller than he, so they cantered along happily. Seeing an attractive hedge ahead, the Prince urged his mount into a gallop and sailed the hedge proudly. He turned to see her appreciation, only to find the Princess doing the same, and holding her seat quite gracefully. Truthfully, he felt like leaving again.

'Didn't anyone ever tell you,' he said coldly, 'that ladies ride side-saddle?' Well, of course they had, but the Princess always thought that that was a silly, unbalanced position that took all the fun out of riding.

Now she apologized prettily and swung her legs around.

At length the Prince hurdled another fence, even more dashingly than before, and turned to see the Princess attempting to do the same thing. But riding sidesaddle, she did not have a sure seat, and tumbled to the ground.

'Girls shouldn't jump,' the Prince told the air, as he helped her up. But on her feet, she was again a head taller than he. She saw the dim displeasure in his eyes. Then, with truly royal impulsiveness, she made a decision to sacrifice for love. She crumpled to the ground.

'My legs,' she said, 'I can't stand.' The Prince swelled with pride, picked her up, and carried her back to the castle.

There the Royal Physician, the Wizard, and even the Witch examined her legs, with the nobility in attendance.

She was given infusions and teas and herbs and packs, but nothing worked. She simply could not stand.

'When there is nothing wrong but foolishness,' the Witch muttered, 'you can't fix it.' And she left. She had no patience with lovesickness.

The prince lingered on day after day, as a guest of the King, while the Princess grew well and happy, although she did not stand. Carried to the window seat, she would sit happily and watch him stride around the room, describing his chivalric exploits, and she would sigh with contentment. The loss of the use of her legs seemed a small price to pay for such a man. The dog observed her without comment.

Since she was often idle now, the Princess practised witty and amusing sayings. She meant only to please the Prince, but he turned on her after one particularly subtle and clever remark and said sharply, 'Haven't you ever heard that women should be seen and not heard?'

The Princess sank into thought. She didn't quite understand the saying, but she sensed that it was somehow like her tallness. For just as he preferred her sitting, not standing, he seemed more pleased when she listened, and more remote when she talked.

The next day when the Prince came to her chambers he found the royal entourage gathered around her bed.

'What's the matter?' he asked. They told him the Princess could not speak, not for herbs or infusions or magic spells. And the Prince sat by the bed and held her hand and spoke to her gently, and she was given a slate to write her desires. All went well for several days. But the Prince was not a great reader, so she put the slate aside, and made conversation with only her eyes and her smile. The Prince told her daily how lovely she was, and then he occupied himself with princely pastimes. Much of the time her only companion was the dog.

One morning the Prince came to see her before he went hunting. His eyes fixed with disgust on the dog, who lay comfortably over her feet.

'Really,' the Prince said, 'sometimes you surprise me.' He went to strike the dog from the bed, but the Princess stayed his hand. He looked at her in amazement.

That night the Princess lay sleepless in the moonlight, and at last, hearing the castle fall silent, and knowing that nobody would catch her talking, she whispered to the dog. 'I don't know what I would do without you.'

'You'd better get used to the idea,' said the dog. 'The Prince doesn't like me.'

'He will never take you away.' The Princess hugged the dog fiercely. The dog looked at her skeptically and gave a little doggy cough.

'He took everything else away,' he said.

'No,' she said. 'I did that. I made myself . . . someone he could love.'

'I love you, too,' the dog said.

'Of course you do.' She scratched his ears.

'And,' said the dog, 'I loved you *then*.' The Princess lay a long time thinking before she finally slept.

The next morning the Prince strode in more handsome and dashing than ever, although oddly enough, the Princess could have sworn he was getting shorter.

As he leaned down to kiss her, his smile disappeared. She frowned a question at him: What's the matter?

'You've still *got* that thing,' he said, pointing to the dog. The Princess grabbed her slate.

'He is all I have,' she wrote hastily. The lady-in-waiting read it to the Prince.

'You have *me,*' the Prince said, his chin high, 'I believe you love that smelly thing more than you love me.' He strode (he never walked any other way) to the door.

'I *was* going to talk to you about the wedding feast,' he said, as he left. 'But now, never mind!'

The Princess wept softly and copiously, and the dog licked a tear from her trembling hand.

'What does he *want* ?' she asked the dog.

'Roast dog for the wedding feast, I'd imagine,' he said. The Princess cried out in horror.

'Oh, not literally,' the dog said. 'But it follows.' And he would say no more.

At last the Princess called the Wizard and wrote on her slate what the dog had said. The Wizard sighed. How awkward. Talking animals were always so frank. He hemmed and hawed until the Princess glared to remind him that Wizards are paid by royalty to advise and interpret — not to sigh.

'All right,' he said at last. 'Things always come in threes. Everything.'

The Princess looked at him blankly.

'Wishes always come in threes,' the Wizard said. 'And sacrifices, too. So far, you've given up walking. You've given up speech. One more to go.'

'Why does he want me to give up the dog?' she wrote.

The Wizard looked sorrowfully at her from under his bushy brows. 'Because you love it,' he said.

'But that takes nothing from him!' she scribbled. The Wizard smiled, thinking that the same thing could be said of her height and her speech.

'If you could convince him of that, my dear,' he said, 'you would be more skilled in magic than I.'

When he was gone, the Princess reached for her cards and cast her own fortune, muttering to herself. The dog watched bright-eyed as the wands of growth were covered by the swords of discord. When the ace of swords fell, the Princess gasped. The dog put a delicate paw on the card.

'You poor dumb thing,' she said, for it is hard to think of a dog any other way, whether it talks or not.'You don't understand. That is death on a horse. Death to my love.'

'His banner is the white rose,' said the dog, looking at the card intently. 'He is also rebirth.' They heard the Prince's striding step outside the door.

'Quick,' the Princess said. 'Under the bed.' The dog's large brown eyes spoke volumes, but he flattened and slid under the bed. And the Prince's visit was surprisingly jolly.

After some time the Prince looked around with imitation surprise. 'Something's missing,' he said. 'I know. It's that creature of yours. You know, I think I was allergic to it. I feel much better now that it's gone.' He thumped his chest to show how clear it was. The Princess grabbed her slate, wrote furiously, and thrust it at the Royal Physician.

' "He loved me," ' the Royal Physician read aloud.

'Not as I love you,' the Prince said earnestly. The Princess gestured impatiently for the reading to continue.

'That's not all she wrote,' the Royal Physician said. 'It says, "The dog loved me *then*." '

When everyone was gone, the dog crept out to find the Princess installed at her window seat thinking furiously.

'If I am to keep you,' she said to him, 'we shall have to disenchant you with the spells book.' The dog smiled, or seemed to. She cast dice, she drew pentagrams, she crossed rowan twigs and chanted every incantation in the index. Nothing worked. The dog was still a dog, silken, elegant, and seeming to grin in the heat. Finally the Princess clapped shut the last book and sank back.

'Nothing works,' she said. 'I don't know what we shall do. Meanwhile, when you hear anyone coming, hide in the cupboard or beneath the bed.'

'You're putting off the inevitable,' the dog told her sadly.

'I'll think of something,' she said. But she couldn't.

At last it was the eve of her wedding day. While the rest of the castle buzzed with excitement, the Princess sat mute in her despair.

'I can't give you up and I can't take you!' she wailed. And the dog saw that she was feeling grave pain.

'Sometimes,' the dog said, looking beyond her shoulder, 'sometimes one must give up everything for love.' The Princess's lip trembled and she looked away.

'What will I *do*?' she cried again. The dog did not answer. She turned toward him and then fell to her knees in shock, for the dog lay motionless on the floor. For hours she sat weeping at his side, holding his lifeless paw.

At last she went to her cupboard and took out her wedding dress, which was of the softest whitest velvet. She wrapped the dog in its folds and picked him up gently.

Through the halls of the castle the Princess walked, and the nobility and chambermaids and royal bishops stopped in their busy preparations to watch her, for the Princess had not walked now for many months. To their astonished faces she said, 'I am going to bury the one who really loved me.'

On the steps of the castle she met the Prince, who was just dismounting and calling out jovial hearty things to his companions. So surprised was he to see her walking that he lost his footing and tumbled to the ground. She paused briefly to look down at him, held the dog closer to her body, and walked on. The Prince got up and went after her.

'What's going on here?' he asked. 'What are you doing? Isn't that your wedding dress?' She turned so he could see the dog's head where it nestled in her left arm.

'I thought you got rid of that thing weeks ago,' the Prince said. It was difficult for him to find an emotion suitable to this complex situation. He tried feeling hurt.

'What you call "this thing",' the Princess said, 'died to spare me pain. And I intend to bury him with honor.' The Prince only half-heard her, for he was struck by another realization.

'You're talking!'

'Yes.' She smiled.

Looking down at him, she said, 'I'm talking. The better to tell you good-bye. So good-bye.' And off she went. She could stride too, when she wanted to.

'Well, my dear,' the Queen said that night, when the Princess appeared in the throne room. 'You've made a proper mess of things. We have alliances to think of. I'm sure you're aware of the very complex negotiations you have quite ruined. Your duty as a Princess...'

'It is not necessarily my duty to sacrifice everything,' the Princess interrupted. 'And I have other duties: a Princess says what she thinks. A Princess stands on her own two feet. A Princess stands tall. And she does not betray those who love her.' Her royal parents did not reply. But they seemed to ponder her words.

The Princess lay awake that night for many hours. She was tired from the day's exertions, for she let no other hand dig the dog's grave or fill it but she could not sleep without slippers and stole through the silent castle ot the gravesite. There she mused upon love, and what she had given for love, and what the dog had given.

'How foolish we are,' she said aloud. 'For a stupid Prince I let my wise companion die.'

At last the Princess dried her tears on her hem and stirred herself to examine the white rose she had planted on the dog's grave. She watered it again with her little silver watering can. It looked as though it would live.

As she slipped to the castle through the ornamental gardens, she heard a quiet jingling near the gate. On the bridge there was silhouetted a horseman. The delicate silver bridles of his horse sparkled in the moonlight. She could see by his crested shield that he must be nobility, perhaps a Prince. Well, there was many an empty room in the castle tonight, with the wedding feast canceled and all the guests gone home. She approached the rider.

He was quite an attractive fellow, thin with silky golden hair. She smiled up at him, admiring his lean and elegant hand on the reins.

'Where have you come from?' she asked.

He looked puzzled. 'Truthfully,' he replied. 'I can't remember. I know I have traveled a long dark road, but that is all I know.' He gave an odd little cough.

The Princess looked past him, where the road was bright in the moonlight.

'I see,' she said slowly. 'And what is your banner?' For she could not quite decipher it waving above him. He moved it down. A white rose on a black background.

'Death,' she breathed.

'No, no.' he said, smiling. 'Rebirth. And for that, a death is sometimes necessary.' He dismounted and bent to kiss the Princess's hand. She breathed a tiny prayer as he straightened up, but it was not answered. Indeed, he was several inches shorter than she was. The Princess straightened her spine.

'It is a pleasure to look up to a proud and beautiful lady,' the young Prince said, and his large brown eyes spoke volumes. The Princess blushed.

'We're still holding hands,' she said foolishly. The elegant Prince smiled, and kept hold of her hand, and they went toward the castle.

In the shadows the Wizard watched them benignly until they were out of sight. Then he turned to the fluffy black cat at his feet.

'Well, Mirabelle,' he said. 'One never knows the ways of enchantments.' The cat left off from licking one shoulder for a moment and regarded him, but said nothing. Mirabelle never had been much of a conversationalist.

'Ah, well.' the Wizard said. 'I gather from all this — I shall make a note — that sometimes one must sacrifice for love.'

Mirabelle looked intently at the Wizard. 'On the other hand,' the cat said at last, 'sometimes one must *refuse* to sacrifice.'

'Worth saying.' said the Wizard approvingly. 'And true. True.' And then, because he had a weakness for talking animals, he took Mirabelle home for an extra dish of cream.

2 Prince Amilec

Tanith Lee

In a palace by the sea lived a beautiful princess. She had eyes as green as apples, long red hair, and a very nasty temper indeed.

One day, her father said that she should think about getting married. Lots of princes had thought they would like to marry her in the past, but once she had flown into a rage with them a few times, they changed their minds and went off to find someone a bit quieter.

'I don't want to get married,' said the princess 'And I won't!' And she picked up a china dog to throw at her father.

He dodged out of the room, just in time.

'I'm getting too old for all this running about,' he said to his secretary. 'I really must get her married off, and then her husband can deal with her.'

'Don't worry,' said the secretary. 'I'll get some messengers to ride around the other kingdoms with the princess's portrait. A lot of people will be interested, and they won't know till they get here what she's like.'

Now, in one of the kingdoms that the messenger visited there lived a handsome young prince named Amilec. When the portrait was brought in, the prince immediately fell in love with the princess in the picture. No sooner were the messengers out of the room than Amilec grabbed his cloak and was riding full speed up the road toward the sea.

When he reached the palace, he found a good many suitors there already. They were waiting for a glimpse of the princess, who was supposed to appear at one of the palace windows and graciously wave to them.

Suddenly a window shot up and a red head appeared.

'Go *away*!' bawled the princess, and went in again.

'Ha, ha!' cried the king, who was leaning anxiously out of another window. 'She will have her little joke!'

The suitors laughed uneasily, and the butler came and showed them to their rooms.

'My dear,' said the king cautiously, 'couldn't you just try? All those nice young men have come such a long way.'

'Don't worry,' said the princess. 'I'll soon get rid of them. I'm going to set them such impossible tasks that they'll give up and go home inside a week.'

Sure enough, when all the suitors had gathered in the dining room, the princess's page came down, asked for silence, and took out a scroll.

'The princess,' read the page, 'wishes to inform you that she has thrown her ruby bracelet out the tower window into the sea. Before any of you think of asking for her hand, you must dive down and get it back for her.'

None of the suitors felt like eating their dinner after that. Some went out immediately and began to pack their bags; others flew into a rage and banged their fists on the table. Prince Amilec put his head in his hands and groaned. The page felt rather sorry for Amilec, who was the only suitor who had not been rude to him.

'If I were you, I should just go home and forget about the princess,' whispered the page. 'She's frightful!'

'I can't,' said Amilec sorrowfully. 'I shall have to look for her bracelet, even if I drown in the attempt.'

'I'll tell you what, then,' said the page. 'Farther up the beach lives a witch in a cave. Nobody's ever seen her, but she's supposed to be very clever. She might help you, if you asked her nicely.'

Prince Amilec wasn't too keen on visiting a witch, but he thanked the page, and went and thought about it. Eventually he decided that it was a lot safer than diving into the sea on his own.

When the palace clock struck twelve, he went quietly out and down the path to the beach. At last he came to a cave with a big front door set in it, covered over by a lot of seaweed. Prince Amilec knocked, feeling rather nervous.

'The witch will probably be horribly ugly, with three eyes and a wart on the end of her nose,' Amilec said to himself. 'But I mustn't let her see that I'm not completely used to people with three eyes and warts, or she may be offended and not help me.'

Just then the door opened, and there stood a very pretty girl holding a lantern.

'Can I help you?' asked the girl.

'Oh—er, yes. I was looking for the witch,' said Amilec, brushing off the seaweed that had fallen on him when the door opened.

'I *am* the witch,' said the girl. 'Do come in.'

She took him down a long cave-corridor, and at the end was another door. The witch hung the lantern on a hook in the wall, opened the door, and led the prince into a small cozy room, where a fire was burning on the hearth.

'I thought,' said Amilec, 'that witches were old and ugly, and lived in ruined castles full of bats.'

'Well,' said the girl, 'I do have a bat.' She pointed and Amilec saw a furry shape with folded wings hanging upside down in a armchair on the other side of the fire.

'Do sit down,' said the witch. 'I'll just hang Basil on the mantelpiece.' Which she did. 'Now tell me what the trouble is.'

So Amilec told her about the red-haired princess, and how he wanted very much to marry her, and about the ruby bracelet that he had to try to find.

'I don't mind helping you,' said the witch when he had finished, 'but the princess will never marry you, you know. And she has a dreadful temper. I can hear her down here sometimes when she starts shouting.'

Prince Amilec sighed and said he thought that might be the case but he just couldn't help being in love with the princess, however awful she was.

'All right,' said the witch. 'Leave everything to me. You just stay here and look after Basil, and see that the fire doesn't go out.'

So saying, she left the room, and a minute later Amilec heard the cave door shout. He couldn't help being curious and as there was a small round window in the cave wall, he looked out of it to see where she had gone. The witch was walking along some rocks that ran into the sea. Suddenly she changed into a dolphin, leaped forward, and vanished in the water.

Amilec tried not to be too surprised. He put some more wood on the fire and hung Basil a bit farther along the mantelpiece, so the smoke wouldn't get into his fur.

Not long after, the cave door opened and the witch, no longer looking a bit like a dolphin, came back into the room. She held a ruby bracelet in her hand.

'Sorry I was so long,' said the witch, 'but a sea serpent had got his tail stuck in it, and I had to pull him out.'

'How can I ever thank you?' gasped Amilec.

'Don't give it a second thought,' said the witch. 'I haven't had an excuse to change into a dolphin for ages.'

Next morning, the princess called all the suitors into a big room and asked them if they had had any luck. Of course, none of them had, although some of them had been swimming about since dawn, and most of them had caught bad colds.

Just then Amilec came in. He walked up to the princess, bowed, and handed her the ruby bracelet.

'Oh!' screamed the princess. 'This can't be the right one,' she added hysterically. However, the king, who had given it to her in the first place, came up and had a look, and declared that it was.

'Well done, my boy,' he added to Amilec.

'Yes, well done,' said the princess quickly. 'Now that you've succeeded with the first task, you can go on and do the second. Everybody else is disqualified.'

So the other suitors snuffled and coughed and complained their way out, and went home.

'The second task,' said the princess, smiling a nasty smile, 'is to find my golden girdle. I have tied it to the arrow of one of the bowmen, and when he fires, goodness only knows where it will end up.'

'Perhaps I could tell him where to aim,' whispered the king's secretary.

'Certainly not!' cried the princess, who had overheard, and she went to the window and gave a signal to the bowman.

When Prince Amilec went out to look for the golden girdle, he found that there was a forest growing at the back of the palace, full of thick fern. He searched till dusk, and then he sat down on a stone, because he was worn out.

'I'll never find it,' he said. 'I might just as well go home right now.'

Just then a figure came through the forest toward him, carrying a lantern and a bat.

'Hello,' said the witch. 'I've just been taking Basil for a fly. You look unhappy. Is it that princess again?'

'I'm afraid it is,' said Amilec.

'I thought so,' said the witch. 'What does she want now?'

Amilec told her about the golden girdle which had been fired into the forest.

'Oh, that's easy,' said the witch. 'Hold Basil, and I'll see what I can do.'

So Amilec sat on the stone with the lantern and Basil. One by one the stars came out, and the sea sounded very drowsy, as if it were going to sleep. Prince Amilec closed his eyes and dreamed that he had won the hand of the red-haired princess and she had just thrown her crown at him. He woke up with a start and found an owl sitting on the ground, a golden girdle in its beak.

'Here we are,' said the owl, changing back into the witch. 'Sorry I was so long, but some doves had got it tangled up in their nest and I had to get it out and put the nest back for them afterward.'

'How can I ever repay you?' implored Amilec.

'Come and have a cup of tea with me,' said the witch. So he did.

The next morning the princess called him into the big room and sneered at him.

'There's no need to say anything,' said the princess. 'Just pack your things and go home. Of course, if you'd care to send me a golden girdle to replace the old one, I might give you a kiss.'

Prince Amilec took out the girdle and handed it to her. The princess screamed, 'I don't believe it! It's not mine—it isn't!'

'Oh, yes, it is,' said the king. 'Well done, my boy.'

'Yes,' said the princess. 'Well done. You can now go on to the third task.'

Amilec paled.

'You see this pearl necklace,' said the princess with a ghastly smile. 'On it are one hundred and fifty pearls.'

The king realized what was coming and tried to stop her, but it was too late. The princess tugged on the silver chain and it broke, and the pearls flew everywhere.

'I want you to find them all, and return them to me in one hour's time.' And she glided out.

'We can help,' cried the king and the secretary.

'No, you can't!' cried the princess, rushing back. The king and the secretary hurried away.

'Now what am I to do?' Amilec wondered. He looked out the window, and who should be walking along the seashore below the palace, gathering seaweed in a basket, but the witch. The prince leaped downstairs and out through the garden gate and along the beach.

'Hello!' said Amilec. 'How's Basil?'

'Basil's very well, thank you,' replied the witch. 'How are you getting on with the princess?'

Amilec sighed deeply and told her about the pearl necklace.

'Wouldn't it be simpler to forget all about it and go home?' asked the witch.

'I'm afraid I love the princess much too much to do that,' murmured Amilec.

'All right,' said the witch. 'You collect me some seaweed in the basket, and I'll go and do what I can.' And she changed into a mouse and ran through the palace gate.

About half an hour later, the witch came back and handed Amilec a velvet bag.

'You said one hundred and fifty pearls, but I found one hundred and fifty-one, so your princess can't count.'

'Here's your seaweed. I can never thank you enough,' said Amilec.

'That's all right,' said the witch. 'Come down and tell me what happens.'

When Prince Amilec went back into the palace, the princess was already sitting waiting. Amilec went forward and tipped all the pearls into her lap.

'Count them!' shouted the princess.

The secretary hurriedly obeyed. 'One hundred and fifty-one,' he declared at last. The princess shrieked and fainted with fury.

'This is the happiest day of my life,' beamed the king. 'At last – you can marry her.'

Just then the princess revived.

'Very well,' she snapped. 'I'm yours, you pest, but before I marry you I want a splendid wedding dress, and if I don't like it, I shall change my mind.'

By this time Amilec was getting a bit fed up with her tantrums, but he thought that, of all her demands, this was the most reasonable. So he bowed and said that he'd do his best.

'See that you do!' yelled the princess, and flounced out.

That night the prince made his way down the path to the witch's cave and knocked. The witch let him in, hung Basil on the mantelpiece, and sat him in the armchair.

'She wants a wedding dress now,' said Amilec, as the witch put on the kettle.

'Oh, does she?' said the witch. 'Well, how would you like me to make her a special magic one?'

'You're marvelous!' said Amilec.

The witch smiled and lifted Basil down for a moment while she got out the teapot. 'I'll bring it up to the castle first thing tomorrow morning.'

'How can I ever thank you enough?' said Amilec.

'I'll think of something,' said the witch.

The next morning the whole court gathered worriedly.

When Amilec came in, the princess jumped up and demanded, 'Where is it?'

'A friend of mine is bringing it,' said the prince. 'She'll be here any moment.'

Just then the doors opened and in came the most beautiful girl the prince had ever seen. The court sighed with wonder, the secretary dropped his pen, and even the princess forgot to be rude.

The girl came up to the prince, curtsied, and said, 'Here is the dress. I thought it would look better with someone wearing it. It's made of moonlight and starglow, and the glitter on a mermaid's tail. I hope you like it.'

'But who are you?' gasped Amilec.

'I am the witch.'

Then, in front of the court, the king, and the princess, Amilec bowed to the witch and said, 'How can I have been so blind! You are the most beautiful girl I have ever met. You are also the kindest. May I humbly ask you to be my wife? I promise to look after Basil, and I'll live in the cave, if it will make things easier.'

'Dear Amilec,' said the witch. 'Basil and I both love you very much, and will be delighted to accept.'

So Amilec and the witch got married and lived happily ever after with Basil, although Basil was asleep most of the time.

As for the red-haired princess, when she had finished shouting and screaming, she told the king that what she really wanted to do was travel. The king was only too glad to see her go, and packed her off as soon as possible.

One day, however, the princess came to a kingdom where there was a very handsome prince, and she thought he was just the kind of young man who would be good enough for her. So she went and knocked on the door of his palace.

'Come in, my dear,' said the queen. 'How pretty you are! I should like my son to marry someone like you. The only trouble is, he always makes princesses complete dreadful tasks before he'll even look at them. The latest thing he wants done is for somebody to make an apple tree grow upside down from his bedroom ceiling. However, I've heard that there's a wizard who lives in the wood, and he might help you, if you asked him nicely.'

'Oh, well,' thought the princess, setting off for the wood. 'The wizard will probably be horribly ugly, with three eyes, and a wart on the end of his nose, but it can't be helped.'

3 Petronella

Jay Williams

In the kingdom of Skyclear Mountain, three princes were always born to the king and queen. The oldest prince was always called Michael, the middle prince was always called George, and the youngest was always called Peter. When they were grown, they always went out to seek their fortunes. What happened to the oldest prince and the middle prince no one ever knew. But the youngest prince always rescued a princess, brought her home, and in time ruled over the kingdom. That was the way it had always been. And so far as anyone knew, that was the way it would always be.

Until now.

Now was the time of King Peter the twenty-sixth and Queen Blossom. An oldest prince was born, and a middle prince. But the youngest prince turned out to be a girl.

'Well,' said the king gloomily, 'we can't call her Peter. We'll have to call her Petronella. And what's to be done about it, I'm sure I don't know.'

There was nothing to be done. The years passed, and the time came for the princes to go out and seek their fortunes. Michael and George said good-bye to the king and queen and mounted their horses. Then out came Petronella. She was dressed in traveling clothes, with her bag packed and a sword by her side.

'If you think,' she said, 'that I'm going to sit at home, you are mistaken. I'm going to seek my fortune, too.'

'Impossible!' said the king.

'What will people say?' cried the queen.

'Look,' said Prince Michael, 'be reasonable, Pet. Stay home. Sooner or later a prince will turn up here.'

Petronella smiled. She was a tall, handsome girl with flaming red hair and when she smiled in that particular way it meant she was trying to keep her temper.

'I'm going with you,' she said. 'I'll find a prince if I have to rescue one from something myself. And that's that.'

The grooms brought out her horse, she said good-bye to her parents, and away she went behind her two brothers.

They traveled into the flatlands below Skyclear Mountain. After many days, they entered a great dark forest. They came to a place where the road divided into three, and there at the fork sat a little, wrinkled old man covered with dust and spiderwebs.

Prince Michael said haughtily, 'Where do these roads go, old man?'

'The road on the right goes to the city of Gratz,' the man replied. 'The road in the center goes to the castle of Blitz. The road on the left goes to the house of Albion the enchanter. And that's one.'

'What do you mean by "And that's one"?' asked Prince George.

'I mean,' said the old man, 'that I am forced to sit on this spot without stirring, and that I must answer one question from each person who passes by. And that's two.'

Petronella's kind heart was touched. 'Is there anything I can do to help you?' she asked.

The old man sprang to his feet. The dust fell from him in clouds.

'You have already done so,' he said. 'For that question is the one which releases me. I have sat here for sixty-two years waiting for someone to ask me that.' He snapped his fingers with joy. 'In return, I will tell you anything you wish to know.'

'Where can I find a prince?' Petronella said promptly.

'There is one in the house of Albion the enchanter,' the old man answered.

'Ah,' said Petronella, 'then that is where I am going.'

'In that case I will leave you,' said her oldest brother. 'For I am going to the castle of Blitz to see if I can find my fortune there.'

'Good luck,' said Prince George. 'For I am going to the city of Gratz. I have a feeling my fortune is there.'

They embraced her and rode away.

Petronella looked thoughtfully at the old man, who was combing spiderwebs and dust out of his beard. 'May I ask you something else?' she said.

'Of course. Anything.'

'Suppose I wanted to resuce that prince from the enchanter. How would I go about it? I haven't any experience in such things, you see.'

The old man chewed a piece of his beard. 'I do not know everything,' he said, after a moment. 'I know that there are three magical secrets which, if you can get them from him, will help you.'

'How can I get them?' asked Petronella.

'Offer to work for him. He will set you three tasks, and if you can do them you may demand a reward for each. You must ask him for a comb for your hair, a mirror to look into, and a ring for your finger.'

'And then?'

'I do not know. I only know that when you rescue the prince, you can use these things to escape from the enchanter.'

'It doesn't sound easy,' said Petronella.

'Nothing we really want is easy,' said the old man. 'Look at me — I have wanted my freedom, and I've had to wait sixty-two years for it.'

Petronella said good-bye to him. She mounted her horse and galloped along the third road.

It ended at a low, rambling house with a red roof. It was a comfortable-looking house, surrounded by gardens and stables and trees heavy with fruit.

On the lawn, in an armchair, sat a handsome young man with his eyes closed and his face turned to the sky.

Petronella tied her horse to the gate and walked across the lawn.

'Is this the house of Albion the enchanter?' she said.

The young man blinked up at her in surprise.

'I think so,' he said. 'Yes, I'm sure it is.'

'And who are you?'

The young man yawned and stretched. 'I am Prince Ferdinand of Firebright,' he replied. 'Would you mind stepping aside? I'm trying to get a suntan and you're standing in the way.'

Petronella snorted. 'You don't sound like much of a prince,' she said.

'That's funny,' said the young man, closing his eyes. 'That's what my father always says.'

At that moment the door of the house opened. Out came a man dressed all in black and silver. He was tall and thin, and his eyes were as black as a cloud full of thunder. Petronella knew at once that he must be the enchanter.

He bowed to her politely. 'What can I do for you?'

'I wish to work for you,' said Petronella boldly.

Albion nodded. 'I cannot refuse you,' he said. 'But I warn you, it will be dangerous. Tonight I will give you a task. If you do it, I will reward you. If you fail, you must die.'

Petronella glanced at the prince and sighed. 'If I must, I must,' she said. 'Very well.'

That evening they all had dinner together in the enchanter's cozy kitchen. Then Albion took Petronella out to a stone building and unbolted its door. Inside were seven huge black dogs.

'You must watch my hounds all night,' said he.

Petronella went in, and Albion closed and locked the door. At once the hounds began to snarl and bark. They bared their teeth at her. But Petronella was a real princess. She plucked up her courage. Instead of backing away, she went toward the dogs. She began to speak to them in a quiet voice. They stopped snarling and sniffed at her. She patted their heads.

'I see what it is,' she said. 'You are lonely here. I will keep you company.'

And so all night long, she sat on the floor and talked to the hounds and stroked them. They lay close to her, panting.

In the morning Albion came and let her out. 'Ah,' said he, 'I see that you are brave. If you had run from the dogs, they would have torn you to pieces. Now you may ask for what you want.'

'I want a comb for my hair,' said Petronella.

The enchanter gave her a comb carved from a piece of black wood.

Prince Ferdinand was sunning himself and working at a crossword puzzle. Petronella said to him in a low voice, 'I am doing this for you.'

'That's nice,' said the prince. 'What's "selfish" in nine letters?'

'You are,' snapped Petronella. She went to the enchanter.

'I will work for you once more,' she said.

That night Albion led her to a stable. Inside were seven huge horses.

'Tonight,' he said, 'you must watch my steeds.'

He went out and locked the door. At once the horses began to rear and neigh. They pawed at her with their iron hoofs.

But Petronella was a real princess. She looked closely at them and saw that their coats were rough and their manes and tails full of burrs.

'I see what it is,' she said. 'You are hungry and dirty.'

She brought them as much hay as they could eat, and began to brush them. All night long she fed them and groomed them, and they stood quietly in their stalls.

In the morning Albion let her out. 'You are as kind as you are brave,' said he. 'If you had run from them they would have trampled you under their hoofs. What will you have as a reward?'

'I want a mirror to look into,' said Petronella.

The enchanter gave her a mirror made of silver.

She looked across the lawn at Prince Ferdinand. He was doing exercises leisurely. He was certainly handsome. She said to the enchanter, 'I will work for you once more.'

That night Albion led her to a loft above the stables. There, on perches, were seven great hawks.

'Tonight,' said he, 'you must watch my falcons.'

As soon as Petronella was locked in, the hawks began to beat their wings and scream at her.

Petronella laughed. 'That is not how birds sing,' she said. 'Listen.' She began to sing in a sweet voice. The hawks fell silent. All night long she sang to them, and they sat like feathered statues on their perches, listening.

In the morning Albion said, 'You are as talented as you are kind and brave. If you had run from them, they would have pecked and clawed you without mercy. What do you want now?'

'I want a ring for my finger,' said Petronella.

The enchanter gave her a ring made from a single diamond.

All that day and all that night Petronella slept, for she was very tired. But early the next morning, she crept into Prince Ferdinand's room. He was sound asleep, wearing purple pajamas.

'Wake up,' whispered Petronella. 'I am going to rescue you.'

Ferdinand awoke and stared sleepily at her. 'What time is it?'

'Never mind that,' said Petronella. 'Come on!'

'But I'm sleepy,' Ferdinand objected. 'And it's so pleasant here.'

Petronella shook her head. 'You're not much of a prince,' she said grimly. 'But you're the best I can do.'

She grabbed him by the wrist and dragged him out of bed. She hauled him down the stairs. His horse and hers were in a separate stable, and she saddled them quickly. She gave the prince a shove, and he mounted. She jumped on her own horse, seized the prince's reins, and away they went like the wind.

They had not gone far when they heard a tremendous thumping. Petronella looked back. A dark cloud rose behind them, and beneath it she saw the enchanter. He was running with great strides, faster than the horses could go.

'What shall we do?' she cried.

'Don't ask me,' said Prince Ferdinand grumpily. 'I'm all shaken to bits by this fast riding.'

Petronella desperately pulled out the comb. 'The old man said this would help me!' she said. And because she didn't know what else to do with it, she threw the comb on the ground. At once a forest rose up. The trees were so thick that no one could get between them.

Away went Petronella and the prince. But the enchanter turned himself into an ax and began to chop. Right and left he chopped, slashing, and the trees fell before him.

Soon he was through the wood, and once again Petronella heard his footsteps thumping behind.

She reined in the horses. She took out the mirror and threw it on the ground. At once a wide lake spread out behind them, gray and glittering.

Off they went again. But the enchanter sprang into the water, turning himself into a salmon as he did so. He swam across the lake and leaped out of the water on to the other bank. Petronella heard him coming— *thump! thump!* —behind them again.

This time she threw down the ring. It didn't turn into anything, but lay shining on the ground.

The enchanter came running up.And as he jumped over the ring, it opened wide and then snapped up around him. It held his arm tight to his body, in a magical grip from which he could not escape.

'Well,' said Prince Ferdinand, 'that's the end of him.'

Petronella looked at him in annoyance. Then she looked at the enchanter, held fast in the ring.

'Bother!' she said. 'I can't just leave him here. He'll starve to death.'

She got off her horse and went up to him. 'If I release you,' she said, 'will you promise to let the prince go free?'

Albion stared at her in astonishment. 'Let him go free?' he said. 'What are you talking about? I'm glad to get rid of him.'

It was Petronella's turn to look surprised. 'I don't understand,' she said. 'Weren't you holding him prisoner?'

'Certainly not,' said Albion. 'He came to visit me for a weekend. At the end of it, he said, "It's so pleasant here, do you mind if I stay on for another day or two?" I'm very polite and I said, "Of course." He stayed on, and on, and on. I didn't like to be rude to a guest and I couldn't just kick him out. I don't know what I'd have done if you hadn't dragged him away.'

'But then —' said Petronella, 'but then — why did you come running after him this way?'

'I wasn't chasing him,' said the enchanter. 'I was chasing *you*. You are just the girl I've been looking for. You are brave and kind and talented and beautiful as well.'

'Oh,' said Petronella. 'I see.'

'Hmm,' said she. 'How do I get this ring off you?'

'Give me a kiss.'

She did so. The ring vanished from around Albion and reappeared on Petronella's finger.

'I don't know what my parents will say when I come home with you instead of a prince,' she said.

'Let's go and find out, shall we?' said the enchanter cheerfully.

He mounted one horse and Petronella the other. And off they

trotted, side by side, leaving Prince Ferdinand of Firebright to walk home as best he could.

4 The Donkey Prince

Angela Carter

Many, many years ago, a Queen went for a walk on a mountain. After a while, she grew tired and sat down to rest under a white stone among the tufts of heather. A donkey came up to her and gazed at her with mournful eyes.

'Give me the apple in your pocket,' said the donkey. 'I've a great craving come upon me for an apple.'

The apple the Queen carried in her pocket was no ordinary fruit but a magic apple from the orchard of her father, the King of the West, which he had given her for a wedding present. 'Keep the apple safe, and you'll never lose your looks or have a day's illness,' he told her. Then he sailed away across the sea in his ship with green sails to attend to his own affairs, which were very extensive.

The Queen felt in her pocket for the apple and wondered how the donkey knew it was there. She smelled magic and was a little uneasy.

'Much as I'd like to, I can't give you my apple because it was a wedding present from my father,' she said. 'But if you come back to the palace with me, I'll give you a whole barrelful of fruit.'

'It is only the one apple I want,' said the donkey. He threw back his head and brayed loudly. Over the rocks came a whole troop of donkeys, jingling with silver bells, and the first one had a white leather saddle on his back.

The donkey who wanted the apple said politely, 'Mount and ride, madam. I cannot go with you, so you must come with me.'

The Queen saw nothing for it but to climb into the white saddle, and all the donkeys trotted over the heather until they came to a gray place where it was neither night nor day but in-between times. There they saw a hut thatched with turf that was the Donkey Parliament. The hut was lit with storm lanterns and there was a heap of old sacks beside a fire. The smoke from the fire went up through a hole in the ceiling.

The donkey who wanted the apple was the President of the Donkey

Parliament, and the heap of sacks was his chair of office, so he sat on it. The hut was crowded with donkeys, and when they saw the Queen riding in, they bellowed and roared. They led her to a bale of clean straw and saw that she was settled comfortably, and then there was a silence.

'Madam,' said the President, 'though you see us in the shapes of donkeys, my company and I are, in fact, Brown Men of the Hills. Your father transformed us into this shape by a cruel enchantment after my son accidentally transfixed him with an arrow while he was out hunting. If you had given your father's apple to me of your own free will, because of my need, we should have returned to our natural forms at the very first bite I took from it.'

At this, the donkeys wept great tears that trickled down their muzzles, and the Queen was so grieved to see their sorrow, she wept with them. She took out the apple and offered it to the President gladly, but he shook his head.

'It is no use now,' he said. 'Now you want to give us the apple from pity and not of your own free will, and that won't do at all.'

'What can I do to help you?' asked the Queen. 'There must be something.'

'Excuse us while we have a conference,' said the President. The three eldest and most venerable donkeys in the gathering rose up and sat beside him on the sacks. While they conversed together in whispers, the Queen sat unhappily in the firelight, for she knew she had failed a test her father had set her to see if her generosity was stronger than her vanity. She had always been excessively proud of her good looks and abundant health.

Finally, the donkey President rose and came to the Queen.

'It is a very great favor we must ask of you,' he said. 'Such a great favor only our desperate need prompts us to ask.'

'I will do all that I can,' she said.

'Would you bring up one of our children as your own, in your own palace, as a prince among men?'

She knew it was her father's plan, and she felt so angry with him for trying her so hard that she almost said no. But the donkey eyes around her were so beseeching, she finally said, 'Yes, I will, no matter what my husband the King says.'

They brought a newborn foal wrapped in a woolen shawl and placed it in her arms.

'The day he finds a man and a woman willing to go through fire and water for him, we shall return to our proper forms,' said the President. 'You will have to bring him up very well to make him worthy of such devotion. And we shall never be able to thank you enough.'

The Queen mounted her white saddle, and the donkeys took her home to the palace. She went into the hall and her ladies flocked around her to peer inside the shawl. They were very much surprised to see a baby with such long ears, such melancholy eyes and such a loud, discordant voice.

'He shall live in the royal nursery and grow up as a prince,' said the Queen.

Everybody was astonished but did not say a word aloud, guessing there was some good explanation. She laid the foal in the King's arms.

'This is the heir to the kingdom,' she said. 'I've promised it will be so, and I can't go back on my word.'

Though the King was extremely disconcerted, he accepted his adopted son with good grace, for he respected his wife's strength of mind. Time passed and the donkey went about the palace with cloth of gold on his back. He learned geometry, trigonometry and Greek, since that formed a prince's education in those days, but he never could learn how to hold a pen in his hoof. So he never knew how to write his name, which was Bruno.

He was of such a sweet disposition, so modest and gentle, that he was greatly loved in spite of his unconventional appearance. The King and Queen never had any children of their own, so no ugly problems of succession were raised, and they loved Prince Bruno quite as well as if he were their own flesh and blood.

When Bruno was almost full grown, the Queen lost her magic apple. If fell from her pocket when she was out walking one day, and she did not know where it went. At once the color faded from her face, and besides losing her looks, she became so ill that everyone said she would die. Physicians and surgeons came from many neighboring countries to try to cure her, but nothing brought her back to health.

All day long she lay on her bed with her face to the wall, staring at the wallpaper as if there were wonderful patterns on it that she alone could see.

As the King and the Prince sat sadly together, a bird flew in through the window and perched on the arm of the King's throne.

'The Queen needs her magic apple back again. That's plain to see,' said the bird. He had feathers of a startling cherry color flecked with gold.

'But where's her apple? That's the question,' said the King.

'A Wild Man found it and took it back to the Savage Mountain where the Wild Men live in mud huts,' said the bird.

'Where is the Savage Mountain?' asked the King.

'How should I know?' demanded the bird. 'I'm not omniscient.' He was a learned bird with a large vocabulary, but he said no more and flew away.

'Wherever it is, I shall find it,' said Bruno. So he went out by himself onto the high road out of the kingdom to look for the Savage Mountain, leaving a message to tell the King where he was going. He met a child who sat on a boulder beside the road, plaiting straw for hats.

'Good morning,' said Bruno. 'Could you tell me the way to the Savage Mountain?'

The child bit on a straw and stared, but not rudely, only out of curiosity. Bruno realized he was no common sight, with his hairy ears and coat of cloth of gold, so he did not take offense. It was a girl child, but she was so dirty and her rags so nondescript that it was difficult, at first, to tell. Her name was Daisy.

'I heard my mother speak of the Savage Mountain, but she's dead now,' said Daisy. 'If I think hard, I shall probably remember the way.'

'Could you take me there?'

'I daresay. I live with an old woman who works my fingers to the bone with the straw-plaiting, and I'd just as soon go off with you. But we must go down this road to the very end.'

With that, she threw her straw away and walked off with him. Soon her feet grew tired.

'May I ride on your back?' she asked. 'My legs are getting weary.'

Nobody had ever ridden on Bruno's back before because he was a prince. But he did not hesitate, for he saw her feet were bare and the road was very rough.

'With pleasure,' he said. She climbed on his back.

'Now I remember the way perfectly,' she said. 'I recall it in full. But soon the road goes into a bog.'

'That's inconvenient,' said Bruno.

'We shall see what we shall see,' said Daisy.

Just as she had said, they soon arrived at a bog full of mist and smells of decay. Bruno thought they could follow the road no farther. But Daisy got down and gathered rushes and plaited them and laid them on the treacherous ground, which seemed to quake and shiver as they looked at it.

'We shall walk safe now, anyway,' she said.

Bruno set his little hooves gingerly on the rushes, and the fragile path held firm. As he went forward, the rush-bridge spread out in front of him and rolled itself up behind, and Daisy wound it up into a ball. By the time they crossed the bog, this ball was very large.

'That is a trick worth knowing,' said Bruno.

'A working girl learns a trick or two,' said Daisy. 'Before us lies a river no man can cross.'

'Then how can we cross it?' asked Bruno, almost in despair. She laughed, but not unkindly.

'I'm not a man, I'm a girl. And as for you, you're neither — you're a donkey.'

'That's perfectly true,' said Bruno bowing his head. 'I'd never have thought of that.'

'A working girl learns to use her common sense, you know.'

They swam the river with ease. On the other side of the river stretched a desolate country where cold winds rushed through grim chasms, and a few trees and bushes, gnarled and stunted by the violence of the elements, clung to the stony soil as if clutching it for dear life with their roots. And still the road went on, though now it was so rough, it was hard to tell the road from the moorland.

'We are approaching the foothills of the Savage Mountain,' said Daisy. 'Listen and you can hear the Wild Men howl.'

Bruno pricked up his enormous ears and heard, carried on the roaring winds, uncouth voices singing outlandish songs in strange harmonies. Since his hearing was extraordinarily good, he also caught another sound. This was the whirr of Wild Men sharpening their knives on grinding stones. But he did not mention this to Daisy, as he thought it would frighten her. Instead, he said, 'I think it would be best if you turned back for home now. The Savage Mountain is no place for little girls.'

'Nor for foolish donkeys either!' said Daisy angrily. Then they saw by one another's expressions that each had hurt the other's feelings equally, and both were equally sorry. Daisy flung her arms around Bruno's neck.

'I'd rather go on with you than turn back, no matter what the danger,' she said. And they went on as before, though often hungry and cold.

They went up steep paths and down narrow valleys where daylight struggled with darkness. Rain clouds drenched them, and then the rain froze. Bruno had a poor diet of heather and scanty grass, and Daisy found only a few withered roots and berries to eat. But the road still showed no signs of coming to an end.

One morning, as they ate their miserable breakfast, thinking themselves lost and alone in this inhospitable place, a huge knife came flashing through the air and buried itself up to the hilt in the earth beside them.

They saw an enormous figure leaning on an ax and gazing at them from huge red eyes that seemed to spit fire. His long hair was done up in many plaits knotted with strips of leather and hung down to his waist. His beard and moustache were also plaited and reached to the middle of his chest, which was covered with an intricate interlaced pattern of blue-and red-tattooing.

A leather sack was slung over his shoulder. He wore trousers of wolfskin, and his belt was stuck with many more knives and also daggers. Beside him a mastiff, almost the size of Bruno, sat panting, showing a pink tongue that lolled out for what seemed yards. The newcomer, clearly a Wild Man, was accompanied by his dog, whose name was Hound.

'I see you've noticed my visiting card,' said the Wild Man in a menacing voice, showing teeth as white and pointed as splinters of fresh wood.

'Yes, indeed,' said Bruno courteously. He and Daisy were not at all afraid, as they were anxious for news of the Wild Men's village.

'I'm sorry, I seem to have interrupted your breakfast,' said the Wild Man, who grew less hostile when they showed no fear.

'Such as it is, you are very welcome to share it,' invited Daisy, spreading out a handful of greenish blackberries as appetizingly as possible. 'But this is all we have, and I'm afraid it's not very nice.'

This offer melted the Wild Man's heart. He was not accustomed to generosity from strangers.

'These are friends, Hound,' he said to his dog, who at once leaped forward and licked Daisy's face. Then he licked Bruno's muzzle.

'I'd be glad to eat breakfast with you if you allow me to provide the food,' said the Wild Man. From his leather sack, he took some oatcakes and a cheese. He sliced them up with one of his wicked knives, and they made a hearty breakfast, for Bruno was fond of oatcakes, too.

'We Wild Men have a bad reputation, but our bark is worse than our bite,' said the Wild Man, who was called Hlajki. All the Wild names were full of flinty, uncomfortable j's and k's.

'We live on a harsh mountain and have no time for the soft ways of the valley people. In return, they always expect the worst from us. There's no love lost, I can tell you, and we soon scare them off when they come creeping up to spy on us, full of curiosity to see our Wild ways. But I can tell that you two are different.'

Bruno took an instant liking to Hlajki because the Wild Man neither stared at him because he was a donkey, nor cringed and groveled because he was a prince. Hlajki also treated Daisy with beautiful politeness, giving her the largest piece of cheese.

'We're on a mission,' confided Bruno.

Hlajki looked grave. 'Is it a matter of life and death?'

'My mother's life hangs by a thread.'

'Then I'm your man,' said Hlajki, swearing by his ax.

'My mother lost her magic apple, and now she is very ill. If she doesn't have her apple back again, they say she'll die. One of the Wild Men found the apple and took it home to his mud dwelling. We have come to fetch it back.'

'My own cousin, who is called Klajj, found this apple,' said Hlajki. 'He brought it into our village, and we clustered around to stare. None of us had seen an apple before, for apple trees won't bear fruit in our climate. Now the apple lies among the other treasures of the Wild Men in the iron safe of our leader, whose name is Terror.'

'Do you think he would give it to me if I told him how much depended on it?' asked Bruno.

'No,' said Hlajki. 'He would kill you with his spear, tan your hide and make himself a pair of trousers from it.'

'We shall have to acquire the apple by guile,' said Daisy, who was a practical girl. 'I shall think of a way. A working girl knows how to use her wits.'

She walked up and down, thinking, while Hlajki and Bruno played two-handed whist, for there was a pack of cards at the bottom of Hlajki's sack. Hound sat on the alert in case anyone approached them secretly, for the Wild Men were a very suspicious people. At last Daisy came back, smiling.

'Let me borrow your golden saddlecloth, Bruno,' she said.

She wrapped the marvelous stuff around her like a robe and decorated her hair with his gold and jeweled ornaments until she looked like a princess herself, and Bruno, stripped of his finery, looked like any common donkey. You would never have thought she was a girl who plaited straw for a living or that Bruno would inherit a kingdom.

'You are the most beautiful thing I've ever seen upon the Savage Mountain,' said Hlajki.

'Take me to your village,' she said. 'I will beard Terror in his den.'

She mounted on Bruno's back, and Hlajki led them to the village, with Hound following them like a dog struck with wonder. The road went right up to the village of the Wild Men and stopped outside Terror's front door, which was surrounded by the skulls of beasts. Their arrival caused considerable commotion among the mud huts of the Wild Men. The Wild Women, with Wild Babies wrapped up in furs, and Wild Children covered with tattooing, all came out to see them, uttering barbaric cries. They gathered about Daisy, fingering her golden robe, their eyes round with awe.

Soon Terror came out of his hut. He was a fearsome sight. He was a head and a half taller then Hlajki and much hairier. His teeth were filed to points as sharp as needles, to show how savage he was. He wore a mantle of bearskin and the antlers of a stag upon his head.

'I am a great magician and will show you some magic tricks,' said Daisy.

She took three of the little leather balls the Wild Children played with and began to juggle them so fast you would have thought you saw a hundred of them in the air at the same time. The Wild People fell silent with astonishment and then cheered and applauded loudly.

'Any twopenny-halfpenny conjurer could do as well as that,' said Terror. His voice was as dreadful as the beginnings of a storm. 'You may impress my wild company who have seen nothing but the Savage Mountain; however, I am a man of travel, and you certainly don't impress me.'

Daisy took one of the stone pots in which the Wild People cooked their food and covered it with a fold of her robe. When she brought the pot into the light again, a pink geranium blossomed there. She broke off the flower and gave it to Terror, but he said with a sneer, 'It's all done with mirrors. Astonish me. Go on, astonish me. I am so bored with hard times on the Savage Mountain that I'll give you anything you ask for — if you make me astonished.'

'Will you give me the apple Hlajki's cousin Klajj found, that is now locked up in you iron safe?' said Daisy.

'How do you know about my treasures?' he asked, his face a picture of surprise.

'Because I am the greatest magician in the world,' she said. And she took a little wooden whistle from the bosom of her robe.

She began to play a tune of such sweetness that all the Wild People began to cry with pleasure, and even Terror found tears of joy were trickling down his tattooed cheeks. Then a flock of birds appeared, strange and beautiful birds with cherry-colored feathers flecked with gold, and Bruno recognized amongst them the bird who had come to the palace before his travels started.

The birds began to weave a mazy dance in the sky to the music Daisy played, and as they flew they dropped down feathers which turned to rubies when they touched the ground. The Wild People picked up the rubies and treasured them greatly. Then Daisy put down her whistle, and the birds all flew away.

'Bring out the apple,' said Terror. 'I would give my name, my rank and my reputation as a warrior to possess even a quarter of your magic.'

So Daisy took the magic apple, and they went back the way they had come. Now they had plenty of cold meat, oatcakes and cheese which the

Wild Men had given them and also the company of Hlajki and Hound, who had vowed by the ax never to leave them. But when the conjuring was over, Terror decided it was a fleeting pleasure compared with the possession of a unique magic apple, and he sent out men to fire the heather and burn the strangers alive.

All the moor behind them became a sea of flame which surged toward them faster than they could run away from it. Hlajki cried out, covered his eyes and began to mutter spells of the Wild Men to protect them, but Daisy said, 'I'll make a firebreak.' She took matches from her pocket and quickly burned a wide strip of heather. They stood on the charred ground in the heart of a wild fire which roared around them but did not harm them and finally burned itself out.

In this way, Hlajki and Daisy went through fire for Bruno.

So they passed the fire safely, though some sparks singed Hlajki's trousers, and Hound was so shocked at the blaze that he was a much gentler dog in the future and jumped nervously at the slightest sound. They went forward over the fire-blackened country until they reached the river no man could cross. Here the waves washed Hlajki back onto the bank as soon as he tried to swim.

'I shall have to stay on the Savage Mountain all my life and never see you both again,' he said, 'nor hear the music of your whistle.'

Man and dog began to cry, but Bruno said, 'Jump on my back.' Hlajki sat astride the donkey, though he had never ridden horse nor pony before, and his seat was very shaky. In this fashion, they entered the water. But it was hard going, for Hlajki was of immense stature and his weight pulled Bruno down until it was clear they would both drown if he continued to ride.

'Good night, sweet Prince,' said Hlajki simply when he realized what was happening, and he slipped off Bruno's back. He would have sunk beneath the waves straight-away if Bruno had not clasped his beard between his teeth, while Daisy clutched his hair and Hound took hold of his belt. In this manner, they kept him on the surface between them.

So Hlajki and Daisy went through water for Bruno, but it was nearly the death of them all.

As they floundered there, a sudden current in the water threw them high in the air, and Daisy gasped, 'I see a ship upon the river.'

Floating toward them on the tide came a barge with sails as green as grass. Sailors in green uniforms manned the rigging, and a very old man whose white beard reached to the ground sat on the poop in a chair of carved oak and looking glass. When the barge reached Bruno, Daisy, Hlajki and Hound, the sailors lowered a dinghy and drew them on board. In a few minutes, they stood before the old man, who rose to welcome them.

'I am the King of the West,' he said.

Bruno went down on his front legs before him, Daisy curtseyed as she had been taught to do to rich old men, and Hlajki inclined his wild head slightly, for the Wild Men were too proud to bow to anyone. But the dog wagged his tail, sending water everywhere, and the old man smiled.

'Give me the apple, for it is from my own orchard,' he said. When he had it safe, he took them into his sumptuous cabin and showed them a mirror.

First this mirror reflected nothing but mist. But soon the mist cleared, and Bruno saw his foster mother in her royal bed at home, waking as if from a refreshing sleep, then taking strong broth hungrily from a cup.

'She's on the high road to health, I'm glad to say,' said the King her father. 'I can see everything in my magic mirror, but unfortunately my powers of intervention are limited. You had to go through fire and water yourselves.'

'Daisy did all the hard work,' said Bruno. 'A donkey finds it hard to cope with human beings.'

But already he was beginning to look more like a man than a donkey.

'I am a greater magician than you, but your talents are certainly wasted in the hat-making industry,' said the King to Daisy. 'Look in the mirror again.'

A fresh cloud of mist blotted out the Queen, and when it blew away, two words in Gothic script appeared in the depths of the glass: *The Future.* Then it showed a young prince in a suit of green velvet, who was plainly Bruno in his true shape. He held Daisy by the hand, and she was wearing a wedding dress. Hlajki in his fur trousers stood beside them as best man, and Hound had his paw on the marriage register, making his mark as a witness. Over their heads, a flock of red-and-gold birds formed a canopy, and the couple was surrounded by a cheering throng of Wild Men, Brown Men of the Hills in their true shapes (small of stature and brown of hue) and the men and women of Bruno's kingdom.

Well, all this came true in the course of time. After Bruno and Daisy were married, the Brown Men returned to their native hills and took up market gardening, for they had given up hunting forever. They always allowed their beasts of burden to wander where they pleased, treating them as equals, which was only right and proper.

Terror's cruelty caused a revolution among the Wild Men, and he was stoned off the Savage Mountain. Hlajki became their new leader, and under his influence, they became gentler by degrees, built themselves houses of wood and thatch, and started eating with knives and forks, which they had never done before.

But all this happened long ago, in another country, and nothing is the same now, of course.

5 ...And Then the Prince Knelt Down and Tried to Put the Glass Slipper on Cinderella's Foot

Judith Viorst

I really didn't notice that he had a funny nose.
And he certainly looked better all dressed up in fancy clothes.
He's not nearly as attractive as he seemed the other night.
So I think I'll just pretend that this glass slipper feels too tight.

6 Snow White

The Merseyside Fairy Story Collective

High above a far off kingdom, carved into the rock of a mountainside, there once stood a mighty castle. It was so high that the people working on the distant plain could look up and see it among the clouds and when they saw it they trembled, for it was the castle of the cruel and powerful Queen of the Mountains.

The Queen of the Mountains had ten thousand soldiers at her command. She sat upon a throne of marble dressed in robes weighed down with glittering jewels, and holding in her hand a magic mirror. This mirror could answer any question the Queen asked it and in it the Queen could see what was happening anywhere in her kingdom. When she looked into the mirror and saw any of her subjects doing things which displeased her she sent soldiers to punish them.

Night and day her soldiers stood guard on the walls of the castle and every day they watched as people from all over the kingdom toiled up the steep pathway carrying heavy loads: iron to shoe the royal horses; weapons to arm the royal soldiers; food to be cooked in the royal kitchens; cloth to clothe the royal servants. The procession wound on and on up the mountainside to the castle. The people were carrying with them all the useful and beautiful things that had been made in the kingdom, for everything they made belonged to the Queen and they were allowed to keep only what was left over or spoiled.

No one could save anything from the Queen of the Mountains for no place was hidden from her magic mirror. Every day the riches of the kingdom were brought to her and every night she asked the mirror:

> Mirror, mirror in my hand,
> Who is the happiest in the land?

Then in a silvery voice the mirror always replied:

> Queen, all bow to your command,
> You are the happiest in the land.

And the Queen would smile.

One day, among the procession climbing the steep path to the castle were a pale little girl called Snow White and seven little men, dwarfs, even smaller than her. Snow White and the dwarfs were carrying between them a heavy chest bound with metal bands. They had travelled all the way from the diamond mines beside the distant sea. There, far underground, often in danger, they and many other men, women and children worked long and weary hours. Every year they must send a chestful of diamonds to the Queen of the Mountains or they would be cruelly punished.

When the other people in the procession reached the castle gates the lovely things they had been carrying were taken from them and they were sent away, but Snow White and the seven dwarfs were surrounded by soldiers and brought to the throne room of the Queen herself.

'Open the chest,' ordered the Queen as they bowed low before her.

Two dwarfs lifted the lid. The chest was full of glittering diamonds and on top of them lay a necklace shaped like branches of ice. The Queen held the necklace up to the light.

'Did you make this?' she asked Snow White.

'Yes Majesty,' said the girl.

'It is well made,' said the Queen. 'You are to stay in the castle as a jewellery maker.'

Snow White's pale cheeks turned red and she opened her mouth to cry 'No!' but each of the seven dwarfs put a crooked finger to his lips, warning her to be silent.

'Take her to the workshop!' ordered the Queen.

The soldiers led Snow White and the dwarfs out of the throne room and up a twisting stairway to a small room at the top of a tower. In the room there was a work bench with jeweller's tools laid out on it. All around the walls, stored in tall glass jars, gleamed jewels of many colours: amethysts, emeralds, rubies, sapphires, topaz. Little light came through the one small window but the jewels shone so brightly that when Snow White looked at them her eyes were dazzled and her head began to ache.

Snow White and the dwarfs took the diamonds from the chest and put them into empty glass jars. Then, one by one, the seven little men kissed Snow White goodbye. There were tears in their eyes for she was their dearest friend. They shouldered the empty chest and went slowly down the twisting staircase.

'You are very lucky,' said one of the soldiers to Snow White. 'You will no longer be poor and lead a hard life toiling undergound in the mine. Here servants will wait on you. You will sleep in a soft, scented bed and be brought whatever delicious food and drink you want. And, if the Queen is especially pleased with your work she will give you rich rewards.'

'But my friends will still be toiling in the mine,' said Snow White and her heart felt like a stone with sorrow.

In the long days and weeks which followed Snow White grew more and more skilful at making beautiful pieces of jewellery out of the precious stones and metals in the workshop. The jewellery pleased the Queen of the Mountains. One evening she summoned Snow White to the throne room.

'This brooch pleases me,' said the Queen. 'You may choose a reward.'

'Oh, Majesty,' answered Snow White, falling on her knees, 'please let me go home.'

The Queen was angry. She turned her mirror towards Snow White and in it the little girl could see the dwarfs and all her other friends digging in the mine and dragging heavy loads along its narrow tunnels.

'You could have anything your heart desires and yet you ask to return to that miserable life!' the Queen exclaimed. 'Go back to your work and think hard before you enter my presence again.'

So, as she deftly twisted the metal and fitted the precious stones, Snow White thought long and hard. She thought of the sufferings she had shared with her friends in the distant mines; of how they and all the people of the land spent their whole lives working to make lovely things for the Queen of the Mountains while they themselves had barely enough to live on. And Snow White knew what she would ask for.

'I will make a jewelled belt so beautiful that the Queen will call me before her again,' she thought and at once set to work.

'Well, Snow White,' said the Queen as the girl stood before her throne a second time, 'you have had time to think. Tell me your heart's desire and I will grant it, for what you have made is more beautiful than anything in my treasure chambers.' As she spoke the Queen ran her fingers along the red and purple gems of the jewelled belt.

'Majesty,' said Snow White, 'I have thought and what I ask for is this: take only what you need from the people of the kingdom and let them keep the rest so that they will no longer be cold and hungry and miserable.'

The Queen's eyes glittered with rage and her hand tightened on the jewelled belt, but when she spoke her voice was as sweet as honey.

'Snow White, if anyone but you had spoken such treachery, I would have ordered my soldiers to throw them from the walls of the castle onto the rocks below. But you have a rare skill and are young enough to change your thoughts. Come close and look in my mirror.'

Snow White looked into the magic mirror and saw herself reflected there, but strangely. She was wearing working clothes and yet in the mirror she was dressed in a richly embroidered gown, pearls and rubies were entwined in her long hair and on her head was a golden crown, 'You see, Snow White,' said the Queen, 'you could be a princess. Now go.'

Snow White went back to the workshop. She stood gazing out of the tiny window and thinking of how she had looked in the mirror, adorned with jewels and gold. Far below her she could see the daily procession of people carrying up the mountainside all the things they had made and must give to the Queen. Beyond them the green plain stretched out until it reached the distant hills. On the other side of the hills was the sea and Snow White's home. The words of a song which she and her friends used to sing when the long day's work in the mine was over came back to her mind.

> Emerald's green but grass is greener
> Sapphires pale beside the sea.
> No jet as black as the wild night sky,
> No ruby red
> No ruby red
> No ruby red as hearts which cry to be free.

'What my friends long for is my heart's desire too,' thought Snow White, 'but the Queen of the Mountains will never set us free.'

Soon the Queen summoned Snow White before her throne a third time.

'No flower in all my gardens is as delicately shaped as these ear-rings you have made,' she said. 'What reward do you want?'

'Nothing, Majesty,' said Snow White quietly.

'Foolish girl!' cried the Queen, 'I know you are unhappy, yet you only have to ask and you can become a princess. Very well, you will continue to make jewellery for me, but from now on soldiers will stand guard at the foot of the tower where you work and unless you choose to be a princess you will never leave the tower again.'

The months passed by. Still Snow White remained alone in the tower and did not ask for her reward. Quiet and pale, she sat at her work, thinking and waiting.

When a whole year had passed Snow White looked from her tiny window and saw below, among the people toiling up the pathway to the castle, seven little figures carrying between them a heavy chest. It was her friends the dwarfs at last.

Snow White waited for the dwarfs to bring the chest of diamonds to the workshop but when the chest was brought in it was carried by some of the Queen's soldiers.

'The Queen has given orders that you are not to see your friends from the mine,' said one of the soldiers. 'She is watching them in her mirror all the time they are here.'

'Please go back to the foot of the stairs and leave me alone,' said Snow White in a sad voice. 'I will fill the glass jars with diamonds and put the empty chest outside the door.'

The soldiers did as she asked, for they liked Snow White and secretly admired her for daring to displease the Queen.

An hour later they returned and took the chest away, down the twisting stairway and into the courtyard where the dwarfs were waiting. The little men swung it onto their shoulders and carried it out of the castle gates and down the mountainside.

All that day the Queen of the Mountains sat on her throne and watched in her mirror as the dwarfs went further and further away. By the time that evening came they had crossed the distant hills. The Queen smiled to herself and asked the mirror her usual question:

> Mirror, mirror in my hand
> Who is happiest in the land?

In its silvery voice, the mirror replied:

> Though all bow to your command,
> Snow White is happiest in the land.

'Snow White!' hissed the Queen, 'Show me Snow White!'

Then, in the mirror, she saw the seven dwarfs lifting the lid off the chest and out of the chest climbed Snow White, her face full of joy.

The Queen's rage was terrible. She ordered that the soldiers who had let Snow White escape were to be thrown from the castle walls. Throughout the night she sat on her throne speaking to no one. Then, as the sun rose, she gave orders to her soldiers.

'Go to the diamond mines,' she commanded. 'Seal up the entrance while Snow White and her companions are working so that they will all die underground.'

Many of the soldiers were filled with horror but they dared not disobey. The Queen watch in her mirror as they sealed up the way out of the mine and when it was done, she laughed.

Word of the terrible thing done at the Queen's command spread quickly through the land. Many people came to where the Queen's soldiers stood guard beside the sealed up entrance to the mine. As the day wore on, more and more people arrived. They stood there quietly at a little distance from the soldiers, as if they were waiting for something to happen. By evening, a great crowd had gathered. They lit fires to keep themselves warm through the night and talked in low voices about all the people trapped underground and about the cruelty of the Queen of the Mountains. They knew that by now there must be little air left to breathe down in the mine. Soon Snow White and her friends would be dead as the Queen of the Mountains had commanded.

Suddenly, among some rocks on the outskirts of the crowd, a tapping sound could be heard. As the people looked at each other in bewilderment, one of the rocks began to move and then was pushed aside from behind to reveal a narrow shaft going deep into the earth. Climbing from this passage was one of the dwarfs.

'Just in time,' wheezed the dwarf. 'I do not think we could have gone on digging much longer. My oldest brother remembered that when he was very young there was another way out of the mine. He led us to the place and we dug in the dark until the way was opened up.'

One by one, helping each other, the workers from the diamond mine climbed out into the fresh night air. Some were faint, some were bruised and many had torn and bleeding hands, but every child, woman and man was safe. Among them was Snow White.

The great crowd of people round the fires and the soldiers stared in amazement. Then the people began to cheer. Some of the soldiers joined in the cheering but others drew their weapons. One of these called out to Snow White.

'Snow White,' he ordered, 'you must come with us at once back to the castle.'

'No,' answered Snow White, 'I will not go back to the castle and we will send no more diamonds to the Queen. Everyone will keep the things they make and send nothing to the Queen of the Mountains.'

As she spoke the cheers grew louder and louder.

'Then we will kill you,' said the soldier.

'You may kill some of us,' said Snow White, 'but in the end you will lose for there are far more people than there are soldiers.'

The people realised that this was true and they surrounded the soldiers determined to take their weapons from them, whatever the cost.

Far away on her marble throne, the Queen of the Mountains took the jewellery Snow White had made and broke it into pieces. In her magic mirror she could see all that was happening. She knew that the people of the land were rising up against her.

Mirror, mirror in my hand
Make them bow to my command,

she ordered her mirror. But the mirror answered:

Queen who was so rich and grand
The people cast you from their land.

The magic mirror misted over and when the mist had gone, the Queen could see nothing reflected there but her own face.

Still grasping the mirror in her hand, the Queen of the Mountains rose from her throne and climbed the stone steps to the highest battlements of the castle. From there she could look out and see with her own eyes the crowds of people gathering on the distant plain. In fear and fury she lifted the mirror above her head and flung it from the castle wall.

The mirror would not leave her hand. She fell with it and hurtled screaming down and down until she was shattered into fragments on the rocks below.

7 The Moon Ribbon

Jane Yolen

There was once a plain but good-hearted girl named Sylva whose sole possession was a ribbon her mother had left her. It was a strange ribbon, the color of moonlight, for it had been woven from the gray hairs of her mother and her mother's mother and her mother's mother's mother before her.

Sylva lived with her widowed father in a great house by the forest's edge. Once the great house had belonged to her mother, but when she died, it became Sylva's father's house to do with as he willed. And what he willed was to live simply and happily with his daughter without thinking of the day to come.

But one day, when there was little enough to live on, and only the great house to recommend him, Sylva's father married again, a beautiful widow who had two beautiful daughters of her own.

It was a disastrous choice, for no sooner were they wed when it was apparent the woman was mean in spirit and meaner in tongue. She dismissed most of the servants and gave their chores over to Sylva, who followed her orders without complaint. For simply living in her mother's house with her loving father seemed enough for the girl.

After a bit, however, the old man died in order to have some peace, and the house passed on to the stepmother. Scarcely two days had passed, or maybe three, when the stepmother left off mourning the old man and turned on Sylva. She dismissed the last of the servants without their pay.

'Girl,' she called out, for she never used Sylva's name, 'you will sleep in the kitchen and do the charring.' And from that time on it was so.

Sylva swept the floor and washed and mended the family's clothing. She sowed and hoed and tended the fields. She ground the wheat and kneaded the bread, and she waited on the others as though she were a servant. But she did not complain.

Yet late at night, when the stepmother and her own two daughters were asleep, Sylva would weep bitterly into her pillow, which was nothing more than an old broom laid in front of the hearth.

One day, when she was cleaning out an old desk, Sylva came upon a hidden drawer she had never seen before. Trembling, she opened the drawer. It was empty except for a silver ribbon with a label attached to it. *For Sylva* read the card. *The Moon Ribbon of Her Mother's Hair.* She took it out and stared at it. And all that she had lost was borne in upon her. She felt the tears start in her eyes, and, so as not to cry, she took the tag off and began to stroke the ribbon with her hand. It was rough and smooth at once, and shone like the rays of the moon.

At that moment her stepsisters came into the room.

'What is that?' asked one. 'Is it nice? It is mine.'

'I want it. I saw it first,' cried the other.

The noise brought the stepmother to them. 'Show it to me,' she said.

Obediently, Sylva came over and held the ribbon out to her. But when the stepmother picked it up, it looked like no more than strands of gray hair woven together unevenly. It was prickly to touch.

'Disgusting,' said the stepmother dropping it back into Sylva's hand. 'Throw it out at once.'

'Burn it,' cried one stepsister.

'Bury it,' cried the other.

'Oh, please. It was my mother's. She left it for me. Please let me keep it,' begged Sylva.

The stepmother looked again at the gray strand. 'Very well,' she said with a grim smile. 'It suits you.' And she strode out of the room, her daughters behind her.

Now that she had the silver ribbon, Sylva thought her life would be better. But instead it became worse. As if to punish her for speaking out for the ribbon, her sisters were at her to wait on them both day and night. And whereas before she had to sleep by the hearth, she now had to sleep outside with the animals. Yet she did not complain or run away, for she was tied by her memories to her mother's house.

One night, when the frost was on the grass turning each blade into a silver spear, Sylva threw herself to the ground in tears. And the silver ribbon, which she had tied loosely about her hair, slipped off and lay on the ground before her. She had never seen it in the moonlight. It glittered and shone and seemed to ripple.

Sylva bent over to touch it and her tears fell upon it. Suddenly the ribbon began to grow and change, and as it changed the air was filled with a woman's soft voice speaking these words:

Silver ribbon, silver hair,
Carry Sylva with great care,
Bring my daughter home.

And there at Sylva's feet was a silver river that glittered and shone and rippled in the moonlight.

There was neither boat nor bridge, but Sylva did not care. She thought the river would wash away her sorrows. And without a single word, she threw herself in.

But she did not sink. Instead, she floated like a swan and the river bore her on, on past houses and hills, past high places and low. And strange to say, she was not wet at all.

At last she was carried around a great bend in the river and deposited gently on a grassy slope that came right down to the water's edge. Sylva scrambled up onto the bank and looked about. There was a great meadow of grass so green and still it might have been painted on. At the meadow's rim, near a dark forest, sat a house that was like and yet not like the one in which Sylva lived.

'Surely someone will be there who can tell me where I am and why I have been brought here,' she thought. So she made her way across the meadow, and only where she stepped down did the grass move. When she moved beyond, the grass sprang back and was the same as before. And though she passed larkspur and meadowsweet, clover and rye, they did not seem like real flowers, for they had no smell at all.

'Am I dreaming?' she wondered, 'or am I dead?' But she did not say it out loud, for she was afraid to speak into the silence.

Sylva walked up to the house and hesitated at the door. She feared to knock and yet feared equally not to. As she was deciding, the door opened of itself and she walked in.

She found herself in a large, long, dark hall with a single crystal door at the end that emitted a strange glow the color of moonlight. As she walked down the hall, her shoes made no clatter on the polished wood floor. And when she reached the door, she tried to peer through into the room beyond, but the crystal panes merely gave back her own reflection twelve times.

Sylva reached for the doorknob and pulled sharply. The glowing crystal knob came off in her hand. She would have wept then, but anger stayed her; she beat her fist against the door and it suddenly gave way.

Inside was a small room lit only by a fireplace and a round white globe that hung from the ceiling like a pale, wan moon. Before the fireplace stood a tall woman dressed all in white. Her silver-white hair was unbound and cascaded to her knees. Around her neck was a silver ribbon.

'Welcome, my daughter,' she said.

'Are you my mother?' asked Sylva wonderingly, for what little she remembered of her mother, she remembered no one as grand as this.

'I am if you make me so,' came the reply.

'And how do I do that?' asked Sylva.

'Give me your hand.'

As the woman spoke, she seemed to move away, yet she moved not at all. Instead the floor between them moved and cracked apart. Soon they were separated by a great chasm which was so black it seemed to have no bottom.

'I cannot reach,' said Sylva.

'You must try,' the woman replied.

So Sylva clutched the crystal knob to her breast and leaped, but it was too far. As she fell, she heard a woman's voice speaking from behind her and before her and all about her, warm with praise.

'Well done, my daughter. You are halfway home.'

Sylva landed gently on the meadow grass, but a moment's walk from her house. In her hand she still held the knob, shrunk now to the size of a jewel. The river shimmered once before her and was gone, and where it had been was the silver ribbon, lying limp and damp in the morning frost.

The door to the house stood open. She drew a deep breath and went in.

'What is that?' cried one of the stepsisters when she saw the crystalline jewel in Sylva's hand.

'I want it,' cried the other, grabbing it from her.

'I will take that,' said the stepmother, snatching it from them all. She held it up to the light and examined it. 'It will fetch a good price and repay me for my care of you. Where did you get it?' she asked Sylva. Sylva tried to tell them of the ribbon and the river, the tall woman and the black crevasse. But they laughed at her and did not believe her. Yet they could not explain away the jewel. So they left her then and went off to the city to sell it. When they returned, it was late. They thrust Sylva outside to sleep and went themselves to their comfortable beds to dream of their new riches.

Sylva sat on the cold ground and thought about what had happened. She reached up and took down the ribbon from her hair. She stroked it, and it felt smooth and soft and yet hard, too. Carefully she placed it on the ground.

In the moonlight, the ribbon glittered and shone. Sylva recalled the song she had heard, so she sang it to herself:

Silver ribbon, silver hair,
Carry Sylva with great care,
Bring my daughter home.

Suddenly the ribbon began to grow and change, and there at her feet was a silver highway that glittered and glistened in the moonlight. Without a moment's hesitation, Sylva got up and stepped out onto the road and waited for it to bring her to the magical house.

But the road did not move.

'Strange,' she said to herself. 'Why does it not carry me as the river did?'

Sylva stood on the road and waited a moment more, then tentatively set one foot in front of the other. As soon as she had set off on her own, the road set off, too, and they moved together past fields and forests, faster and faster, till the scenery seemed to fly by and blur into a moon-bleached rainbow of yellows, grays, and black.

The road took a great turning and then quite suddenly stopped, but Sylva did not. She scrambled up the bank where the road ended and found herself again in the meadow. At the far rim of the grass, where the forest began, was the house she had seen before.

Sylva strode purposefully through the grass, and this time the meadow was filled with the song of birds, the meadowlark and the bunting and the sweet jug-jug-jug of the nightingale. She could smell fresh-mown hay and the pungent pine.

The door of the house stood wide open, so Sylva went right in. The long hall was no longer dark but filled with the strange moonglow. And when she reached the crystal door at the end, and gazed at her reflection twelve times in the glass, she saw her own face set with strange gray eyes and long gray hair. She put up her hand to her mouth to stop herself from crying out. But the sound came through, and the door opened of itself.

Inside was the tall woman all in white, and the globe above her was as bright as a harvest moon.

'Welcome, my sister,' the woman said.

'I have no sister,' said Sylva, 'but the two stepsisters I left at home. And you are none of those.'

'I am if you make me so.'

'How do I do that?'

'Give me back my heart which you took from me yesterday.'

'I did not take your heart. I took nothing but a crystal jewel.'

The woman smiled. 'It was my heart.'

Sylva looked stricken. 'But I cannot give it back. My stepmother took it from me.'

'No one can take unless you give.'

'I had no choice.'

'There is always a choice,' the woman said.

Sylva would have cried then, but a sudden thought struck her. 'Then it must have been your choice to give me your heart.'

The woman smiled again, nodded gently, and held out her hand.

Sylva placed her hand in the woman's and there glowed for a moment on the woman's breast a silvery jewel that melted and disappeared.

'Now will you give me your heart?'

'I have done that already,' said Sylva, and as she said it, she knew it to be true.

The woman reached over and touched Sylva on her breast, and her heart sprang out onto the woman's hand and turned into two fiery red jewels. 'Once given, twice gained,' said the woman. She handed one of the jewels back to Sylva. 'Only take care that you give each jewel with love.'

Sylva felt the jewel warm and glowing in her hand, and at its touch felt such comfort as she had not had in many days. She closed her eyes and a smile came on her face. And when she opened her eyes again, she was standing on the meadow grass not two steps from her own door. It was morning, and by her feet lay the silver ribbon, limp and damp from the frost.

The door to her house stood open.

Sylva drew in her breath, picked up the ribbon, and went in.

'What has happened to your hair?' asked one stepsister.

'What has happened to your eyes?' asked the other.

For indeed Sylva's hair and eyes had turned as silver as the moon.

But the stepmother saw only the fiery red jewel in Sylva's hand. 'Give it to me,' she said, pointing to the gem.

At first Sylva held out her hand, but then quickly drew it back. 'I *can*not,' she said.

The stepmother's eyes became hard. 'Girl, give it here.'

'I *will* not,' said Sylva.

The stepmother's eyes narrowed. 'Then you shall tell me where you got it.'

'That I shall, and gladly,' said Sylva. She told them of the silver ribbon and the silver road, of the house with the crystal door. But strange to say, she left out the woman and her words.

The stepmother closed her eyes and thought. At last she said, 'Let me see this wondrous silver ribbon, that I may believe what you say.'

Sylva handed her the ribbon, but she was not fooled by her stepmother's tone.

The moment the silver ribbon lay prickly and limp in the stepmother's hand, she looked up triumphantly at Sylva. Her face broke into a wolfish grin. 'Fool,' she said, 'the magic is herein. With this ribbon there are jewels for the taking.' She marched out of the door, and the stepsisters hurried behind her.

Sylva walked after them, but slowly, stopping in the open door. The stepmother flung the ribbon down. In the early morning sun it glowed as if with a cold flame.

'Say the words, girl,' the stepmother commanded.

From the doorway Sylva whispered:

> Silver ribbon, silver hair,
> Lead the ladies with great care,
> Lead them to their home.

The silver ribbon wriggled and writhered in the sunlight, and as they watched, it turned into a silver-red stair that went down into the ground.

'Wait,' called Sylva. 'Do not go.' But it was too late.

With a great shout, the stepmother gathered up her skirts and ran down the steps, her daughters fast behind her. And before Sylva could move, the ground had closed up after them and the meadow was as before.

On the grass lay the silver ribbon, limp and dull, Sylva went over and picked it up. As she did so, the jewel melted in her hand and she felt a burning in her breast. She put her hand up to it, and she felt her heart beating strongly beneath. Sylva smiled, put the silver ribbon in her pocket, and went back into her house.

After a time, Sylva's hair returned to its own color, except for seven silver strands, but her eyes never changed back. And when she was married and had a child of her own, Sylva plucked the silver strands from her own hair and wove them into the silver ribbon, which she kept in a wooden box. When Sylva's child was old enough to understand, the box with the ribbon was put into her safekeeping, and she has kept them for her own daughter to this very day.

8 Russalka *or* The Seacoast of Bohemia

Joanna Russ

Russalka might be alive today (the book said) if she had lived in the deep sea. But the Bay of Bohemia is a backwater, with only a small community of the sea-people in it and life is easy and pleasant, and it was there that Russalka was born. She was a sea-girl, or mermaid as they're called. The sea-folk don't have fish-tails, as some stories tell you, but look very like people, with cold blood and webs between their fingers, with flat, webbed feet and gills and pale green skins and flat noses, and with glaucous eyes with an extra eyelid under the usual ones, which comes up like a film and covers their eyes when they want it to. 'Glaucous' means iridescent, like mother-of-pearl. This is what Russalka looked like.

She was an heiress among the sea-folk and this made her an awful snob. She would never leave gifts for a mer-youth who had pleased her because none of them pleased her, and she stuck her flat nose up at the old mer-matrons' wisdom, and was rude to the old mer-gentlemen when they told her they remembered her handsome father (who had been dead for years; so had her mother, in fact). She only said, 'Nonsense!'

Then she began to read books, and that was fatal.

In the deep sea this would have brought no harm, for they have their own books there, and the sea-colleges and sea-laboratories and sea-universities, and she could have become anything she liked. But the sea-people in the Bay of Bohemia are pleasant and dull and don't write books, so Russalka read land books and began to daydream about the land. Nobody knew where the books came from — either they had fallen off a boat or come down with a drowned human family — but once Russalka began to read them she became more impossible than ever. She despised the sea-people and everything in the sea. When the mer-youths and mer-maids came in the mornings asking her to go picking sea-grapes with them, or minding the sea-cattle, she wouldn't, and when they told jokes and stories she was always somewhere else. In the deep sea they would have known at once what was happening to her and would have sent her off to negotiate treaties with the great whales or chart the cold currents in the abyssal* depths where there is hardly anything to breathe, even for sea-folk, and the cold makes them sluggish, and it's dark and perilous. But the Bay of Bohemia was warm and shallow and life was dull, so Russalka became a romantic.

She would gaze all day from beneath the water at the sun, which looks from below like a wavering flower on top of the waves. We expect people who get like this to look at the moon a lot and so call it 'mooning', but the sea-folk call it 'sunning'. She also spent hours looking at the skeletons of drowned humans that the sea-people had set up in a graveyard surrounded by pretty plantings of sea-anemones (which look like flowers but are really animals) and sea-kelp. If we fall into their element the sea-people are sorry for us and carry us to land (when they can) or push us up into the air so we can breathe, but after we're drowned there's nothing they can do. Russalka thought that the skeletons, even without their flesh, were handsomer than her own people. She read her books over and over again, to memorize them before they could rot. (One was a book of fairy tales and one was *Captain Capek's Guide to Coastal Navigation,* which she didn't understand at all). She daydreamed about love, but not about youths of her own nation, for she had conceived a prejudice against green skins, flat noses, and webbed hands and feet. She daydreamed about land-men.

In short, nothing would do for Russalka but a human lover with white skin and yellow hair. Then one day the Prince of Bohemia rode along the edge of the beach with his retinue behind him, and Russalka saw him. She had met her fate.

Some say it was the banners and splendid trappings on the horses and that Russalka was ambitious, but don't you believe it. It was worse than that. She had caught the human disease — which is wanting what you can't have — and at bottom she despised her own kind. She was a daring and stubborn girl. She thought about the Prince for a day, then buried her books in the ooze at the sea-bottom, sold her sea-cattle and her family's lands, and with the wealth in both hands (sea-folk use shells for money) she went to bargain with the great sea-witch.

'Make me a human girl,' she said.

The sea-witch refused. She was a stooped, old, blunt-spoken woman

---

*'Abyssal' means deep in the abyss.

and told Russalka that she was being a fool. She offered to send her to the Finnish coast to learn magic, to Labrador to be an explorer, to the University on the edge of the great Pacific Trench, where they study everything and one can meet mer-folk from every nation.

Russalka said, 'I shall throw myself on the sand and die at his feet,' for the sea-people drown in air just as we do in water.

'By Bottom, child!' said the old witch (swearing by the seabottom as we do by the sky when we say, 'By Heaven'), 'all this for a freakish monster you've seen once and whose body you've never even touched!'

But Russalka was determined. As the old sea-witch said, she was afire with love and something worse. For the fire of the body can be quenched with a pleasant person and the fire of the heart with a dear friend, but the fire of the imagination is the very devil. And the end of it was that the old mer-matron had to agree and tell Russalka what to do and when. And the witch told her what to do if she wanted to change back, but she must do it near the sea and jump in at once, or she would drown in the air. It was all titration, distillation, radiation, hydration, and oxidation, for the person you and I call an old witch was really a distinguished scientist. But she refused to take the shells, telling Russalka to put them in the bank or lend them to someone, for she would need them when she got tired of 'that bleach-faced ninny' (as the sea-witch called the Prince) and came back to the sea.

So Russalka did it. Most of it was boring and she had to write it down on sea-paper to remember it. The ingredients took her a whole week to get, and putting them together took the better part of a day. She did it in the shallows, so as not to drown (either way), and when it was over she stood on the sand of the beach in the horrible, bright emptiness of the air, tired, feeling dreadfully heavy because she was out of the water, and shaky with hunger. The witch had given her human feet to walk on, lungs to breath the air, her gills and webs were gone, and her shape was somewhat changed. But Russalka's skin was still pale, her blood was still cold, and her long hair was still pale green. There was a limit to what the witch could do. Also she still had her extra eyelids, her features were flat and slanted, and she smelled of salt water. but by the Bohemian standards of the land, she was a pretty woman.

She walked towards the Prince's castle, which stood on a promontory overlooking the sea. It wasn't far, but Russalka was faint with hunger, and the chill of the night was coming on, which always makes the sea-folk clumsy and slow. She tried to catch mice for food, but her fingers were too slow and her body heavy with being out of the water. Sometimes she walked and sometimes she tried to run. On the last part of her trip she got down on her hands and knees and crawled. So it was past midnight when a strange, beautiful, naked woman, dressed in nothing but her own long, green hair, walked into the court-yard of the castle and fainted dead away on the stones.

Of course the Prince took a fancy to her at once. She was good-looking and she had appeared out of the night in a romantically mysterious way. Perhaps he had a touch of the same disease as Russalka and loved anything exotic and different. And different she remained, since her voice — made for the thick sea — hurt her so badly in the thin, empty air that she was forced to be silent.(She kept trying to write, 'I am a sea-maid who did this for love of you', on pieces of paper, but nobody in the castle could read.) Having your feet hurt when you walk is nothing compared to losing your voice. And writing notes that nobody can read and nobody cares about. But it all seemed worth it when she heard the Prince say that he had fallen in love with the strange Princess (he supposed her to be royal, like himself) and that he intended to marry her.

They were married within the week. Russalka was dressed in a land-lady's dress, with white fur around the neck and pearls sewn over the white satin skirt, and the Prince had an entire wardrobe sewn for her, of white or pale green dresses so that she would always look like a mermaid or a snow-angel.

It is customary, in telling this kind of story, to describe the Prince and the Princess's first kiss on their wedding night (if not the entire love-making), so I will tell you that as soon as the lovers were left alone in the splendid bridal chamber, they did kiss, and they expected it to be grand and beautiful.

It wasn't.

To him she felt cold and slimy; to her he felt hot and rough. Each of them smelled wrong. He almost let go of her when he saw her third eyelid slide up. He tried to go on making love, for he was a goodhearted and kindly man and she was, after all, his bride, whom he had chosen, but he couldn't. He was perplexed and unhappy. Russalka scribbled endless notes which he couldn't read and which the chambermaid swept up the next day.

Things got worse. It remained unnerving to him to see her eyes turn into blank pearls, which happened whenever she was tired or bored or thinking. Her habit of dining on cold fish — for anything cooked or hot nauseated her — upset him. The way she slowed down and became almost motionless after sunset terrified him. And as for Russalka herself, her fine clothes itched intolerably, her skirts weighed too much, and staying indoors in one place and doing embroidery bored her horribly. She would wait for the Prince all day among her ladies' maids, whose coarse skins and hot smell repelled her and whose chatter was loathsome, and when he came, the fire of love that had been in her heart for him all day would die. She tried to remember how she'd felt when she'd glimpsed him from under the sea, but it was no good. And then when he wasn't there it would all come back to her and she would love him passionately.

Some stories say that at this point the Prince turned his affections to a woman of his own people, but that's not true. He was still trying to love Russalka because he felt that he ought to, and besides, he was goodhearted. As for Russalka, she hadn't any other friend in the castle than he (the court ladies were too terrified of her to make friends) and she hated to admit that she'd been wrong. So they kept trying. Besides, closer acquaintance had made them feel the beginnings of something else for each other: a distant courtesy, a careful politeness, a puzzled and despairing pity, as you'd feel towards anyone in trouble.

Then one day the Prince saw his beautiful, pale bride sitting in a courtyard of the castle near an ornamental pond full of goldfish. (She liked to sit there because the pond reminded her of the sea, but nobody knew this.) She looked sad and drooping and he remembered how she had appeared out of the night only a few weeks before. His heart was moved. Then this lovely, sad lady in her shimmering, pale-green, satin gown dipped her ermine-trimmed sleeve in the pond, caught a goldfish with her bare hand, and ate it raw.

You can imagine what the Prince felt. He wanted very badly to get rid of Russalka and never see her again. But he was an honorable man and had bound himself to her in marriage. Then a solution came to him, a beautiful and simple idea, and although it was wrong (as most beautiful and simple ideas are) it consoled him wonderfully.

She was under a spell.

He was right, of course, although he'd got it all backwards: Russalka's paleness, her sluggishness in the cold, her slippery skin, her odd smell, and her strange eating habits — these were not the work of enchantment (as the Prince thought) but the only things left about her that were natural. The enchantment was all the other way. But the Prince thought he could transform her into a lovely, human bride, and in the joy of this discovery he sent post-haste for the court wizard. The wizard felt Russalka's pulse, tapped her knees, looked down her throat, peered into her ears, and counted her teeth. Then he pronounced a mighty spell over her.

Nothing happened.

Then the wizard tried necromancy,[1] cheiromancy,[2] geomancy,[3] aeluromancy,[4] and megalopolisomancy.[5] Nothing worked. Russalka kept writing on pieces of paper, 'I am not an enchanted land-princess, I am an enchanted sea-creature, please leave me alone!' but nobody paid any attention. The wizard could read, but only a little, and he couldn't make sense out of her handwriting. So eventually all her writing materials were taken away from her on the grounds that 'compulsive graphomania' (scribbling all the time) was part of the spell.

Other wizards were sent for. The Prince scoured the length and breadth of the land. Russalka tried to escape out the window of her room, but they caught her. Then she tried to barricade herself in her room, but she was constantly watched. It's notable that the spell the sea-witch had put on Russalka so easily couldn't be taken off by even the greatest land-wizards, but finally the Prince sent clear to Translyvania (which means 'across the forests') for the greatest land-wizard of all.

He was an old, old man with an immensely long, white beard, a fearful temper, a long, blue gown, and a conical hat. He was exactly what wizards are supposed to be. He knew at once that he was faced with a fantastically powerful spell, but he also knew how to remove it. He had Russalka brought naked before him in front of the whole court and said to her (she had gone past the stage of biting people and fighting; she was now very tired):

'We will make you into a real woman.'

She wrung her hands.

'Yes, yes,' said the old wizard, 'I know you don't like being what you are. I know that you are strange and sad and cold.'

Russalka fell to her knees. She meant, *Let me go back to the sea,* but of course nobody understood her.

'Yes, yes, we know that you want the spell removed,' said the old wizard.

Russalka opened her mouth to scream at him, but no sound came out.

'Yes, yes,' said the old wizard soothingly. 'We will fix all that.' From his pouch he took out a white powder, which he had spent all day preparing from his magical equipment: his flasks and tubing, his fires, his knives and staves, his pieces of dead animals, his gunpowder and mushrooms. He flung the white powder at Russalka and immediately she was enveloped in a pale cloud, like the fog on the sea at night. Through it the Prince could see something shimmer and change. He waited eagerly for the cloud to disappear and show him his beautiful human bride, but when the cloud did fade — and he saw Russalka at last — she didn't look beautiful or human to him at all.

She looked like a giant frog.

The Prince was shocked. He thought Russalka was a she-demon who had enchanted herself in order to destroy him. He thought her green skin was horrible and the webs between her fingers and toes disgusting. He thought her gills were a lace collar until they began to open and shut, and then he realized they were part of her and turned his face away. He couldn't bear to look at her. Later on he would realize what he had done and would feel profoundly sorry for Russalka. He was a good man, and the idea of a sea-maid dying for love of him gave him no pleasure. Only when he was very old and getting a bit silly would he hug himself in secret and say, 'I am the *only* Prince in the whole, wide world who had a sea-maid die for love of him.' He would marry, of course, not just because a Prince ought to but because he would want to; but he would have a memorial built around the goldfish pond, with columns, a roof, and a low wall, and he would have the wall decorated with paintings of all the creatures of the sea. He would have songs and stories invented about her, and would wonder if her sea-friends grieved — they did, for a while, remembering her as 'Russalka, you know, the one who was cracked' — and he would never let her memory die.

He forced himself to look at her. Russalka's gills were opening and shutting wildly. She was staggering over the marble floor of the throne room, jerking about the way a fish will flop around when you take it out of water. He tried to say something to her: that he was really sorry, that they could start over, that she could change back if she liked, that at last he saw her as she was and that he knew she was beautiful among her own people.

He took hold of her arm. Her extra eyelid went up, leaving her eyes blank. She tried to speak in the thin, bright air, but all that came out was a feeble, hissing sound; then in spite of the pain (for she was drowning in the air) Russalka managed to say one word, the only word she had ever spoken to him. She meant it for both of them.

'Fool!' she said.

And at his feet she bowed, she fell, she lay down; at his feet she bowed, she fell, she lay down dead.

Notes

1   'Necromancy' means performing magic by means of the dead.
2   'Cheiromancy' means performing magic by means of birds.
3   'Geomancy' is magic by means of the earth.
4   'Aeluromancy' is magic by means of cats (I don't know whether you use the cats or the cats do it themselves.)
5   'Megalopolisomancy' is magic by means of very large cities.

9 A Fairy Tale for Our Time

Jack Zipes

Steffie awoke with such a jolt that she fell out of bed. It was true, she thought. It must be. Her dreams never lied. The fairy tale had been kidnapped, and if she did not find it by nightfall, there would be silence, eternal silence, like the dreadful darkness that surrounded her room.

Haunted by her dream, Steffie got dressed as quickly as she could, and without realizing it she was soon outside the house and heading toward the country. When she reached the forest, she was overwhelmed by the devastating silence. It had already begun just as the sun was making its appearance felt. And yet, the sun was no help to her now. So she went straight to the massive oak trees and asked if they had seen the fairy tale. Without warning they all began to sob and told her that the magic had left their leaves. The entire forest was in danger. The dwarfs no longer worked in the caves, the nixies no longer swam in the ponds, the witches had thrown away their brooms, and the giants were scared of their own shadows. All of them had left the forest, but the trees could not tell her why.

So Steffie wandered deeper into the forest and gradually became aware that the birds had stopped chirping. Most of the animals looked ragged and sad, and the bushes seemed limp and paralysed. It was almost as if the entire forest had turned pale out of fright, and yet, Steffie did not see anything frightening. The only animal she encountered was a tiny rabbit who stood his ground when she approached him.

'So, you've come at last,' the rabbit sighed and let his ears droop to the ground.

'Me?' Steffie responded.

'Well, get it over with,' he said morosely.

'Get what over with?'

'Kill me!'

'What?' Steffie could not believe her ears.

'You've poisoned the fairy tale. You're destroying my home with

sprays and guns,' the rabbit asserted. 'The least you could do would be
to kill me right away!'

'Never,' Steffie replied.

Then the rabbit stuck out his tongue at her and darted into some
nearby bushes. Steffie hung her head and bumbled through a thicket.
As she wandered into an open field wondering why the rabbit had
picked on her, a huge cow with chocolate spots came trotting toward
her.

'Hey you!' the burly cow bellowed.

'Me?' Steffie was surprised.

'What have you done with the fairy tale?'

'I haven't done a thing.'

'You must have done something. We can hardly breathe here,' the
cow scowled. 'First you bring these tools and instruments to torture us
and steal our milk. Then you inject long needles into us to make us grow
fat. You put chemicals into our food. You use all my friends in the
farmyard for experiments. And you're telling me that you haven't
killed the fairy tale, too!'

'That's not true,' Steffie protested. 'I'm looking for ... '

'Get out of here, or else I'll call my friends,' and she nodded to
tremendous, sleek and powerful bulls and cows grazing at the other end
of the field. 'Moooove your self! Be quick!'

'But ... '

'Mooooooooove!'

The cow started to nudge her, and Steffie began to run. She ran past
the animals in the fields and heard taunts 'Go baaaaaaaack home,
baaaack! Cluck, cluck, cluck, cluck!' The howls and shrill sounds sent
shivers up her spine. She felt like a criminal on the run, and she kept
running until she reached the city.

Though the city was already at full speed, she had an eerie feeling that
it, too, was in danger. As she walked through the streets, the people
pushed and shoved her. And, whenever she tried to tell them what had
happened to the fairy tale, nobody seemed to care. At one point she
burst out crying, and a young woman dressed in an elegant business suit
stopped by her side: 'What's the matter, dear? Are you lost?'

'No, not really.' Steffie dried her tears.

'Well, what's the matter?'

'It's the fairy tale. They've kidnapped it.'

The young woman stared at Steffie as if she were crazy and moved
on.

Just at that moment Steffie noticed a movie theater across the street
with a big sign on the marquee: SLEEPING BEAUTY. Her eyes lit up,

and she dodged the cars as she crossed the street.

'Watch out, you lunatic!' a driver yelled at her. But Steffie did not even hear him. She went up to the box office and asked the mousy-looking man who sold tickets whether she could go in and look for the fairy tale.

'Scram! I ain't got time to fool with kids like you!' the man threatened her with his fist.

'But, but . . .' Steffie stuttered and suddenly became aware of the pictures of nude sleeping beauties that lined the entrance to the theater.

The man made a motion as if he were going to run out after her, and Steffie scooted away. Now she walked aimlessly through the city with her bright eyes vacant and her shoulders slumped. After a while she became tired and sat down on a bench in the middle of a small park strewn with litter. Next to her was an old lady twirling a cane between her legs. She was dressed in a long, tattered calico gown, army boots, and a fancy, broad-brimmed hat with a navy blue veil.

'You're a sight!' the lady said to Steffie.

Steffie knew that she should not talk to the lady, but something inside her prompted her to smile.

'What are you looking at?' the lady pouted.

'Nothing, nothing,' Steffie became afraid.

'Oh, don't become afraid.' There was something tender now in the lady's face, a mournful but sympathetic look in her eyes.

'What's the matter?' Steffie asked.

'Oh, nothing, except that they're going to put me away tomorrow.'

'Put you away? Why? Have you done something wrong?'

'No, not that I know of. I just don't have anyone. No money, no friends, and the boss people are kicking me out of my apartment, and some other boss people are going to cart me off.'

'But where will they take you?'

'I don't know. Some home, maybe. I'm not sure,' the lady suddenly began to sob.

'Please don't,' Steffie tried to calm the old lady. 'If I could, I'd take you home with me, but we don't have much money either, and I don't think that my mom and dad would like it. They've been in a terrible mood ever since my dad got fired.'

'I know.'

'You know?'

'I mean, I can imagine. I know what it's like to be without work,' the lady bowed her head.

'Are you sure there's nothing I can do?' Steffie touched her arm.

'Maybe.'

'I could help you find a hideout.'

'No, no. I have to go. The boss people will find me. They always track you down.'

'There must be something I can do,' Steffie hoped.

'Well,' the lady had a twinkle in her eye.

'Well, tell me.' Steffie was getting impatient.

'No. You tell me. Tell me a story.'

'But I can't,' Steffie replied. 'I don't know how.'

'I'll bet you can,' the lady looked square into Steffie's eyes.

'You don't understand,' the girl resisted. 'I've been searching for the fairy tale the entire day, and, if I can't find it pretty soon, then . . .'

'You said you wanted to help me, didn't you?' the old woman seemed upset.

So Steffie thought for a few seconds, and before she knew it, she began telling the lady a tale about a young woman in a calico dress who lived all alone in the city. 'Nobody knew she had magic powers. But she did, you know. And one day she went into the forest, and she met a rabbit and a cow. They were dying. The trees, too. And all she had to do, you see, was touch them, and music exploded. It broke right through the dead silence, and they were well again. The young woman liked the forest so much that she decided to stay there for many years, and the animals and the trees loved her. Finally, when she became old, I mean, not all that old, she went back into the city. But, you see, nobody liked her magic powers. Nobody cared about her. So they didn't work anymore. She tried to get people to talk to each other and help each other. But they laughed at her. Nobody knew how wonderful she was, and . . .' Steffie fumbled for words. Then she said: 'I'm not sure how the story ends.' She blushed. 'I mean, I'm sorry. I can't finish it.'

There was silence for a moment. Then the lady leaned over and gave her a kiss. 'That's all right, Steffie. You're my fairy tale.' The old lady smiled. 'You're the fairy tale. I'm sure of it.'

The lady stood up. She was a tall woman, and she glanced at Steffie with an impish grin. Then she turned from the girl, who remained seated on the bench, and she used her cane to propel herself down the path. In the twilight it seemed that a slight breeze twirled the calico gown and whisked the lady forwards. Steffie watched the large figure grow smaller, and at one point it seemed as if the lady had pushed herself into the air with her cane and was now riding on it like a broom. Steffie stood up, looked to make sure, and her heart told her that at that moment she had finally found the fairy tale.

II Feminist Fairy Tales for Old (and Young) Readers

10 The Green Woman

Meghan B. Collins

April had been chill and stormy this year, so on the first day that truly felt like spring I was happy to go outdoors in the gentle sunshine to work in my garden. After a long winter under my low, dark roof, it lightened me to see young leaves arching in airy layers overhead. I often paused in my digging to look up through them to the newborn blue sky beyond.

I was shaking soil from a clump of roots before tossing it into the barrow when the geese began to scurry about their pen with a din of honking. Geese are much better watchdogs than my old shaggy True, who now only raised his head with good-natured interest to look toward the road. If ever the villagers come to get me, the geese might warn me in time to run away into the forest. Still, old True is ferocious against rats and mice, and I would not dare to keep a cat. You never know what small thing might be brought against you later.

Now I heard the sound of wheels creaking toward my gate. I stood up to look, shading my eyes with my trowel. Whoever it was could only be coming here, for this was the end of the road.

My house is set in a clearing in the woods. There is enough open space to give sunlight for the garden, but the forest crowds in close, right to the fence that keeps deer from eating my herbs. Thus, trees hid the carriage from view until it was almost beside my front gate.

When I saw it was a closed carriage drawn by two fine roans, my heart gave a horrid lurch within me, for I knew of only one such in all the countryside, and it belonged to the Governor. In that first moment, I thought surely he was sending some men after me. I picked up the front of my skirt and half-turned to run before I noticed the shadowy head of a woman behind the carriage windows.

The equipage tilted to a halt, with one wheel in a rut. A driver in Kendal green livery jumped from the box to open the carriage door. A brightly colored figure within furled herself up like a morning glory to fit through the narrow doorframe.

When she had stepped forth onto the roadside, I recognized her from certain descriptions of Parson Wicker to be the Governor's lady. The coachman opened the gate for her, then leaned upon the gatepost with a frank and impudent interest to watch Milady stroll toward me, herself gazing about curiously.

I tossed my trowel into the barrow and brushed dirt from my fingers as best I could. I wondered what could be bringing me such a visitor. Few from the village dare approach my house by daylight. They don't want anyone to know they come to me, those dropsical old folk who creep up my path in the gloaming to be dosed with foxglove, or the young girls who come seeking a charm to make someone love them.

Now and again, someone will knock on my door in the night to fetch me to the village. The midwife there is skilled, but the one thing beyond her is a breech birth. At such times she sends for me, for I have the art of turning the baby within the womb, which I learned from my mother.

Whatever their distress, though, the sun is well down before any of these good folk slip from behind the trees toward my house. The sawyer would come by day if he wished, for he fears neither God nor the devil, but as it happens, the moonlight shines down on most of his visits. The sawyer — well, the sawyer has a sickly wife. He is a big man, and his eyes are a very clear dark blue, and that is all I care to say about that.

Parson Wicker is sure enough of his soul's safety to visit me by daylight. Many an afternoon he sits by the hour at my table, drinking cider and talking to me as I work. I am sure he tells his parishioners that he seeks to cure my own wretched soul by his visits. Perhaps he thinks so himself. I know better.

As we know, the priests of Rome are not allowed to marry. I have sometimes thought it is because they must stay empty in their own lives to keep space within for all the human woe they carry away from the confessional. But Parson Wicker is no priest, and when the weight of all he knows about the villagers grows too heavy for his heart, he brings it to me because he knows it is perfectly safe to do so.

Yes, he has told me much that he should not, that spry little pink-cheeked man. I keep silent, and often find it useful in my work to know more about the village of Starwater than the busiest gossip in it, though I seldom cross the green myself.

What chagrin would have filled the breast of this fine young lady who now approached me if she knew how much I had heard about her! Her great mansion with its gardens and lake, her extravagance in the purchase of table porcelain, her quarrels with her handsome sulky husband.

She was wearing a long cloak of soft blue wool like a jay's wing, lined in darker blue. The hood had fallen back from her head. She was so fair that it was hard to see her brows, or where her broad forehead left off and the fine pale hair began.

The path was not very long, yet she seemed to take a long time to reach me, like a boat's sail you see from afar that looms toward you slowly. When she came closer, I could see a strangeness and strength to the beauty of her face. For all she was so soft and fair, you would hesitate to cross her will.

I made her a curtsy and said, 'Madam Governor, how do you do.'

She inclined her head, accepting without question that I knew who she was. I suppose she was used to being recognized by all. She spoke no greeting in reply, but said at once, 'I have business with you, Miss. May we go into your house?'

She did not wait for me to answer, but walked straight past me toward the open doorway. My house is such a little gray weathered box; most peculiar it seemed to watch her elegant figure disappear inside, like a doll-lady on a foreign clock.

I followed her inside and gave her the chair to sit on while I took a bench facing her. She settled down with a little shake of her shoulders, as a bird settles its feathers, and gazed calmly about the room for a few moments before speaking. My notice was caught by the delicate shoes she was wearing, of softest pewter-gray leather, as fine as glove leather, with shoe roses at the instep and scarlet heels. I drew my clogs under the bench and pulled my eyes away.

Sunshine coming through the open door cast a bright square on the floor planks, and dust motes quivered in the falling rays like a veil of light. Tiny points of light twinkled from the shelves of crocks and jars; otherwise the room was shadowy and cool, with a tang in the air from bunches of dried plants hanging among the rafters.

A long silence fell while the lady scrutinized my face and uncovered head.

'They say,' she remarked in a clear, almost joyful tone of accusation, 'that witches have red hair.'

I sat quietly, looking at her. Then I shrugged. *'They say,'* I answered, repeating her emphasis, 'that looking at the new moon in a mirror will drive you mad — but it isn't so.'

She considered this for a moment with her lips pursed, and then countered, 'Well, but I have heard you can read and write!'

'As my mother taught me before she died, Madam. We must be able to read the herbals, and write labels for our mixtures, you see. And I write down new things that I learn, so as not to forget them myself, and to pass on that knowledge to my own daughter when I have one. Many men know how to read — there is no witchcraft in it just because a woman can.'

'Then what do you call yourself if not a witch?' she asked slyly.

'I call myself a green woman, Milady. If anything is wrong with you that plants can cure, I may be able to help you, for that has been my life study.' I paused and searched her face, trying to read her thought. 'Are you ailing? Tell me about it.'

She looked down into her lap and sat twisting the wedding band on her white finger.

'I have heard that if a woman is with child and does not want to be, you are able to — well, you know — make an end to it.' She shot me a keen glance from under her fair lashes and looked down again. I frowned, thinking hard.

It is true they come to me sometimes, young girls half crazy with fear, or exhausted young wives with a child in the cradle and one on the floor, and three or four in sizes up from there. How they weep, poor souls, with their heads in my lap. How they have waited and prayed, looking by night and by day for signs that do not come!

They have no fear of me then, no, no. Most gratefully they take the Contessa's powder. But afterward, when their bodies and hearts are light once more, they draw off from me with strange looks. The devil must be in it, they think, that I can in this manner turn aside from them the hand of God.

Has one of these women now, I thought, been tormenting herself in the night with fears of hellfire? Gone to the Governor, perhaps, and complained of me, so that he has sent his lady here to entrap me with questions?

I took a deep breath and ventured, 'I am wondering why such rumors would interest you, Madam Governor, a married lady like yourself, with no children of your own, I believe?'

'That is just it,' she replied. 'Three years now we have been wed, and still no children. I was thinking, you see, that since you know how to make an end, you must know how to make a beginning, too.' She turned up her palms in an expressive gesture of appeal.

'Ah, that is another trouble entirely,' I said, thinking of a certain almost empty jar on the upper shelf. 'I am afraid I cannot help you there.'

At these words, her fair softness congealed at once into a substance much harder and colder. Her lips set in a line, and the pupils of her eyes were tiny blank points in circles of gray ice.

'If I were in your place, I should think very carefully before refusing,' she said. She leaned forward in her chair and added almost in a whisper,

'It has been a long, long time since we have had a witch's trial in these parts.'

A hush fell between us now that almost had a thickness to it. It was like the moment when you drop a stone down a well and wait for the sound of its striking.

'To make a life,' I mused. 'As I told you, that is another thing, much harder than the other. Suppose I do try to help you and nothing comes of it?'

'A long, long time,' she repeated. 'Since your grandmother's day, if I recall correctly.'

I showed my teeth at her in a grin or a snarl, she could take her choice. 'You use strong persuasions, Madam. I hope your rewards are equally weighty!'

'Oh yes, I will pay in gold,' she assured me, her voice becoming lighter, almost eager, as she felt sure her will had pierced through to me.

'All right,' I said slowly. I went on to question her at some length about her health and habits, to get a better idea of what might be amiss. At last I added, 'You will have to give me some time to make up the medicine. A week, say. Shall I bring it to you, or will you come back here?

'I will come back here, I think. It would be as well for my husband not to know of this.'

I nodded. A memory came to mind of the one time I had seen the Governor. He was walking into the inn, but paused on the steps to turn around at someone's call. He was a handsome fellow, though just inclining to stoutness. The glistening salt-white of his shirt and his suit of fine black serge well became his pale complexion and glinting dark eyes. (I also recalled Parson Wicker's complaint that the church might install a new pew each year with the money the Governor spent on linen alone.) A certain droop of the Governor's mouth and the lackadaisical manner of his turn spoke of a constitution perhaps not altogether virile.

'Just a moment,' I said as Milady rose to leave. 'There is something I want you to take with you.'

I went to the shelves, took down a jar, and began to spoon some of its contents into a small packet for her.

'Starting from today, try to have your husband take some of this each day. Make it up into a tea for him, a spoonful to the cup.'

She laughed shortly. 'It would be quite a trick to make my husband drink anything but ale. Yes, one would have to be a magician, I think.'

'Put it in a toddy, then, with rum and honey, and give it to him for a bedtime drink. It will work just as well that way.'

'Yes, that he would take. What is the stuff?' she looked curiously at the jar I was restoppering.

'Oh, sarsaparilla and other things. It is a tonic.'

'And might I take it too?'

I smiled. 'No, just your husband. It is in my mind that the press of office might be fatiguing the Governor. This will build up his manly vigor.'

A curious half-smile crossed her face and was gone. I could not guess its meaning.

'You do look pale,' I observed. 'Perhaps your blood is thin. Take some molasses every day to strengthen yourself. I will have your other medicine ready when you come back.'

She took the packet without further question and began to saunter toward the door. 'I shall return next Wednesday, then. My, what a great stack of firewood you have, and you with no man around the place. Do you have to cut it yourself?'

'No, the sawyer brings it to me from the mill.'

'Ah, the sawyer. I have seen him, I think. A big man, with blue eyes?' She stood still, gazing at the wood in a deep reverie, then pulled herself up with a shake of the head, as if gnats were pestering her.

'Good-bye for the present, then,' she said.

I bowed to her in the doorway but did not follow her outside. I stood and watched her walk away down the path toward her waiting carriage. Above her head, a jay flew down from the treetops to perch on a lower branch. He called at me with his jeering cry.

'Haw!' he seemed to be laughing. 'Haw-haw!'

When the last rattle of carriage wheels had died away, when the sheltering woods were once again silent of all but their own sounds, I turned away from the doorsill and sat down in the chair with my grandmother's old handwritten herbal in my lap. It was a long, narrow gray book with 'Journal' printed on the cover in dull maroon letters. I myself had pasted new cloth along its spine to strengthen the binding. I did not trouble to open the book at first. I suppose I just wanted to hold it in my hands to feel the healing presence of that little aged creature whose bright face I can barely remember.

My mother and I had searched through the book so many times before, searching for this particular formula, but it was one of the very few Grandmother had not written down. Nor did she, before they came to take her away, show my mother how it was made. Perhaps she herself had bought the mixture from somewhere, as I must buy stoneseed from the Indian trader and Peruvian bark from the apothecary. If that were so, she may not have known how to compound it herself; I don't know.

The times we needed to give out such a medicine, and these came but seldom, Mother and I always just took from the jar the small amount needed. As the level sank down, we grew ever more cautious and thrifty about measuring it. Even so, the last full dose we could eke out had been given three years ago, and since my mother died I have not even admitted to knowing such a cure. What was left in the jar were just flakes that you could hold in your palm — so old that there was probably no power in them anymore, for virtue cannot last forever in plants, no more than in women.

The rest of that day and part of the next I read through all the ledgers that had been handed down to me from those two wise women now gone from my life; Grandmother, whose manner of death I do not dare to think of right now, and Mother, who died quite young of a tumor not all her mandrake extracts could diminish. Partly, as I said, I just wanted to feel their company — to bring back a sense of their real persons, which handwriting seems to call up so strongly. But partly I hoped one formula or another might jump together in a pattern to give me a new idea.

I took down the jar with its few leaves and spread them out on a piece of paper to smell them and taste them. I carried them over to a good light by the window and looked at them under my mother's strong glass, with the gold bumblebee for its handle, that the fine gentleman gave her so long ago.

The mixture contained motherwort, of that I was sure, and wormwood. There appeared to be water nerveroot, and water betony also, and something else that might be black horehound. I remembered that when my mother gave out the cure she did not give the dried mixture itself, but boiled it up in water and strained off an infusion.

Still, I was ringed about with unanswered questions. The time of year when herbs are gathered often makes a difference in their properties. Was I to use the leaves, the roots, the stems? And most important, in what proportion must I mix the different kinds?

One late afternoon, while I sat at table with pen and paper writing out a receipt for possible use, Parson Wicker arrived for a visit, announced by screaming from the geese. I could tell he was troubled, for he did not sit down with his usual eagerness to sip and nibble at the little meal of cider, bread, and cheese that I rose to set out for him. Instead, he walked about the room and stood by the window, thoughtfully tapping his teeth with his forefinger. When he spoke, it was in a manner he had when ill at ease, adding a little humming sound before certain words: 'How have you been? I hope you are hmmmwell?'

'I am well enough. But you seem restless today. Are you upset about something?'

'Truth to tell, I am a little. Mrs. Jacob Taylor tells me that the Governor's lady drove past their farm Wednesday in her carriage. So, she must have come here — there is no other house beyond the Taylors'.

'That is true. She was here.'

'Oh dear,' his ruddy face puckered unhappily. 'And I suppose she wanted you to hmmtreat her for some ailment?'

'No, it was just a sociable visit,' I replied lightly, but the poor man was altogether too heavy-minded to understand pleasantry. A struggle to imagine the Governor's wife paying a social call to the likes of me began to warp his features into the most comical expression, so I quickly added, 'I'm teasing, I'm teasing. But you must understand I cannot tell you why she came to me.'

'Oh, I think I can guess that. Not long ago, she was lamenting to me about her childless state, and at the same time she questioned me very closely about your skills. That is why I am so sorely troubled. To think I may have been the cause of her coming here!'

He fiddled with the handle of his mug in silence for a time, and then burst out, '*Why* can you not give this up? You shall only end by being hanged or burned one day. Can you not set aside these magics and medicines and live like ordinary folk?'

I thought of the village green, that pleasant oval, with the little houses set around it. There people smiled when they met in the road, and the women called greetings to each other while they hung out their linens to dry in the sun. Thinking of such friendly neighbors made me pull a wry face at the parson.

'And will I have a kindly welcome, dear sir, when I move into my little cottage on the green? Will the good and trusting folk of Starwater rush to buy the pies I shall bake from my famous secret receipts to earn my living? Will the good wives invite me to tea?'

His eyes rolled up to the rafters to avoid meeting mine.

'Well, but this is not the only village in the world,' he demurred. 'You could go to another where nobody knows you. You are young still, and hmmpleasing to look at. You might even marry, if you could learn to bridle that sharp tongue of yours.'

'We do not marry,' I told him haughtily.

'And why not, I should like to know?'

'I don't know. It is a tradition. In a way, I suppose we are like the priests of Rome — we have to keep our own lives empty to be free to cure others.'

'Hush, woman! What blasphemy!'

'Well, you asked me,' I murmured, smiling to turn his mood. 'As for going away, we have been living in this house since time out of mind.

Am I now to be run off like a homeless dog because the fine lady might take a whim against me?'

'She is a danger; never doubt it. Did you know that she works her farms and gardens with prisoners' labor? Yes, and has them flogged at her displeasure. A heart of marble, truly.'

He hunched his shoulders and looked so wretched that I reached out and patted his hand.

'Please, don't distress yourself so. It is true that I sometimes think with longing of the life you describe, to be safe and sheltered, and part of a friendly, homely world. But it always comes back to this, that what I know cannot be unlearned. Nor would I wish to know less than I do. Whatever the risk, I will not be less than what my life has made me.'

I paused to look at him earnestly and added, 'It is my own choice, you see. However it turns out, there is no reason you should feel accountable.'

He sat looking down at the table for a short while and at last nodded his head several times in acceptance. Without further word or look, he rose and, picking up his tall hat that was covered with road dust, walked slowly out the door.

The next days were long and weary for me. Although many useful plants grow in my home garden — sage, poppy, foxglove, and the like — I also make daily use of wild herbs from the woods and meadows. It may sound like dainty work to wander about with a willow basket, picking flowers and rare greens, but remember, I must go in any weather. Dusty and sun scorched, or windy and raining ice, no matter. Sometimes I must walk many miles to find what I am looking for, and still there is the day's work to do when I get home.

For some of life's needs I can barter. I keep no cow, for instance, since the farm wives of our district pay me in butter and cheese. But there is much I must do for myself, and living alone as I do with no one to help, just the chores of staying alive pare many precious hours from my day.

The only work I truly hate, though, is hunting the bogs for water plants. There, my flesh crawls with the nearness of snakes I cannot see. I am always in dread of a false step on that quaking ground, which would suck me down slowly, screaming, into the ooze. Sometimes I wake up in the night, drenched in sweat but also shivering cold, having dreamed of that.

So it was good, after a day spent in the bog late that week, to have the sawyer's company in the night. I was drying plants on a screen over the fire when he came in. My hair was sticking to my face in tendrils from the heat, and I felt tired and unkempt, but I was glad to see him. I smiled a greeting and fetched him a mug of ale to sit with while I finished my work.

Later, when all had been tidied away and the hearth swept, I took up the ale jug and carried it to where he was sitting. He threw an arm around my knees.

'Do you know what I like about you?' he muttered, nuzzling his face against my belly. 'You make me feel that it pleases you to feed me and love me. I hate that feeling that everything I need wears a body to death.'

Surprised and touched, I cradled his dark head in my hands. It was seldom he was so tender. That night he was a gentle breeze lifting me up, not the wild wind or bluff gale I was accustomed to. At some point the thought came to me to worry about all the mixtures I had been tasting, and a fear jumped in my gullet like the sudden leap of a frog. But then, almost as clearly as if she had been there, I could hear my mother's firm voice in my ear: 'Dear heart, it is time you had a daughter of your own.' At these words, a pure well of peacefulness filled within me, and I feared no more.

Just as she had promised, in the afternoon of the seventh day Milady once more approached my house with her slow, swaying walk like a boat at anchor or a wind-tilted bell. I had already set out for her on the table a stoneware bottle containing the potion I had brewed for her. Seeing it, she picked it up at once and turned it curiously in her hands.

I made her reckon up her monthly dates, which she had trouble remembering. Then I made some calculations on a piece of paper, while she watched me with uneasy interest, as if I were writing sorcerers' signs.

'Here is what you must do,' I told her, when I finished writing. 'From the time the moon is in its last quarter you must not have anything to do with your husband. If he presses you, pretend you are ill. In the dark of the moon, begin to take this liquid. Take half a wine goblet both morning and night. From the third day after the new moon, lie with your husband as often as he will for a few days. Can you remember that?'

'Yes.'

I stood up so that I could look down on her.

'Now, my pay for this. I want two gold pieces now and three more when you find yourself full.'

'When?' she repeated with mocking challenge. 'You are so sure, then, of your merit?'

I gathered up all the strength of my being and fixed my eyes on her like a mighty beam of light. Pressing the heels of my hands on the table,

I leaned across it toward her and asked in a measured, chiming voice:
'Do you now believe I have powers to do it?'

She swallowed and bent her head.

'Then trust what I tell you.'

I let the aftertones of my words circle out in the silent room until they
died away. Then, resuming my normal voice, I said, 'Here, I shall wrap
your bottle in a bit of cloth to guard it against breaking. Keep it
somewhere cool at home, for heat will rob its power.'

She stirred in her chair. Opening a little netted purse, she took out
two gold pieces and placed them on the table, meticulously pushing
them side by side with her tapered forefinger. As if the act of payment
had restored her proper rank, she too now rose and looked about her
with an arrogant tilt of her head.

'More firewood!' she exclaimed. 'The handsome sawyer treats you
well.'

'Yes, he is good to me.'

'You are so fortunate.' She gave a little laugh, sharp as broken glass,
and walked away. 'Good-bye, then. I hope your potion works as
promised. For both our sakes, eh?'

Once she was gone, I should have felt some ease. I should have been
able to say to myself, 'It is done now. There is nothing more but to
wait.'

There was something, though, an unnameable shadow in my mind
that would not let me settle. During the next days, if I were at sweeping,
I would stop and lean on the broom, staring with vacant eyes. Digging
in the garden was the same — I would start out of a dream and find that
I had been idly drawing lines on the ground with the edge of my trowel.

Thus driven by unrest, I paced and thought. I wished for the wisdom
of King Solomon himself, to tell me what else I should do to preserve
my life and the one perhaps to come. At length I called to True and set
out on the road toward the sawmill.

When we had come near to the bridge, I took a side path through the
woods and stood among trees on the edge of the stream, just across
from the sawmill. He was working the big saw that is run by the water-
wheel, and the noise of it drowned out every other sound in the world.
I wondered how he could abide such a din in his ears all day. I waited
until I was sure he had seen me, then withdrew into the woods to sit on
a stump until he should come. The sound of the saw faded in a dying
whine, and before long the flicker of his blue shirt showed through the
underbrush.

'Is something wrong?' he asked, for I had never before approached
the mill.

'No, I just have a favor to ask, and I wasn't sure when you might come back to my house.'

'Ah,' he said, squatting down with his back against a tree and reaching out to scratch the dog's head.

'I need some white Solomon's seal to make up a salve, and the nearest place to find it is Vannever's Lake. It must be eleven miles to walk there. Will you take one of your horses and ride over to get it for me?'

He raised his head and gave me a curious look, without answering for a moment.

'Don't you want to take the horse and go yourself? How can you be sure I would get the right plant?'

'I couldn't do that. Everyone in the countryside knows the sawmill horses by sight. Do you want to scandalize your name?'

That made him twitch. I pressed on: 'I can show you a picture of white Solomon's seal in a herbal before you go. It is not hard to recognize. And I will show you how to pack it so it will stay fresh.'

'Vannevar's Lake is on the Governor's land. Suppose he has me up for trespass?'

'Go to the mansion and ask permission of the Governor's lady. Ask her pleasantly and I'm sure she will not refuse you. The stuff grows wild in the woods there, after all.'

He looked up at me in pure male mischief.

'The Governor's lady, eh? She has a wanton look in her eye, that one. Suppose she will be following me into the woods?'

I smiled. 'Well, if the Governor will not do his duty, I'm sure you can make up the lack.'

He scowled. 'And wouldn't you care?'

'Of course I would care!' I cried out, and then recovered my light tone. 'I am just wise like King Solomon, who knew that true love will bear any cost to guard the child.'

'You talk riddles,' he said impatiently.

'But will you go?'

'All right, then.'

'And one thing more. Can you arrange your work to make the trip next Monday? Tuesday at the latest? The time of the moon is very important in these matters, you see.'

Again he gave me a peculiar look, but made no objection. And so we parted, after a brief embrace. When he turned his back and started to walk away, though, I felt such a wave of desolation that I followed a few steps after him in spite of myself.

'John!' I called. He turned around, puzzled. 'You will come back to me, after?'

A smile creased his cheek, and his blue gaze steadied my heart. 'How could I not?' he said simply, and was gone.

So now I have come back to my house all alone. This week I shall turn out all my drawers and cupboards to tidy them. Such a pastime will keep my mind busy. Besides, if they should be coming to get me soon, I do not want the virtuous women of Starwater to be clucking over my housekeeping afterward, saying, 'Look, what a sloven she was.'

But there is no need for me to worry about that. I have staked all the skill of my mind, and thrown my heart's dear desire in after it. Now there is no more to be done, indeed, but to wait and see what tidings the full moon shall bring.

11 Briar Rose (Sleeping Beauty)

Anne Sexton

Consider
a girl who keeps slipping off,
arms limp as old carrots,
into the hypnotist's trance,
into a spirit world
speaking with the gift of tongues.
She is stuck in the time machine,
suddenly two years old sucking her thumb,
as inward as a snail,
learning to talk again.
She's on a voyage.
She is swimming further and further back,
up like a salmon,
struggling into her mother's pocketbook.
Little doll child,
come here to Papa.
Sit on my knee.
I have kisses for the back of your neck.
A penny for your thoughts, Princess.
I will hunt them like an emerald.
Come be my snooky
and I will give you a root.
That kind of voyage,
rank as honeysuckle.

Once
a king had a christening
for his daughter Briar Rose
and because he had only twelve gold plates
he asked only twelve fairies

to the grand event.
The thirteenth fairy,
her fingers as long and thin as straws,
her eyes burnt by cigarettes,
her uterus an empty teacup,
arrived with an evil gift.
She made this prophecy:
The princess shall prick herself
on a spinning wheel in her fifteenth year
and then fall down dead.
Kaputt!
The court fell silent.
The king looked like Munch's *Scream*.
Fairies' prophecies,
in times like those,
held water.
However the twelfth fairy
had a certain kind of eraser
and thus she mitigated the curse
changing that death
into a hundred-year sleep.
The king ordered every spinning wheel
exterminated and exorcized.
Briar Rose grew to be a goddess
and each night the king
bit the hem of her gown
to keep her safe.
He fastened the moon up
with a safety pin
to give her perpetual light
He forced every male in the court
to scour his tongue with Bab-o
lest they poison the air she dwelt in.
Thus she dwelt in his odor.
Rank as honeysuckle.

On her fifteenth birthday
she pricked her finger
on a charred spinning wheel
and the clocks stopped.
Yes indeed. She went to sleep.
The king and queen went to sleep,

the courtiers, the flies on the wall.
The fire in the hearth grew still
and the roast meat stopped crackling.
The trees turned into metal
and the dog became china.
They all lay in a trance,
each a catatonic
stuck in the time machine.
Even the frogs were zombies.

Only a bunch of briar roses grew
forming a great wall of tacks
around the castle.
Many princes
tried to get through the brambles
for they had heard much of Briar Rose
but they had not scoured their tongues
so they were held by the thorns
and thus were crucified.
In due time
a hundred years passed
and a prince got through.
The briars parted as if for Moses
and the prince found the tableau intact.
He kissed Briar Rose
and she woke up crying:
Daddy! Daddy!
Presto! She's out of prison!
She married the prince
and all went well
except for the fear—
the fear of sleep.

Briar Rose
was an insomniac ...
She could not nap
or lie in sleep
without the court chemist
mixing her some knock-out drops
and never in the prince's presence.
If it is to come, she said,
sleep must take me unawares

while I am laughing or dancing
so that I do not know that brutal place
where I lie down with cattle prods,
the hole in my cheek open.
Further, I must not dream
for when I do I see the table set
and a faltering crone at my place,
her eyes burnt by cigarettes
as she eats betrayal like a slice of meat.

I must not sleep
for while asleep I'm ninety
and think I'm dying.
Death rattles in my throat
like a marble.
I wear tubes like earrings.
I lie as still as a bar of iron.
You can stick a needle
through my kneecap and I won't flinch.
I'm all shot up with Novocain.
This trance girl
is yours to do with.
You could lay her in a grave,
an awful package,
and shovel dirt on her face
and she'd never call back: Hello there!
But if you kissed her on the mouth
her eyes would spring open
and she'd call out: Daddy! Daddy!
Presto!
She's out of prison.

There was a theft.
That much I am told.
I was abandoned.
That much I know.
I was forced backward.
I was forced forward.
I was passed hand to hand
like a bowl of fruit.
Each night I am nailed into place
and I forget who I am.

Daddy?
That's another kind of prison.
It's not the prince at all,
but my father
drunkenly bent over my bed,
circling the abyss like a shark,
my father thick upon me
like some sleeping jellyfish.

What voyage this, little girl?
This coming out of prison?
God help —
this life after death?

12 Little Red Riding Hood

Olga Broumas

I grow old, old
without you, Mother, landscape
of my heart. No child, no daughter between my bones
has moved, and passed
out screaming, dressed in her mantle of blood

as I did
once through your pelvic scaffold, stretching it
like a wishbone, your tenderest skin
strung on its bow and tightened
against the pain. I slipped out like an arrow, but not before

the midwife
plunged to her wrist and guided
my baffled head to its first mark. High forceps
might, in that one instant, have accomplished
what you and that good woman failed
in all these years to do: cramp
me between the temples, hobble
my baby feet. Dressed in my red hood, howling, I went —

evading
the white-clad doctor and his fancy claims: microscope,
stethoscope, scalpel, all
the better to see with, to hear,
and to eat — straight from your hollowed basket
into the midwife's skirts. I grew up
good at evading, and when you said,
'Stick to the road and forget the flowers, there's
wolves in those bushes, mind

where you got to go, mind
you get there,' I
minded. I kept

to the road, kept
the hood secret, kept what it sheathed more
secret still. I opened
it only at night, and with other women
who might be walking the same road to their own
grandma's house, each with her basket of gifts, her small hood
safe in the same part. I minded well. I have no daughter

to trace that road, back to your lap with my laden
basket of love. I'm growing
old, old
without you. Mother, landscape
of my heart, architect of my body, what other gesture
can I conceive

to make with it
that would reach you, alone
in your house and waiting, across this improbable forest
peopled with wolves and our lost, flower-gathering
sisters they feed on.

13 Rapunzel

Sara Henderson Hay

Oh God, let me forget the things he said.
Let me not lie another night awake
Repeating all the promises he made,
Freezing and burning for his faithless sake;
Seeing his face, feeling his hand once more
Loosen my braided hair until it fell
Shining and free; remembering how he swore
A single strand might lift a man from Hell . . .

I knew that other girls, in Aprils past,
Had leaned, like me, from some old tower's room
And watched him clamber up, hand over fist . . .
I knew that I was not the first to twist
Her heartstrings to a rope for him to climb.
I might have known I would not be the last.

14 Wolfland

Tanith Lee

1

When the summons arrived from Anna the Matriarch, Lisel did not wish to obey. The twilit winter had already come, and the great snows were down, spreading their aprons of shining ice, turning the trees to crystal candelabra. Lisel wanted to stay in the city, skating fur-clad on the frozen river beneath the torches, dancing till four in the morning, a vivid blonde in the flame-bright ballrooms, breaking hearts and not minding, lying late next day like a cat in her warm, soft bed. She did not want to go traveling several hours into the north to visit Anna the Matriarch.

Lisel's mother had been dead sixteen years, all Lisel's life. Her father had let her have her own way, in almost everything, for about the same length of time. But Anna the Matriarch, Lisel's maternal grandmother, was exceedingly rich. She lived thirty miles from the city, in a great wild château in the great wild forest.

A portrait of Anna as a young widow hung in the gallery of Lisel's father's house, a wicked-looking bone-pale person in a black dress, with rubies and diamonds at her throat, and in her ivory yellow hair. Even in her absence, Anna had always had a say in things. A recluse, she had still manipulated like a puppet-master from behind the curtain of the forest. Periodic instructions had been sent, pertaining to Lisel. The girl must be educated by this or that method. She must gain this or that accomplishment, read this or that book, favor this or that cologne or color or jewel. The latter orders were always uncannily apposite and were often complemented by applicable — and sumptuous — gifts. The summons came in company with such. A swirling cloak of scarlet velvet leapt like a fire from its box to Lisel's hands. It was lined with albino fur, all but the hood, which was lined with the finest and heaviest red brocade. A clasp of gold joined the garment at the throat, the two portions, when closed, forming Anna's personal device, a many-petaled flower. Lisel had exclaimed with pleasure, embracing the cloak, picturing herself flying in it across the solid white river like a dangerous blood-red rose. Then the letter fell from its folds.

Lisel had never seen her grandmother, at least, not intelligently, for Anna had been in her proximity on one occasion only: the hour of her birth. Then, one glimpse had apparently sufficed. Anna had snatched it, and sped away from her son-in-law's house and the salubrious city in a demented black carriage. Now, as peremptory as then, she demanded that Lisel come to visit her before the week was out. Over thirty miles, into the uncivilized northern forest, to the strange mansion in the snow.

'Preposterous,' said Lisel's father. 'The woman is mad, as I've always suspected.'

'I shan't go,' said Lisel.

They both knew quite well that she would.

One day, every considerable thing her grandmother possessed would pass to Lisel, providing Lisel did not incur Anna's displeasure.

Half a week later, Lisel, was on the northern road.

She sat amid cushions and rugs, in a high sled strung with silver bells, and drawn by a single black-satin horse. Before Lisel perched her driver, the whip in his hand, and a pistol at his belt, for the way north was not without its risks. There were, besides, three outriders, also equipped with whips, pistols and knives, and muffled to the brows in fur. No female companion was in evidence. Anna had stipulated that it would be unnecessary and superfluous for her grandchild to burden herself with a maid.

But the whips had cracked, the horses had started off. The runners of the sled had smoothly hissed, sending up lace-like sprays of ice. Once clear of the city, the north road opened like a perfect skating floor of milky glass, dim-lit by the fragile winter sun smoking low on the horizon. The silver bells sang, and the fierce still air through which the horses dashed broke on Lisel's cheeks like the coldest champagne. Ablaze in her scarlet cloak, she was exhilarated and began to forget she had not wanted to come.

After about an hour, the forest marched up out of the ground and swiftly enveloped the road on all sides.

There was presently an insidious, but generally perceptible change. Between the walls of the forest there gathered a new silence, a silence which was, if anything, *alive,* a personality which attended any humanly noisy passage with a cruel and resentful interest. Lisel stared up into the narrow lane of sky above. They might have been moving along the channel of a deep and partly frozen stream. When the drowned sun flashed through, splinters of light scattered and went out as if in water.

The tall pines in their pelts of snow seemed poised to lurch across the road.

The sled had been driving through the forest for perhaps another hour, when a wolf wailed somewhere amid the trees. Rather than break the silence of the place, the cry seemed born of the silence, a natural expression of the landscape's cold solitude and immensity.

The outriders touched the pistols in their belts, almost religiously, and the nearest of the three leaned to Lisel.

'Madam Anna's house isn't far from here. In any case we have our guns, and these horses could race the wind.'

'I'm not afraid,' Lisel said haughtily. She glanced at the trees, 'I've never seen a wolf. I should be interested to see one.'

Made sullen by Lisel's pert reply, the outrider switched tactics. From trying to reassure her, he now ominously said: 'Pray you don't, m'mselle. One wolf generally means a pack, and once the snow comes, they're hungry.'

'As my father's servant, I would expect you to sacrifice yourself for me, of course,' said Lisel. 'A fine strong man like you should keep a pack of wolves busy long enough for the rest of us to escape.'

The man scowled and spurred away from her.

Lisel smiled to herself. She was not at all afraid, not of the problematical wolves, not even of the eccentric grandmother she had never before seen. In a way, Lisel was looking forward to the meeting, now her annoyance at vacating the city had left her. There had been so many bizarre tales, so much hearsay. Lisel had even caught gossip concerning Anna's husband. He had been a handsome princely man, whose inclinations had not matched his appearance. Lisel's mother had been sent to the city to live with relations to avoid this monster's outbursts of perverse lust and savagery. He had allegedly died one night, mysteriously and luridly murdered on one of the forest tracks. This was not the history Lisel had got from her father, to be sure, but she had always partly credited the more extravagant version. After all, Anna the Matriarch was scarcely commonplace in her mode of life or her attitude to her granddaughter.

Yes, indeed, rather than apprehension, Lisel was beginning to entertain a faintly unholy glee in respect of the visit and the insights it might afford her.

A few minutes after the wolf had howled, the road took a sharp bend, and emerging around it, the party beheld an unexpected obstacle in the way. The driver of the sled cursed softly and drew hard on the reins, bringing the horse to a standstill. The outriders similarly halted. Each peered ahead to where, about twenty yards along the road, a great black carriage blotted the white snow.

A coachman sat immobile on the box of the black carriage, muffled in coal-black furs and almost indistinguishable from them. In forceful contrast, the carriage horses were blonds, and restless, tossing their necks, lifting their feet. A single creature stood on the track between the carriage and the sled. It was too small to be a man, too curiously proportioned to be simply a child.

'What's this?' demanded the third of Lisel's outriders, he who had spoken earlier of the wolves. It was an empty question, but had been a long time in finding a voice for all that.

'I think it is my grandmother's carriage come to meet me,' declared Lisel brightly, though, for the first, she had felt a pang of apprehension.

This was not lessened, when the dwarf came loping toward them, like a small, misshapen, furry dog and, reaching the sled, spoke to her, ignoring the others.

'You may leave your escort here and come with us.'

Lisel was struck at once by the musical quality of his voice, while out of the shadow of his hood emerged the face of a fair and melancholy angel. As she stared at him, the men about her raised their objections.

'We're to go with m'mselle to her grandmother's house.'

'You are not necessary,' announced the beautiful dwarf, glancing at them with uninterest. 'You are already on the Lady Anna's lands. The coachman and I are all the protection your mistress needs. The Lady Anna does not wish to receive you on her estate.'

'What proof,' snarled the third outrider, 'that you're from Madame's château? Or that she told you to say such a thing. You could have come from any place, from hell itself most likely, and they crushed you in the door as you were coming out.'

The riders and the driver laughed brutishly. The dwarf paid no attention to the insult. He drew from his glove one delicate, perfectly formed hand, and in it a folded letter. It was easy to recognize the Matriarch's sanguine wax and the imprint of the petaled flower. The riders brooded and the dwarf held the letter toward Lisel. She accepted it with an uncanny but pronounced reluctance.

'*Chère*,' it said in its familiar, indeed its unmistakable, characters, '*Why are you delaying the moment when I may look at you? Beautiful has already told you, I think, that your escort may go home. Anna is giving you her own escort, to guide you on the last laps of the journey. Come! Send the men away and step into the carriage.*'

Lisel, reaching the word, or rather the name, Beautiful, had glanced involuntarily at the dwarf, oddly frightened at its horrid contrariness and its peculiar truth. A foreboding had clenched around her young heart, and, for a second, inexplicable terror. It was certainly a dreadful dilemma. She could refuse, and refuse thereby the goodwill, the gifts, the ultimate fortune her grandmother could bestow. Or she could brush aside her silly childish fears and walk boldly from the sled to the carriage. Surely, she had always known Madame Anna was an eccentric. Had it not been a source of intrigued curiosity but a few moments ago?

Lisel made her decision.

'Go home,' she said regally to her father's servants. 'My grandmother is wise and would hardly put me in danger.'

The men grumbled, glaring at her, and as they did so, she got out of the sled and moved along the road toward the stationary and funereal carriage. As she came closer, she made out the flower device stamped in gilt on the door. Then the dwarf had darted ahead of her, seized the door, and was holding it wide, bowing to his knees, thus almost into the snow. A lock of pure golden hair spilled across his forehead.

Lisel entered the carriage and sat on the somber cushions. Courageous prudence (or greed) had triumphed.

The door was shut. She felt the slight tremor as Beautiful leapt on the box beside the driver.

Morose and indecisive, the men her father had sent with her were still lingering on the ice between the trees, as she was driven away.

She must have slept, dazed by the continuous rocking of the carriage, but all at once she was wide awake, clutching in alarm at the upholstery. What had roused her was a unique and awful choir. The cries of wolves.

Quite irresistibly she pressed against the window and stared out, impelled to look for what she did not, after all, wish to see. And what she saw was unreassuring.

A horde of wolves were running, not merely in pursuit, but actually alongside the carriage. Pale they were, a pale almost luminous brownish shade, which made them seem phantasmal against the snow. Their small but jewel-like eyes glinted, glowed and burned. As they ran, their tongues lolling sideways from their mouths like those of huge hunting dogs, they seemed to smile up at her, and her heart turned over.

Why was it, she wondered, with panic-stricken anger, that the coach did not go faster and so outrun the pack? Why was it the brutes had been permitted to gain as much distance as they had? Could it be they had already plucked the coachman and the dwarf from the box and devoured them — she tried to recollect if, in her dozing, she had registered masculine shrieks of fear and agony — and that the horses plunged on. Imagination, grown detailed and pessimistic, soon dispensed with these images, replacing them with that of great peppercolored paws scratching on the frame of the coach, the grisly talons ripping at the door, at last a wolf's savage mask thrust through it, and her own frantic and pointless screaming, in the instants before her throat was silenced by the meeting of narrow yellow fangs.

Having run the gamut of her own premonition, Lisel sank back on the seat and yearned for a pistol, or at least a knife. A malicious streak in her lent her the extraordinary bravery of desiring to inflict as many hurts on her killers as she was able before they finished her. She also took space to curse Anna the Matriarch. How the wretched old woman would grieve and complain when the story reached her. The cleanpicked bones of her granddaughter had been found a mere mile or so from her château, in the rags of a blood-red cloak; by the body a golden clasp, rejected as inedible. . . .

A heavy thud caused Lisel to leap to her feet, even in the galloping, bouncing carriage. There at the door, grinning in on her, the huge face of a wolf, which did not fall away. Dimly she realized it must impossibly be balancing itself on the running board of the carriage, its front paws raised and somehow keeping purchase on the door. With one sharp determined effort of its head, it might conceivably smash in the pane of the window. The glass would lacerate, and the scent of its own blood further inflame its starvation. The eyes of it, doused by the carriage's gloom, flared up in two sudden pupilless ovals of fire, like two little portholes into hell.

With a shrill howl, scarcely knowing what she did, Lisel flung herself at the closed door and the wolf the far side of it. Her eyes also blazed, her teeth also were bared, and her nails raised as it to claw. Her horror was such that she appeared ready to attack the wolf in its own primeval mode, and as her hands struck the glass against its face, the wolf shied and dropped away.

In that moment, Lisel heard the musical voice of the dwarf call out from the box, some wordless whoop, and a tall gatepost sprang by.

Lisel understood they had entered the grounds of the Matriarch's château. And, a moment later, learned, though did not understand, that the wolves had not followed them beyond the gateway.

2

The Matriarch sat at the head of the long table. Her chair, like the table, was slender, carved and intensely polished. The rest of the chairs, though similarly high-backed and angular, were plain and dull, including the chair to which Lisel had been conducted. Which increased Lisel's annoyance, the petty annoyance to which her more eloquent emotions of fright and rage had given way, on entering the domestic, if curious, atmosphere of the house. And Lisel must strive to conceal her ill-temper. It was difficult.

The château, ornate and swarthy under its pointings of snow, retained an air of decadent magnificence, which was increased within. Twin stairs flared from an immense great hall. A hearth, large as a room, and crow-hooded by its enormous mantel, roared with muffled firelight. There was scarcely a furnishing that was not at least two hundred years old, and many were much older. The very air seemed tinged by the somber wood, the treacle darkness of the draperies, the old-gold gleams of picture frames, gilding and tableware.

At the center of it all sat Madame Anna, in her eighty-first year, a weird apparition of improbable glamour. She appeared, from no more than a yard or so away, to be little over fifty. Her skin, though very dry, had scarcely any lines in it, and none of the pleatings and collapses Lisel generally associated with the elderly. Anna's hair had remained blonde, a fact Lisel was inclined to attribute to some preparation out of a bottle, yet she was not sure. The lady wore black as she had done in the portrait of her youth, a black starred over with astonishing jewels. But her nails were very long and discolored, as were her teeth. These two incontrovertible proofs of old age gave Lisel a perverse satisfaction. Grandmother's eyes, on the other hand, were not so reassuring. Brilliant eyes, clear and very likely sharp-sighted, of a pallid silvery brown. Unnerving eyes, but Lisel did her best to stare them out, though when Anna spoke to her, Lisel now answered softly, ingratiatingly.

There had not, however, been much conversation, after the first clamor at the doorway:

'We were chased by wolves!' Lisel had cried. 'Scores of them! Your coachman is a dolt who doesn't know enough to carry a pistol. I might have been killed.'

'You were not,' said Anna, imperiously standing in silhouette against the giant window of the hall, a stained glass of what appeared to be a hunting scene, done in murky reds and staring white.

'No thanks to your servants. You promised me an escort — the only reason I sent my father's men away.'

'You had your escort.'

Lisel had choked back another flood of sentences; she did not want to get on the wrong side of this strange relative. Nor had she liked the slight emphasis on the word 'escort'.

The handsome ghastly dwarf had gone forward into the hall, lifted the hem of Anna's long mantle, and kissed it. Anna had smoothed off his hood and caressed the bright hair beneath.

'Beautiful wasn't afraid,' said Anna decidedly. 'But, then, my people know the wolves will not harm them.'

An ancient tale came back to Lisel in that moment. It concerned certain human denizens of the forests, who had power over wild beasts. It occurred to Lisel that mad old Anna liked to fancy herself a sorceress, and Lisel said fawningly: 'I should have known I'd be safe. I'm sorry for my outburst, but I don't known the forest as you do. I was afraid.'

In her allotted bedroom, a silver ewer and basin stood on a table. The embroideries on the canopied bed were faded but priceless. Antique books stood in a case, catching the firelight, a vast yet random selection of the poetry and prose of many lands. From the bedchamber window, Lisel could look out across the clearing of the park, the white sweep of it occasionally broken by trees in their winter foliage of snow, or by the slash of the track which broke through the high wall. Beyond the wall, the forest pressed close under the heavy twilight of the sky. Lisel pondered with a grim irritation the open gateway. Wolves running, and the way to the château left wide at all times. She visualized mad Anna throwing chunks of raw meat to the wolves as another woman would toss bread to swans.

This unprepossessing notion returned to Lisel during the unusually early dinner, when she realized that Anna was receiving from her silent gliding servants various dishes of raw meats.

'I hope,' said Anna, catching Lisel's eye, 'my repast won't offend a delicate stomach. I have learned that the best way to keep my health is to eat the fruits of the earth in their intended state — so much goodness is wasted in cooking and garnishing.'

Despite the reference to fruit, Anna touched none of the fruit or vegetables on the table. Not did she drink any wine.

Lisel began again to be amused, if rather dubiously. Her own fare was excellent, and she ate it hungrily, admiring as she did so the crystal goblets and gold-handled knives which one day would be hers.

Presently a celebrated liqueur was served — to Lisel alone — and Anna rose on the black wings of her dress, waving her granddaughter to the fire. Beautiful, meanwhile, had crawled onto the stool of the tall piano and begun to play wildly despairing romances there, his elegant fingers darting over discolored keys so like Anna's strong yet senile teeth.

'Well,' said Anna, reseating herself in another carven throne before the cave of the hearth. 'What do you think of us?'

'Think, Grandmère? Should I presume?'

'No. But you do.'

'I think,' said Lisel cautiously, 'everything is very fine.'

'And you are keenly aware, of course, the finery will eventually belong to you.'

'Oh, Grandmère!' exclaimed Lisel, quite genuinely shocked by such frankness.

'Don't trouble yourself,' said Anna. Her eyes caught the fire and became like the eyes of the wolf at the carriage window. 'You expect to be my heiress. It's quite normal you should be making an inventory. I shan't last forever. Once I'm gone, presumably everything will be yours.'

Despite herself, Lisel gave an involuntary shiver. A sudden plan of selling the château to be rid of it flitted through her thoughts, but she quickly put it aside, in case the Matriarch somehow read her mind.

'Don't speak like that, Grandmère. This is the first time I've met you, and you talk of dying.'

'Did I? No, I did not. I spoke of *departure*. Nothing dies, it simply transmogrifies.' Lisel watched politely this display of apparent piety. 'As for my mansion,' Anna went on, 'you mustn't consider sale, you know.' Lisel blanched — as she had feared her mind had been read, or could it merely be that Anna found her predictable? 'The château has stood on this land for many centuries. The old name for the spot, do you known that?'

'No, Grandmère.'

'This, like the whole of the forest, was called the Wolfland. Because it was the wolves' country before ever men set foot on it with their piffling little roads and tracks, their carriages and foolish frightened walls. Wolfland. Their country then, and when the winter comes, their country once more.'

'As I saw, Grandmère,' said Lisel tartly.

'As you saw. You'll see and hear more of them while you're in my house. Their voices come and go like the wind, as they do. When that little idiot of a sun slips away and the night rises, you may hear scratching on the lower floor windows. I needn't tell you to stay indoors, need I?'

'Why do you let animals run in your park?' demanded Lisel.

'Because,' said Anna, 'the land is theirs by right.'

The dwarf began to strike a polonaise from the piano. Anna clapped her hands, and the music ended. Anna beckoned, and Beautiful slid off the stool like a precocious child caught stickying the keys. He came to Anna, and she played with his hair. His face remained unreadable, yet his pellucid eyes swam dreamily to Lisel's face. She felt embarrassed by

the scene, and at his glance was angered to find herself blushing.
'There was a time,' said Anna, 'when I did not rule this house. When
a man ruled here.'
'Grandpère,' said Lisel, looking resolutely at the fire.
'Grandpère, yes, Grandpère.' Her voice held the most awful scorn.
'Grandpère believed it was a man's pleasure to beat his wife. You're
young, but you should know, should be told. Every night, if I was not
already sick from a beating, and sometimes when I was, I would hear
his heavy drunken feet come stumbling to my door. At first I locked it,
but I learned not to. What stood in his way he could always break. He
was a strong man. A great legend of strength. I carry scars on my
shoulders to this hour. One day I may show you.'
    Lisel gazed at Anna, caught between fascination and revulsion. 'Why
do I tell you?' Anna smiled. She had twisted Beautiful's gorgeous hair
into a painful knot. Clearly it hurt him, but he made no sound, staring
blindly at the ceiling. 'I tell you, Lisel, because very soon your father
will suggest to you that it is time you were wed. And however handsome
or gracious the young man may seem to you that you choose, or that is
chosen for you, however, noble or marvelous or even docile he may
seem, you have no way of being certain he will not turn out to be like
your beloved grandpère. Do you know, he brought me peaches on our
wedding night, all the way from the hothouses of the city. Then he
showed me the whip he had been hiding under the fruit. You see what
it is to be a woman, Lisel. Is that what you want? The irrevocable
marriage vow that binds you forever to a monster? And even if he is a
good man, which is a rare beast indeed, you may die an agonizing death
in childbed, just as your mother did.'
    Lisel swallowed. A number of things went through her head now. A
vague acknowledgement that, though she envisaged admiration, she
had never wished to marry and therefore never considered it, and a
starker awareness that she was being told improper things. She desired
to learn more and dreaded to learn it. As she was struggling to find a
rejoinder, Anna seemed to notice her own grip on the hair of the dwarf.
    'Ah,' she said, 'forgive me. I did not mean to hurt you.'
    The words had an oddly sinister ring to them. Lisel suddenly guessed
their origin, the brutish man rising from his act of depravity, of
necessity still merely sketched by Lisel's innocence, whispering,
gloatingly muttering: Forgive me. I did not mean to hurt.
    'Beautiful,' said Anna, 'is the only man of any worth I've ever met.
And my servants, of course, but I don't count them as men. Drink your
liqueur.'
    'Yes, Grandmère,' said Lisel, as she sipped, and slightly choked.

'Tomorrow,' said Anna, 'we must serve you something better. A vintage indigenous to the château, made from a flower which grows here in the spring. For now,' again she rose on her raven's wings; a hundred gems caught the light and went out, 'for now, we keep early hours here, in the country.'

'But, Grandmère,' said Lisel, astounded, 'it's scarcely sunset.'

'In my house,' said Anna, gently, 'you will do as you are told, m'mselle.'

And for once, Lisel did as she was told.

At first, of course, Lisel did not entertain a dream of sleep. She was used to staying awake till the early hours of the morning, rising at noon. She entered her bedroom, cast one scathing glance at the bed, and settled herself to read in a chair beside the bedroom fire. Luckily she had found a lurid novel amid the choice of books. By skimming over all passages of meditation, description or philosophy, confining her attention to those portions which contained duels, rapes, black magic and the firing squad, she had soon made great inroads on the work. Occasionally, she would pause, and add another piece of wood to the fire. At such times she knew a medley of doubts concerning her grandmother. That the Matriarch could leave such a novel lying about openly where Lisel could get at it outraged the girl's propriety.

Eventually, two or three hours after the sun had gone and the windows blackened entirely behind the drapes, Lisel did fall asleep. The excitements of the journey and her medley of reactions to Madame Anna had worn her out.

She woke, as she had in the carriage, with a start of alarm. Her reason was the same one. Out in the winter forest of night sounded the awesome choir of the wolves. Their voices rose and fell, swelling, diminishing, resurging, like great icy waves of wind or water, breaking on the silence of the château.

Partly nude, a lovely maiden had been bound to a stake and the first torch applied, but Lisel no longer cared very much for her fate. Setting the book aside, she rose from the chair. The flames were low on the candles and the f:re almost out. There was no clock, but it had the feel of midnight. Lisel went to the window and opened the drapes. Stepping through and pulling them fast closed again behind her, she gazed out into the glowing darkness of snow and night.

The wolf cries went on and on, thrilling her with a horrible disquiet, so she wondered how even mad Anna could ever have grown accustomed to them? Was this what had driven grandfather to brutishness and beatings? And, colder thought, the mysterious violent death he was supposed to have suffered — what more violent than to be torn apart by long pointed teeth under the pine trees?

Lisel quartered the night scene with her eyes, looking for shapes to fit the noises, and, as before, hoping not to find them.

There was decidedly something about wolves. Something beyond their reputation and the stories of the half-eaten bodies of little children with which nurses regularly scared their charges. Something to do with actual appearance, movement; the lean shadow manifesting from between the trunks of trees — the stuff of nightmare. And their howlings — ! Yet, as it went on and on, Lisel became aware of a bizarre exhilaration, an almost-pleasure in the awful sounds which made the hair lift on her scalp and gooseflesh creep along her arms — the same sort of sensation as biting into a slice of lemon —

And then she saw it, a great pale wolf. It loped by directly beneath the window, and suddenly, to Lisel's horror, it raised its long head, and two fireworks flashed, which were its eyes meeting with hers. A primordial fear, worse even than in the carriage, turned Lisel's bones to liquid. She sank on her knees, and as she knelt there foolishly, as if in prayer, her chin on the sill, she beheld the wolf moving away across the park, seeming to dissolve into the gloom.

Gradually, then, the voices of the other wolves began to dull, eventually falling quiet.

Lisel got up, came back into the room, threw more wood on the fire and crouched there. It seemed odd to her that the wolf had run *away* from the château, but she was not sure why. Presumably it had ventured near in hopes of food, then, disappointed, withdrawn. That it had come from the spot directly by the hall's doors did not, could not, mean anything in particular. Then Lisel realized what had been so strange. She had seen the wolf in a faint radiance of light — but from where? The moon was almost full, but obscured behind the house. The drapes had been drawn across behind her, the light could not have fallen down from her own window. She was turning back unhappily to the window to investigate when she heard the unmistakable soft thud of a large door being carefully shut below her, in the château.

The wolf had been in the house. Anna's guest.

Lisel was petrified for a few moments, then a sort of fury came to her rescue. How dared the old woman be so mad as all this and expect her civilized granddaughter to endure it? Brought to the wilds, told improper tales, left improper literature to read, made unwilling party to the entertainment of savage beasts. Perhaps as a result of the reading matter, Lisel saw her only course abruptly, and it was escape. (She had already assumed Anna would not allow her grandchild to depart until whatever lunatic game the old beldame was playing was completed.) But if escape, then how? Though there were carriage, horses, even coachman, all were Anna's. Lisel did not have to ponder long, however. Her father's cynicism on the lower classes had convinced her that anyone had his price. She would bribe the coachman — her gold bracelets and her ruby eardrops — both previous gifts of Anna's, in fact. She could assure the man of her father's protection and further valuables when they reached the city. A vile thought came to her at that, that her father might, after all, prove unsympathetic. Was she being stupid? Should she turn a blind eye to Anna's wolfish foibles? If Anna should disinherit her, as surely she would on Lisel's flight —

Assailed by doubts, Lisel paced the room. Soon she had added to them. The coachman might snatch her bribe and still refuse to help her. Or worse, drive her into the forest and violate her. Or —

The night slowed and flowed into the black valleys of early morning. The moon crested the château and sank into the forest. Lisel sat on the edge of the canopied bed, pleating and repleating the folds of the scarlet cloak between her fingers. Her face was pale, her blonde hair untidy and her eyes enlarged. She looked every bit as crazy as her grandmother.

Her decision was sudden, made with an awareness that she had wasted much time. She flung the cloak round herself and started up. She hurried to the bedroom door and softly, softly, opened it a tiny crack.

All was black in the house, neither lamp not candle visible anywhere. The sight, or rather lack of it, caused Lisel's heart to sink. At the same instant, it indicated that the whole house was abed. Lisel's plan was a simple one. A passage led away from the great hall to the kitchens and servants' quarters and ultimately to a courtyard containing coachhouse and stables. Here the grooms and the coachman would sleep, and here too another gateway opened on the park. These details she had either seen for herself as the carriage was driven off on her arrival or deduced from the apparent structure of the château. Unsure of the hour, yet she felt dawn was approaching. If she could but reach the servants' quarters, she should be able to locate the courtyard. If the coachman proved a villain, she would have to use her wits. Threaten him or cajole him. Knowing very little of physical communion, it seemed better to Lisel in those moments, to lie down with a hairy peasant than to remain the Matriarch's captive. It was that time of night when humans are often prey to ominous or extravagant ideas of all sorts. She took up one of the low-burning candles. Closing the bedroom door behind her, Lisel stole forward into the black nothingness of unfamiliarity.

Even with the feeble light, she could barely see ten inches before her, and felt cautiously about with her free hand, dreading to collide with ornament or furniture and thereby rouse her enemies. The stray gleams, shot back at her from a mirror or a picture frame, misled rather than aided her. At first her total concentration was taken up with her safe progress and her quest to find the head of the double stair. Presently, however, as she pressed on without mishap, secondary considerations began to steal in on her.

If it was difficult to proceed, how much more difficult it might be should she desire to retreat. Hopefully, there would be nothing to retreat from. But the ambience of the château, inspired by night and the limited candle, was growing more sinister by the second. Arches opened on drapes of black from which anything might spring. All about, the shadow furled, and she was one small target moving in it, lit as if on a stage.

She turned the passage and perceived the curve of the stair ahead and the dim hall below. The great stained window provided a grey illumination which elsewhere was absent. The stars bled on the snow outside and pierced the white panes. Or could it be the initial tinge of dawn?

Lisel paused, confronting once again the silliness of her simple plan of escape, Instinctively, she turned to look the way she had come, and the swiftness of the motion, or some complementary draught, quenched her candle. She stood marooned by this cliché, the phosphorescently discernible space before her, pitch-dark behind, and chose the path into the half-light as preferable.

She went down the stair delicately, as if descending into a ballroom. When she was some twenty steps from the bottom, something moved in the thick drapes beside the outer doors. Lisel froze, feeling a shock like an electric volt passing through her vitals. In another second she knew from the uncanny littleness of the shape that it was Anna's dwarf who scuttled there. But before she divined what it was at, one leaf of the door began to swing heavily inwards.

Lisel felt no second shock of fear. She felt instead as if her soul drifted upward from her flesh.

Through the open door soaked the pale ghost-light that heralded sunrise, and with that, a scattering of fresh white snow. Lastly through the door, its long feet crushing both light and snow, glided the wolf she had seen beneath her window. It did not look real, it seemed to waver and to shine, yet, for any who had ever heard the name of wolf, or a single story of them, or the song of their voices, here stood that word, that story, that voice, personified.

The wolf raised its supernatural head and once more it looked at the young girl.

The moment held no reason, no pity, and certainly no longer any hope of escape.

As the wolf began to pad noiselessly toward Lisel up the stair, she fled by the only route now possible to her. Into unconsciousness.

3

She came to herself to find the face of a prince from a romance poised over hers. He was handsome enough to have kissed her awake, except that she knew immediately it was the dwarf.

'Get away from me!' she shrieked, and he moved aside.

She was in the bedchamber, lying on the canopied bed. She was not dead, she had not been eaten or had her throat torn out.

As if in response to her thoughts, the dwarf said musically to her: 'You have had a nightmare, m'mselle.' But she could tell from a faint expression somewhere between his eyes, that he did not truly expect her to believe such a feeble equivocation.

'There was a wolf,' said Lisel, pulling herself into a sitting position, noting that she was still gowned and wearing the scarlet cloak. 'A wolf which *you* let into the house.'

'I?' The dwarf elegantly raised an eyebrow.

'You, you frog. Where is my grandmother? I demand to see her at once.'

'The Lady Anna is resting. She sleeps late in the mornings.'

'Wake her.'

'Your pardon, m'mselle, but I take my orders from Madame.' The dwarf bowed. 'If you are recovered and hungry, a maid will bring *petit déjeuner* at once to your room, and hot water for bathing, when you are ready.'

Lisel frowned. Her ordeal past, her anger paramount, she was still very hungry. An absurd notion came to her — *had* it all been a dream? No, she would not so doubt herself. Even though the wolf had not harmed her, it had been real. A household pet, then? She had heard of deranged monarchs who kept lions or tigers like cats. Why not a wolf kept like a dog?

'Bring me my breakfast,' she snapped, and the dwarf bowed himself goldenly out.

All avenues of escape seemed closed, yet by day (for it was day, the tawny gloaming of winter) the phenomena of the darkness seemed far removed. Most of their terror had gone with them. With instinctive immature good sense, Lisel acknowledged that no hurt had come to her, that she was indeed being cherished.

She wished she had thought to reprimand the dwarf for his mention of intimate hot water and his presence in her bedroom. Recollections of unseemly novelettes led her to a swift examination of her apparel — unscathed. She rose and stood morosely by the fire, waiting for her breakfast, tapping her foot.

By the hour of noon, Lisel's impatience had reached its zenith with the sun. Of the two, only the sun's zenith was insignificant.

Lisel left the bedroom, flounced along the corridor and came to the stairhead. Eerie memories of the previous night had trouble in remaining with her. Everything seemed to have become rather absurd, but this served only to increase her annoyance. Lisel went down the stair boldly. The fire was lit in the enormous hearth and blazing cheerfully. Lisel prowled about, gazing at the dubious stained glass, which she now saw did not portray a hunting scene at all, but some pagan subject of men metamorphosing into wolves.

At length a maid appeared. Lisel marched up to her.

'Kindly inform my grandmother that I am awaiting her in the hall.'

The maid seemed struggling to repress a laugh, but she bobbed a curtsey and darted off. She did not come back, and neither did grandmother.

When a man entered bearing logs for the fire, Lisel said to him, 'Put those down and take me at once to the coachman.'

The man nodded and gestured her to follow him without a word of acquiescence or disagreement. Lisel, as she let herself be led through the back corridors and by the hub-bub of the huge stone kitchen, was struck by the incongruousness of her actions. No longer afraid, she felt foolish. She was carrying out her 'plan' of the night before from sheer pique, nor did she have any greater hope of success. It was more as if some deeply hidden part of herself prompted her to flight, in spite of all resolutions, rationality and desire. But it was rather like trying to walk on a numbed foot. She could manage to do it, but without feeling.

The coachhouse and stables bulked gloomily about the courtyard, where the snow had renewed itself in dazzling white drifts. The coachman stood in his black furs beside an iron brazier. One of the blond horses was being shod in an old-fashioned manner, the coachman overseeing the exercise. Seeking to ingratiate herself, Lisel spoke to the coachman in a silky voice.

'I remarked yesterday, how well you controlled the horses when the wolves came after the carriage.'

The coachman did not answer, but hearing her voice, the horse sidled a little, rolling its eye at her.

'Suppose,' said Lisel to the coachman, 'I were to ask you if you would take me back to the city. What would you say?'

Nothing, apparently.

The brazier sizzled and the hammer of the blacksmithing groom smacked the nails home into the horse's hoof. Lisel found the process disconcerting.

'You must understand,' she said to the coachman, 'my father would give you a great deal of money. He's unwell and wishes me to return. I received word this morning.'

The coachman hulked there like a big black bear, and Lisel had the urge to bite him viciously.

'My grandmother,' she announced, 'would order you to obey me, but she is in bed.'

'No, she is not,' said the Matriarch at Lisel's back, and Lisel almost screamed. She shot around, and stared at the old woman, who stood about a foot away, imperious in her furs, jewels frostily blistering on her wrists.

'I wish,' said Lisel, taking umbrage as her shield, 'to go home at once.'

'So I gather. But you can't, I regret.'

'You mean to keep me prisoner?' blurted Lisel.

Grandmother laughed. The laugh was like fresh ice crackling under a steel skate. 'Not at all. The road is snowed under and won't be clear for several days. I'm afraid you'll have to put up with us a while longer.'

Lisel, in a turmoil she could not herself altogether fathom, had her attention diverted by the behavior of the horse. It was bristling like a cat, tossing its head, dancing against the rope by which the second groom was holding it.

Anna walked at once out into the yard and began to approach the horse from the front. The horse instantly grew more agitated, kicking up its heels, and neighing croupily. Lisel almost cried an automatic warning, but restrained herself. Let the beldame get a kicking, she deserved it. Rather to Lisel's chagrin, Anna reached the horse without actually having her brains dashed out. She showed not a moment's hesitation or doubt, placing her hand on its long nose, eyeing it with an amused tenderness. She looked very cruel and very indomitable.

'There now,' said Anna to the horse, which, fallen quiet and still, yet trembled feverishly. 'You know you are used to me. You know you were trained to endure me since you were a foal, as your brothers are sometimes trained to endure fire.'

The horse hung its head and shivered, cowed but noble.

Anna left it and strolled back through the snow. She came to Lisel and took her arm.

'I'm afraid,' said Anna, guiding them toward the château door, 'that they're never entirely at peace when I'm in the vicinity, though they are good horses, and well-trained. They have borne me long distances in the carriage.'

'Do they fear you because you ill-treat them?' Lisel asked impetuously.

'Oh, not at all. They fear me because to them I smell of wolf.'

Lisel bridled.

'Then do you think it wise to keep such a pet in the house?' she flared.

Anna chuckled. It was not necessarily a merry sound.

'That's what you think, is it? What a little dunce you are, Lisel. *I* am the beast you saw last night, and you had better get accustomed to it. Grandmère is a werewolf.'

The return walk through the domestic corridors into the hall was notable for its silence. The dreadful Anna, her grip on the girl's arm unabated, smiled thoughtfully to herself. Lisel was obviously also deliberating inwardly. Her conclusions, however, continued to lean to the deranged rather than the occult. Propitiation suggested itself, as formerly, to be the answer. So, as they entered the hall, casting their cloaks to a servant, Lisel brightly exclaimed:

'A werewolf, Grandmère. How interesting!'

'Dear me,' said Anna, 'what a child.' She seated herself by the fire in one of her tall thrones. Beautiful had appeared. 'Bring the liqueur and some biscuits,' said Anna. 'It's past the hour, but why should we be the slaves of custom?'

Lisel perched on a chair across the hearth, watching Anna guardedly.

'You are the interesting one,' Anna now declared. 'You look sulky rather than intimidated at being mured up her with one whom you wrongly suppose is a dangerous insane. No, *ma chère,* verily I'm not mad, but a transmogrifite. Every evening, once the sun sets, I become a wolf, and duly comport myself as a wolf does.'

'You're going to eat me, then,' snarled Lisel, irritated out of all attempts to placate.

'Eat you? Hardly necessary. The forest is bursting with game. I won't say I never tasted human meat, but I wouldn't stoop to devouring a blood relation. Enough is enough. Besides, I had the opportunity last night, don't you think, when you swooned away on the stairs not fifty feet from me. Of course, it was almost dawn, and I *had* dined, but to rip out your throat would have been the work only of a moment. There-after we might have stored you in the cold larder against a lean winter.'

'How dare you try to frighten me in this way!' screamed Lisel in a paroxysm of rage.

Beautiful was coming back with a silver tray. On the tray rested a plate of biscuits and a decanter of the finest cut glass containing a golden drink.

'You note, Beautiful,' said Madame Anna, 'I like this wretched granddaughter of mine. She's very like me.'

'Does that dwarf know you are a *werewolf?'* demanded Lisel, with baleful irony.

'Who else lets me in and out at night? But all my servants know, just as my other folk know, in the forest.'

'You're disgusting,' said Lisel.

'Tut, I shall disinherit you. Don't you want my fortune any more?'

Beautiful set down the tray on a small table between them and began to pour the liqueur, smooth as honey, into two tiny crystal goblets.

Lisel watched. She remembered the nasty dishes of raw meat — part of Anna's game of werewolfery — and the drinking of water, but no wine. Lisel smirked, thinking she had caught the Matriarch out. She kept still and accepted the glass from Beautiful, who, while she remained seated, was a mere inch taller than she.

'I toast you,' said Anna, raising her glass to Lisel. 'Your health and your joy.' She sipped. A strange look came into her strange eyes. 'We have,' she said, 'a brief winter afternoon before us. There is just the time to tell you what you should be told.'

'Why bother with me? I'm disinherited.'

'Hardly. Taste the liqueur. You will enjoy it.'

'I'm surprised that you did, Grandmère.'

'Don't be,' said Anna with asperity. 'This wine is special to this place. We make it from a flower which grows here. A little yellow flower that comes in the spring, or sometimes, even in the winter. There is a difference then, of course. Do you recall the flower of my excutcheon? It is the self-same one.'

Lisel sipped the liqueur. She had had a fleeting fancy it might be drugged or tampered with in some way, but both drinks had come from the decanter. Besides, what would be the point? The Matriarch valued an audience. The wine was pleasing, fragrant and, rather than sweet as Lisel had anticipated, tart. The flower which grew in winter was plainly another demented tale.

Relaxed, Lisel leant back in her chair. She gazed at the flames in the wide hearth. Her mad grandmother began to speak to her in a quiet, floating voice, and Lisel saw pictures form in the fire. Pictures of Anna, and of the château, and of darkness itself. . . .

4

How young Anna looked. She was in her twenties. She wore a scarlet gown and a scarlet cloak lined with pale fur and heavy brocade. It resembled Lisel's cloak but had a different clasp. Snow melted on the shoulders of the cloak, and Anna held her slender hands to the fire on the hearth. Free of the hood, her hair, like marvelously tarnished ivory, was piled on her head, and there was a yellow flower in it. She wore ruby eardrops. She looked just like Lisel, or Lisel as she would become in six years or seven.

Someone called. It was more a roar than a call, as if a great beast came trampling into the château. He was a big man, dark, all darkness, his features hidden in a black beard, black hair — more, in a sort of swirling miasmic cloud, a kind of psychic smoke: Anna's hatred and fear. He bellowed for liquor and a servant came running with a jug and cup. The man, Anna's husband, cuffed the servant aside, grabbing the jug as he did so. He strode to Anna, spun her about, grabbed her face in his hand as he had grabbed the jug. He leaned to her as if to kiss her, but he did not kiss, he merely stared. She had steeled herself not to shrink from him, so much was evident. His eyes, roving over her to find some overt trace of distaste or fright, suddenly found instead the yellow flower. He vented a powerful oath. His paw flung up and wrenched the flower free. He slung it in the fire and spat after it.

'You stupid bitch,' he growled at her. 'Where did you come on that?'

'It's only a flower.'

'Not only a flower. Answer me, where? Or do I strike you?'

'Several of them are growing near the gate, beside the wall; and in the forest. I saw them when I was riding.'

The man shouted again for his servant. He told him to take a fellow and go out. They must locate the flowers and burn them.

'Another superstition?' Anna asked. Her husband hit her across the head so she staggered and caught the mantel to steady herself.

'*Yes,*' he sneered, 'another one. Now come upstairs.'

Anna said, 'Please excuse me, sir. I am not well today.'

He said in a low and smiling voice:

'Do as I say, or you'll be worse.'

The fire flared on the swirl of her bloody cloak as she moved to obey him.

And the image changed. There was a bedroom, fluttering with

lamplight. Anna was perhaps thirty-five or six, but she looked older. She lay in bed, soaked in sweat, uttering hoarse low cries or sometimes preventing herself from crying. She was in labor. The child was difficult. There were other women about the bed. One muttered to her neighbor that it was beyond her how the master had ever come to sire a child, since he got his pleasure another way, and the poor lady's body gave evidence of how. Then Anna screamed. Someone bent over her. There was a peculiar muttering among the women, as if they attended at some holy ceremony.

And another image came. Anna was seated in a shawl of gilded hair. She held a baby on her lap and was playing with it in an intense, quite silent way. As her hair shifted; traceries became momentarily visible over her bare shoulders, and arms, horrible traceries left by a lash.

'Let me take the child,' said a voice, and one of the women from the former scene appeared. She lifted the baby from Anna's lap, and Anna let the baby go, only holding her arms and hands in such a way that she touched it to the last second. The other woman was older than Anna, a peasant dressed smartly for service in the château. 'You mustn't fret yourself,' she said.

'But I can't suckle her,' said Anna. 'I wanted to.'

'There's another can do that,' said the woman. 'Rest yourself. Rest while he is away.' When she said 'he' there could be no doubt of the one to whom she referred.

'Then, I'll rest,' said Anna. She reclined on pillows, wincing slightly as her back made contact with the fine soft silk. 'Tell me about the flowers again. The yellow flowers.'

The woman showed her teeth as she rocked the baby. For an instant her face was just like a wolf's.

'You're not afraid,' she said. '*He* is. But it's always been here. The wolf-magic. It's part of the Wolfland. Wherever wolves have been, you can find the wolf-magic. Somewhere. In a stream or a cave, or in a patch of ground. The château has it. That's why the flowers grow here. Yes, I'll tell you, then. It's simple. If any eat the flowers, then they receive the gift. It comes from the spirit, the wolfwoman, or maybe she's a goddess, an old goddess left over from the beginning of things, before Christ came to save us all. She has the head of a wolf and yellow hair. You swallow the flowers, and you call her, and she comes, and she gives it you. And then it's yours, till you die.'

'And then what? Payment?' said Anna dreamily. 'Hell?'

'Maybe.'

The image faded gently. Suddenly there was another which was not gentle, a parody of the scene before. Staring light showed the bedchamber. The man, his shadow-face smoldering, clutched Anna's baby in his hands. The baby shrieked; he swung it to and fro as if to smash it on some handy piece of furniture. Anna stood in her nightdress. She held a whip out to him.

'Beat me,' she said. 'Please beat me. I want you to. Put down the child and beat me. It would be so easy to hurt her, and so soon over, she's so small. But I'm stronger. You can hurt me much more. See how vulnerable and afraid I am. Beat *me.*'

Then, with a snarl he tossed the child onto the bed where it lay wailing. He took the whip and caught Anna by her pale hair —

There was snow blowing like torn paper, everywhere. In the midst of it a servant woman, and a child perhaps a year old with soft dark hair, were seated in a carriage. Anna looked at them, then stepped away. A door slammed, horses broke into a gallop. Anna remained standing in the snow storm.

No picture came. A man's voice thundered: 'Where? Where did you send the thing? It's mine, I sired it. My property. *Where?*'

But the only reply he got were moans of pain. She would not tell him, and did not. He nearly killed her that time.

Now it is night, but a black night bleached with whiteness, for a full moon is up above the tops of the winter pines.

Anna is poised, motionless, in a glade of the wild northern forest. She wears the scarlet cloak, but the moon has drained its color. The snow sparkles, the trees are umbrellas of diamond, somber only at their undersides. The moon slaps the world with light. Anna has been singing, or chanting something, and though it can no longer be heard, the dew of it lies heavy over the ground. Something is drawn there, too, in the snow, a circle, and another shape inside it. A fire has been kindled nearby, but now it has burned low, and has a curious bluish tinge to it. All at once a wind begins to come through the forest. But it is not wind, not even storm. It is the soul of the forest, the spirit of the Wolfland.

Anna goes to her knees. She is afraid, but it is a new fear, an exulting fear. The stalks of the flowers whose heads she has eaten lie under her knees, and she raises her face like a dish to the moonlight.

The pines groan. They bend. Branches snap and snow showers down from them. The creature of the forest is coming, nearer and nearer. It is a huge single wing, or an enormous engine. Everything breaks and sways before it, even the moonlight, and darkness fills the glade. And out of the darkness Something whirls. It is difficult to see, to be sure — a glimpse of gold, two eyes like dots of lava seven feet in the air, a grey jaw, hung breasts which have hair growing on them, the long hand which is not a hand, lifting — And then every wolf in the forest seems to give tongue, and the darkness ebbs away.

Anna lies on her face. She is weeping. With terror. With —

It is night again, and the man of the house is coming home. He swaggers, full of local beer, and eager to get to his wife. He was angry, a short while since, because his carriage, which was to have waited for him outside the inn, had mysteriously vanished. There will be men to curse and brutalize in the courtyard before he goes up to his beloved Anna, a prelude to his final acts with her. He finds her a challenge, his wife. She seems able to withstand so much, looking at him proudly with horror in her eyes. It would bore him to break her. He likes the fact he cannot, or thinks he does. And tonight he has some good news. One of the paid men has brought word of their child. She is discovered at last. She can be brought home to the château to her father's care. She is two years old now. Strong and healthy. Yes, good news indeed.

They had known better in the village than to tell him he should beware on the forest track. He is not anxious about wolves, the distance being less than a mile, and he has his pistol. Besides, he organized a wolf hunt last month and cleared quite a few of the brutes off his land. The area about the château has been silent for many nights. Even Anna went walking without a servant — though he had not approved of that and had taught her a lesson. (Sometimes it occurs to him that she enjoys his lessons as much as he enjoys delivering them, for she seems constantly to seek out new ways to vex him.)

He is about a quarter of a mile from the château now, and here a small clearing opens off on both sides of the track. It is the night after the full moon, and her disc, an almost perfect round, glares down on the clearing from the pine tops. Anna's husband dislikes the clearing. He had forgotten he would have to go through it, for generally he is mounted or in the carriage when he passes the spot. There is some old superstition about the place. He hates it, just as he hates the stinking yellow flowers that grew in it before he burned them out. Why does he hate them? The woman who nursed him told him something and it frightened him, long ago. Well, no matter. He walks more quickly.

How quiet it is, how still. The whole night like a pane of black-white silence. He can hardly hear his own noisy footfalls. There is a disturbance in the snow, over there, a mark like a circle.

They he realizes something is behind him. He is not sure how he realizes, for it is quite soundless. He stops, and turns, and sees a great and ghostly wolf a few feet from him on the track.

In a way, it is almost a relief to see the wolf. It is alone, and it is a natural thing. Somehow he had half expected something unnatural. He draws his pistol, readies it, points it at the wolf. He is a fine shot. He already visualizes lugging the bloody carcass, a trophy, into the house. He pulls the trigger.

A barren click. He is surprised. He tries again. Another click. It comes to him that his servant has emptied the chamber of bullets. He sees a vision of the park gates a quarter of a mile away, and he turns immediately and runs toward them.

Ten seconds later a warm and living weight crashes against his back, and he falls screaming, screaming before the pain even begins. When the pain does begin, he is unable to scream for very long, but he does his best. The final thing he sees through the haze of his own blood, which has splashed up into his eyes, and the tears of agony and the enclosing of a most atrocious death, are the eyes of the wolf, gleaming coolly back at him. He knows they are the eyes of Anna. And that it is Anna who then tears out his throat.

The small crystal goblet slipped out of Lisel's hand, empty, and broke on the floor. Lisel started. Dazed, she looked away from the fire, to Anna the Matriarch.

Had Lisel been asleep and dreaming? What an unpleasant dream. Or had it been so unpleasant? Lisel became aware her teeth were clenched in spiteful gladness, as if on a bone. If Anna had told her the truth, that man — that *thing* — had deserved it all. To be betrayed by his servants, and by his wife, and to perish in the fangs of a wolf. A werewolf.

Grandmother and granddaughter confronted each other a second, with identical expressions of smiling and abstracted malice. Lisel suddenly flushed, smoothed her face, and looked down. There had been something in the drink after all.

'I don't think this at all nice,' said Lisel.

'Nice isn't the word,' Anna agreed. Beautiful reclined at her feet, and she stroked his hair. Across the big room, the stained-glass window was thickening richly to opacity. The sun must be near to going down.

'*If* it's the truth,' said Lisel primly, 'you will go to hell.'

'Oh? Don't you think me justified? He'd have killed your mother at the very least. *You* would never have been born.'

Lisel reviewed this hypothetical omission. It carried some weight.

'You should have appealed for help.'

'To whom? The marriage vow is a chain that may not be broken. If I had left him, he would have traced me, as he did the child. No law supports a wife. I could only kill him.'

'I don't believe you killed him as you say you did.'

'Don't you, m'mselle? Well, never mind. Once the sun has set, you'll see it happen before your eyes.' Lisel stared and opened her mouth to remonstrate. Anna added gently: 'And, I am afraid, not to myself alone.'

Aside from all reasoning and the training of a short lifetime, Lisel felt the stranglehold of pure terror fasten on her. She rose and squealed: 'What do you mean?'

'I mean,' said Anna, 'that the liqueur you drank is made from the same yellow flowers I ate to give me the power of transmogrification. I mean that the wolf-magic, once invoked, becomes hereditary, yet dormant. I mean that what the goddess of the Wolfland conveys must indeed be paid for at the hour of death — unless another will take up the gift.'

Lisel, not properly understanding, not properly believing, began to shriek wildly. Anna came to her feet. She crossed to Lisel and shook the shrieks out of her, and when she was dumb, thrust her back in the chair.

'Now sit, fool, and be quiet. I've put nothing on you that was not already yours. Look in a mirror. Look at your hair and your eyes and your beautiful teeth. Haven't you always preferred the night to the day, staying up till the morning, lying abed till noon? Don't you love the cold forest? Doesn't the howl of the wolf thrill you through with fearful delight? And why else should the Wolfland accord you an escort, a pack of wolves running by you on the road. Do you think you'd have survived if you'd not been one of their kind, too?'

Lisel wept, stamping her foot. She could not have said at all what she felt. She tried to think of her father and the ballrooms of the city. She tried to consider if she credited magic.

'Now listen to me,' snapped Anna, and Lisel muted her sobs just enough to catch the words. 'Tonight is full moon, and the anniversary of that night, years ago, when I made my pact with the wolf goddess of the north. I have good cause to suspect I shan't live out this year. Therefore, tonight is the last chance I have to render you in my place into her charge. That frees me from her, do you see? Once you have swallowed the flowers, once she has acknowledged you, you belong to her. At death, I escape her sovereignty, which would otherwise bind me forever to the earth in wolf form, phantom form. A bargain: you save me. But you too can make your escape, when the time comes. Bear a child. You will be mistress here. You can command any man to serve you, and you're tolerable enough the service won't be unwilling. My own child, your mother, was not like me at all. I could not bring her to live with me, once I had the power. I was troubled as to how I should wean her to it. But she died, and in you I saw the mark from the first hour. You are fit to take my place. Your child can take yours.'

'You're hateful!' shrieked Lisel. She had the wish to laugh. But someone was flinging open the doors of the hall. The cinnamon light streamed through and fell into the fire and faded it. Another fire, like antique bronze, was quenching itself among the pines. The dying of the sun.

Anna moved toward the doors and straight out onto the snow. She stood a moment, tall and amazing on the peculiar sky. She seemed a figment of the land itself, and maybe she was.

'Come!' she barked. Then turned and walked away across the park.

All the servants seemed to have gathered like bats in the hall. They were silent, but they looked at Lisel. Her heart struck her over and over. She did not know what she felt or if she believed. Then a wolf sang in the forest. She lifted her head. She suddenly knew frost and running and black stillness, and a platinum moon, red feasts and wild hymnings, lovers with quicksilver eyes and the race of the ice wind and stars smashed under the hard soles of her four feet. A huge white ballroom opened before her, and the champagne of the air filled her mouth.

Beautiful had knelt and was kissing the hem of her red cloak. She patted his head absently, and the gathering of the servants sighed.

Presumably, as Anna's heiress, she might be expected to live on in the forest, in the château which would be hers. She could even visit the city, providing she was home by sunset.

The wolf howled again, filling her veins with lights, raising the hair along her scalp.

Lisel tossed her head. Of course, it was all a lot of nonsense.

She hastened out through the doors and over the winter park and followed her grandmother away into the Wolfland.

15 Malagan and the Lady of Rascas

Michael de Larrabeiti

At the time of the crusades and in the land of Provence there were many beautiful castles and one of the finest was the castle of Rascas. High on a mountain peak it stood, built of golden stone and set against a sky which was as blue as the heart of a sapphire. At the foot of the mountain lay a village, its roofs shaded by broad-leaved plane trees and its streets cooled by the waters of a spring that overflowed in the village square. All around stretched a fruitful valley and there the villagers raised sheep and laboured among the olive trees and vines for their sustenance and for the greater pleasure of their lord, the Baron Rascas.

Baron Rascas was a stern and selfish man who lived in great style and luxury and sought pleasure in all the good things that life had to offer him. He was not particularly cruel to his subjects but neither was he particularly kind. For him the common people did not exist. As long as his needs, and those of his courtiers, were satisfied then all was well; but if the Baron were thwarted in any way then he could become brutal and, like the violent soldier he was, he possessed the courage and the means to impose his will on anyone.

For the most part however the Baron bore himself well enough and was content to live his life from day to day, gazing over his domain or seeking happiness with his courtiers. And thus he lived until about the middle time of his life when, without warning, a royal messenger rode up to the castle and commanded the Baron to assemble his men at arms so that he might follow the king to Palestine, there to deliver battle to the Saracens who occupied the Holy City, in an attempt to wrest it from them by force of arms for the glory of God.

The Baron had no alternative but to obey. Like any other feudal lord he held his lands under the king and was sworn to provide soldiers and service to his monarch whenever summoned and for as long as necessary. The Baron cursed but gave orders nevertheless and preparations were made.

Within three weeks all was ready and the day of departure arrived sooner than had been thought possible. On that day there was a great noise and bustle to be observed both in the castle and the village. Pack horses were led from the stables and loaded; chargers were saddled and the Baron's armour, highly polished and reflecting the cloudless sky, was stowed away by his squires, together with his weapons. The Baron too was busy and strode about his courtyard making sure that not one dagger or one mace had been forgotten. From the battlements the courtiers, fine gentlemen exquisitely dressed in silken robes and velvet cloaks, gazed down and bit their lips. These were men too cowardly to follow their lord, and by their sides leant their ladies, desiring only that the Baron would be gone so that they might continue their endless round of amusement and dance.

Of all this the Baron was well aware but he had no wish to take such men to war with him, they would be but a burden and a hindrance. In any event his service to the king did not demand that he take all his followers. He had chosen only his bravest soldiers, about sixty of them, resolute men who knew that they might never survive this adventure, but that if they did they would live from the glory and holiness of it for the rest of their lives.

The Baron glanced up into the battlements; at least those courtiers he left behind would be there to protect the castle and the valley in times of danger. Though he could not trust them to fight well on a foreign campaign he was sure that they would defend their own lives and possessions to the last gasp if called upon to do so. The Baron sighed; would he and his men ever see this valley again? It was unlikely. The very journey to the Holy Land was full of hazards; there would be skirmishes at every frontier, drownings at every river crossing and even when the army embarked aboard its fleet it would be no safer. How many ships would founder beneath the waves? How many would be taken by pirates? And even at the journey's end death lurked in every desert and waited at every crossroad. Diseases that no physician could cure flourished in Palestine and when the king's soldiers reached the battlefield, those that survived, they would find in the Saracen an enemy more implacable and more merciless than any in their previous experience.

The Baron shook his head and tried to clear his mind of such thoughts. He ordered the men at arms to lead their pack horses down the side of the mountain and to wait for him at the village. He settled the sword at his waist and watched as the ladies of his court stepped aside to allow his wife to approach him so that she might speak her farewells.

Of all the ladies in the castle the most beautiful was the Baron's wife, the Lady of Rascas. She was young and stately but the most striking thing about her was the way in which the kindness of her heart showed through the features of her face. All through Provence she was renowned for her generosity and her modesty. The Baron's courtiers could find no fault in her and the common people could not love her enough for the care she took of them.

Again the Baron sighed. He was a brave man, some said there was no man braver, but as he took his wife in his arms he felt his resolve weaken. His spirit quailed. He pressed his wife to him and closed his eyes. She was so beautiful; of all the things he possessed she was what he cherished most and the thought that he might never see her again tormented him and hurt his heart. Perhaps she would weary of waiting for him and someone else, younger, more handsome, would come to the castle and charm her with his poetry, seduce her with a new song, laugh with her in the topmost towers as the sun went down the sky and turned the countryside to gold.

The Baron's face darkened; it was a prospect he could not face. Death and disease would be better.

'My lord,' said the Lady of Rascas, 'be not so sad, the day of your return is even now approaching.' She spoke gently and touched her husband's hand.

The Baron held his wife at arm's length so that he could contemplate her beauty.

'Can you love me this long time I am away?' he asked, his voice thick with feeling. But he did not wait for an answer and turned, forbidding anyone to follow him as he made his way into an arcaded gallery let into the wall of the castle and there he commanded that cool wine be sent to him and that Malagan, the sorcerer, should attend him without delay.

Malagan came, his soft shoes making no sound on the flagstones and he stood silently before his master, his arms folded beneath his scarlet gown. Malagan was young, tall and dark-skinned, there was Saracen blood in his veins. His hair was black and ragged and his nose was a hook in his face and the deep lines in his countenance were lines of suffering and grief.

There were those in the castle who said that Malagan was the most evil magician in Provence, in the world even, but they did not say it loudly. No one knew where he came from or what bound him to the Baron. Some courtiers said that the Lord of Rascas had, by accident, freed the magician from a spell and that in return Malagan had vowed to serve the Baron in everything for a certain number of years, and so far he had remained faithful to that vow.

What was known was that Malagan could change base metals into gold, imprison the souls of men in stone and make flowers bloom in the driest desert. He could also alter his form at will and like a maggot work his way into a man's brain and discover his innermost thoughts. In a word he could do everything that a god might do except restore life. The Baron poured two goblets of wine and bade his sorcerer sit. 'Malagan,' he said, 'I want from you this day strong magic, magic to ease my heart of its jealousy and doubt. You will ensure that my wife is faithful while I am away.'

The magician put down his cup and spoke, his voice full of menace; 'This does not need magic,' he said, 'your lady is faithful and honest, this much I know for truth. No spell of mine can make her more or less so.'

The Baron looked hard into Malagan's eyes; 'It is a command,' he said.

Malagan spoke again; 'I can imprison her in a tree, a cliff. I can change her into a bird.'

'No,' said the Baron. 'There is danger there. A bird may be killed, a tree felled and a cliff struck by a thunderbolt. She must live in the castle, protected. She must see to my lands. I have considered it. Make her hard to look upon, so that no one will desire her, ugly, like a beast.'

'This is my lord's wish?' asked Malagan. He showed no surprise but he was hesitant.

'It is,' said the Baron, 'but I have no mind to see it. You will wait until I have left the castle. Then you will follow me on my journey. I do not want this spell to be undone during my absence.'

Malagan's eyes glowed at the Baron's words but he said nothing, only getting to his feet and bowing slightly as his lord left the gallery and went directly to the courtyard, back to his wife.

Once more he embraced her and enjoined her to be courageous and to endure faithfully the years of separation that lay ahead and to accept with humility whatever life might hold in store. For his part he swore to be brave and loyal.

'I am sure our love will survive,' he said. 'Now I go to join my king, leaving you in charge of my lands and fortune. You are to care for them as if they were your own children.'

At this the Lady of Rascas fell to her knees and watched as her husband, followed by his squires and his bodyguard, rode through the gate, across the drawbridge and into the narrow road that led from the castle and down to the valley below. The courtiers and their fine ladies watched too and waved their hands and handkerchieves, but their attention was soon caught by something other than their lord's departure. Bearing a great book of magic bound in Arabian leather and studded with silver stars, Malagan appeared in the courtyard leading his own savage horse and the sight of the magician rooted everyone to the spot where they stood. Malagan laid his book on the low stone coping of the castle fountain and, speaking in a curious tongue, he made strange passes with his hands while his dark eyes glared all the while into the horrified face of the still kneeling Lady of Rascas.

Malagan spoke for several minutes, his voice rising and falling in a dreamlike chant until at last his hands dropped to his book and he slammed it shut. Then, so sure was he of his magic that he turned without a glance behind him, mounted his horse and followed his master through the castle gates. And the courtiers, immobile, like statues in their fear, stared from the battlements and waited.

They did not wait long; a great moan of anguish rose from their throats as the effects of the magic became apparent. The Lady of Rascas touched her hands to her face and found that it was changing. Hair, close and stiff like fur, began to sprout there. Her eyes grew larger and larger, her lips thickened, her teeth widened and her jaw-bone became long and heavy. Under her fingers she felt her ears take a pointed shape and her nostrils spread and turn into voluminous purses of velvet. It was over and her head was the head of a human being no more; it was the head of a horse. This was the magic of Malagan. This was how her husband had chosen to keep her faithful, and with this fearful realisation the Lady of Rascas screamed, leapt to her feet and ran to her apartments, locking the doors behind her and allowing no one into her presence. For many days her cries and sobs were heard over all the castle and the courtiers and the servants stood in the corridors and galleries in idle groups, unhappy and forlorn, not knowing what to do for their lady or for themselves.

But the Lady of Rascas was a lady of unusual spirit. As the months went by she began to show herself again. First of all to her own servants and then, little by little, to the whole society of the castle. There were good reasons for this apart from her own strength of character. The demands of her husband's estate made it necessary for her to visit all corners of it; to see that everything was as it should be; to make sure that fruit trees were pruned; the vines cultivated; the crops stored and the sheep counted. Gradually, as the months of the Baron's absence became years, the people of Rascas accustomed themselves to their mistress's appearance and as she went amongst them, still clad in her beautiful gowns, so pleasant was her manner, so calm her spirits and so quick her mind, that they hardly noticed that her face was not a human face. To strangers and travellers too she was so welcoming and gracious that after a few hours in her company they completely forgot the forbidding countenance of this stricken chatelaine. There were even troubadours and minstrels who composed songs and poems about the Lady of Rascas and did not even mention her physical aspect, they sang instead of her other qualities; her composure and sensitivity; her good husbandry and learning; and the love and fidelity she bore towards her cruel lord.

And so life went on and the years passed, seven of them. The courtiers served their lady and accepted her judgements and her kindness with happy hearts. Of the Baron there was little news save occasional rumours of fierce battles in the Holy Land; death and disease; long sieges and forced marches; towns taken and cities surrendered. All that was known for sure was that the Baron still lived though many of his followers had perished, sickened by the plague or pierced by Saracen arrows.

One day, when the eighth year of her transformation was almost upon her, while walking on the ramparts the Lady of Rascas saw a plume of dust rising from the distant road near where it crossed the silver river. It was dust that rose from the hooves of a messenger's horse and in less than an hour the breathless courier was at his lady's feet. The Baron had landed in Provence, the crusades were over. He and what was left of his retinue were returning to the castle.

With haste and diligence the Lady of Rascas ordered everything to be made ready for her husband's return. The castle was cleaned, the store houses inspected, the accounts made ready and everyone dressed themselves in their best robes. So pleased was the Lady of Rascas and so delighted the courtiers that they forgot that the Baron had not seen his wife as she now appeared, had not seen her since Malagan had wrought his evil spell and no one gave any thought as to how the Baron would look upon his wife.

The whole population of the castle assembled in the courtyard and waited for the Baron and his men to ride over the drawbridge and through the gate. The Baron had aged more years than he had been absent. His armour was dented and tarnished, its leather straps cracked and broken by the sun. His face was furrowed by the terrible things he had endured, his eyes dulled by the blood of the men he had killed. His heart had grown hard in seven years of war and he remembered nothing of the ways of peace.

Like an old man he dismounted and leaning against his war horse he looked at his wife as she curtsied and held up to him the keys of the castle, stores and treasure. The Baron's lips parted in horror. When last he had seen his wife she had been the most beautiful woman in Provence.

He fell back a step and the courtiers recollected that the Baron had never seen his wife like this and they searched with their eyes and discovered for themselves what the Baron already knew; Malagan no longer followed his lord and there was no one to remove the spell. And, although later they asked, the courtiers could not discover what had become of the sorcerer; dead by disease or vanquished by a stronger magic, no one knew . . . or if they did they would not say.

The Baron could not tolerate the sight of his wife. With a roar of anger he strode past her and pushing his subjects from his path he entered the castle. His lady pursued him and threw herself at his feet but the Baron held his hands before his eyes and commanded his wife to take herself off to the castle's topmost tower and to stay there until she died.

For many days the Baron would speak or listen to no one. He cursed his followers and cuffed his servants unmercifully. Most of his time he spent seated in a dark corner of the great hall, lost in sorrow and self-pity. The results of his cruel behaviour afflicted him deeply and when he learnt of his wife's irreproachable conduct and when he inspected his estates and saw evidence everywhere of her goodness, he regretted more and more what he had caused Malagan to do all those years previously. And he was shamed too by those courtiers who had learnt to love the Lady of Rascas and had the courage to say that her imprisonment was a crime, but although the Baron knew in his heart that they were right he could not bear to release his wife from her prison. He knew that every time he looked upon her his own shame would burn within him.

At last and in despair the Baron sent messengers across the length and breadth of Provence, offering a fine reward to any magician, sorcerer or wizard who could remove the spell from his wife and make him happy again. The reward was great and many strove to win it, but there was not one whose magic was as strong as Malagan's and the Lady of Rascas stayed as she was and lived alone in her tower and as time passed her husband pushed the thought of her from his mind. So much so that as each sorcerer came to the castle to try his skill he was not greeted by the Baron at all but dealt with by the meanest servants, and only by those who still loved their lady and remembered her qualities.

Once more the years passed and the Baron sought happiness in pleasure and the castle of Rascas was soon renowned for mirth and merry-making, poetry and music, and troubadours hastened there from all over Provence to sing of its delights and only a very few faithful courtiers and servants gave a thought to the sadness sitting lonely in the tower.

There came a time too when magicians and sorcerers no longer journeyed to Rascas for the Baron had ceased to send messengers to search for them. He was more selfish than he had ever been; more cruel than in war and more foolish than in youth. The Baron and his flatterers thought only of themselves and the pleasure of the moment while his estates and his subjects, those that his wife had cared for so well, began to suffer and to fall upon hard times.

One summer's evening, when the Baron was at dinner, a servant appeared at the door of the hall and, speaking with mirth in his voice, informed his master that there was someone at the castle gates who begged admittance. This man, said the servant, was aged and riding a spavined mule. He had no retinue and was dressed only in a tattered cloak which had been torn by the winds and burnt threadbare by the sun. Tied to his saddle was a straw basket and that seemed to contain the sum total of his worldly possessions.

The Baron, deep in wine at the head of his table and surrounded by the most beautiful of his ladies, held up his hand to signify that the traveller be received. He did this not out of a feeling of hospitality but in the hope that the newcomer might offer some entertainment. His ladies and courtiers were delighted with the idea and laughed and clapped their hands and called for some more wine, making a great deal of noise as they did so.

But all this din came to a sudden stop and every voice was stilled as a dark shadow fell across the doorway to their chamber and in the yellow light of the torches a forbidding figure slowly advanced. The Baron and his courtiers stared. He was old this traveller and his hair was long and grey and matted with the dust of travel. His face was sombre and its texture was like pitted stone which has been scarred by a thousand years of driven rain. The eyes were pale, like those of a dead man and the mouth was a gash in the stone face with no lines of softness to make it human.

The Baron stirred in his seat and felt forward for his goblet of wine. The silence of the courtiers prolonged itself.

'Laugh,' commanded the Baron, 'do you not laugh when you see an old scarecrow?'

Dutifully a few of the courtiers made as if to laugh but the feeble sound soon died in their throats.

'What is it you seek here,' asked the Baron, 'a night's rest, money? Are you a beggar?'

'I am not a beggar,' said the stranger, and when he spoke his voice was sharp and strong and pierced the air like a lance. 'I bring you the gift of happiness. I have heard tell that there is a reward for whoever can bring your wife, the Lady of Rascas, to happiness again. This I can achieve.'

Now the Baron and the courtiers did laugh in reality. Could this scarecrow perform what the greatest wizards in the land had failed to do?

'Old man,' said the Baron, 'you do not have the power in your blood and the evil knowledge in your spirit to undo what has been done.'

The stranger at the door nodded. 'What you say, my lord, may be true, but old is not always bad and backwards is sometimes forward.'

The Baron laughed long and loud. 'If your magic is as strong as your words are foolish,' he answered, 'then my wife shall indeed be saved. You have amused me and I will strike a bargain. I will give you a room above the kennels for a period of fifteen days. If you achieve nothing in that time then I shall bind you backwards on your mule and the scullions will beat you down the valley. On the other hand if you should succeed in your attempt to bring me happiness then great riches shall be yours. Now leave me, I weary of would-be magicians.'

'I want no riches,' said the stranger as he turned to go. 'My satisfaction lies elsewhere,' and he left the room.

The magician went directly to the place that had been given him and locked himself inside. Those who took him his food reported that he spent most of his time reading in a great book, which he carried in his straw basket, or staring from his window, unblinking, at the sun. Once or twice he had been seen drawing with a stick in the dust of the courtyard or talking to the animals in the stables, but not once did he address a word to any of the Baron's courtiers or servants. At last, on the fifteenth day, he climbed to the topmost tower, opened the door to the chamber where the Lady of Rascas dwelt, even though it was triple locked, and taking her by the hand he led her down the spiral staircase and into the Baron's presence.

There was a gasp from the onlookers. It had been years since anyone there had seen the Baron's wife. Many had never seen her at all, having arrived at the castle since the lady's imprisonment, and these cried out in horror. Even the Baron turned his gaze away, shamed once again by what he had done. Yet the Lady of Rascas moved with such stateliness and grace that her ugliness was in some measure diminished and the courtiers calmed each other and ranged themselves along the walls of the great hall to see what the magician should do.

Firstly he commanded the Baron's wife to sit on a low stool before her husband's throne. Then he stretched his arms in his tattered gown and began to speak, looking straight into the Baron's eyes while the Baron himself tried to look elsewhere but found he could not.

The language used by the magician was unknown to all there save the Baron. It was the Saracen tongue and he had learnt to understand it during his time in the Holy Land. Now, as he listened, he gripped the arms of his chair and trembled with fear.

'I tell the story of Malagan,' said the stranger, 'how he cast this fearful spell on the command of his lord because he too was under a spell at that time. I tell this story because I am Malagan and I have returned to undo the evil I did.'

The Baron roared as if under torture but he did not move and nor did he turn his eyes away from the dreadful sorcerer.

'He bade me follow him to Palestine,' said Malagan, pointing at the Baron, 'and he left me for dead on the field of battle nor bothered himself with my body or deigned to send messengers to see if I was really dead or no. I was sorely injured, captured, enslaved, made the menial of a great magician who drained all my power from me when I was weak, stole my books of magic, discovered the secrets of my charms and ointments, and then when he'd finished with me, sold me into even more abject a bondage. I became so weak that I was left upon the road to die. Somehow I survived as a beggar and was befriended at last by a man of Alexandria who took me into his house as a servant and saw to it that I was nursed back to health. He was a scholar and I studied with him and shared his knowledge and I regained some magic, but never was it as it had been before. After some years this man of Alexandria gave me my freedom and I journeyed back to Christendom, through many more years and many more adventures. Now I have returned to this castle to seek revenge for the years of slavery and toil, revenge on the lord who abandoned me.'

Malagan drew his breath and the Baron slipped low in his chair and his courtiers looked on, wondering at the words that had been said.

'They told me you were dead,' cried the Baron, 'we were hard pressed by the enemy, I could not return to give you burial.'

'You did not even think to try,' said Malagan, 'you did not consider me worthy. I am Malagan and I wish you harm . . . yet would I undo the evil you had me do and make your lady content . . . but, alas, my power is not what it once was. To reverse a spell requires more power than to make one.' And Malagan broke into a chant of ancient Arabic and not one word of it could the Baron understand. Malagan's voice rose and the summer air darkened and in the valley below the castle there was thunder and blackness. The courtiers fell to their knees and crossed themselves and prayed for mercy. Suddenly there was a cry from the Baron and he lifted his hands to his face and found that it was changing. Hair, close and stiff like fur began to sprout there; his eyes grew larger and larger, his lips thickened, his teeth widened and his jaw-bone became long and heavy. Under his fingers he felt his ears take a pointed shape and his nostrils spread and turn into voluminous purses of velvet. Then it was over and his head was the head of a human being no more; it was the head of a horse. The Baron sobbed and fell senseless to the floor. Only his wife, amongst all those present, got to her feet and ran towards him to hold his head in her arms to comfort him.

With his work done Malagan the Magician pulled his cloak around his shoulders and with his tattered gown flowing behind him he strode across the flagstones and passed through the high wooden doors of the great hall and left the castle, never to be seen or heard of again.

Those courtiers who had fortune enough quitted Rascas immediately for other, happier places. Many more drifted away as and when the opportunity presented itself, bearing no loyalty to a Baron who had become so ill-favoured and who was now unable to entertain and please them. Only those who loved the Lady of Rascas for her own sake remained, together with those who were too poor to go elsewhere.

At first a vast sadness settled over the castle and its inhabitants; there was no feasting, no music, no dancing. The Baron, ashamed of his appearance, locked himself in his wife's tower room and would allow none to see him but she. Once more the Lady of Rascas was forced to take charge of the daily business of her husband's estates and in due time this course of events brought its advantages.

The Baron discovered in his wife all those qualities she had developed during his absence and rediscovered those attributes she had possessed before his departure but which he had forgotten. She taught the Baron to accept his misfortune with patience and humility, showing how to take a delight in the beauty of the valley and simple life of its people. The Baron fell in love all over again and much more profoundly than he had the first time. He found in his wife the most loving and intelligent creature he had ever known and in the light of her husband's gaze the Lady of Rascas became happier than she had been in her youth. The people of the castle rejoiced in what they saw and they learned to be happy, watching as a new love bloomed between their master and mistress.

So the Lady of Rascas was made as content as Malagan had wished her to be and her lord became wise and looked after his lands with care. Though they were never seen outside their estates they were renowned throughout Provence in song and in legend for the perfection of their love, the length of their lives and the beauty of their children and grandchildren. And over the castle gate the Lady of Rascas caused to be carved, before she died, the following words;

'Out of evil came good, out of ugliness, beauty.'

The Baron approved of this work but when the stone-mason had finished his task the Baron took him to the postern gate at the rear of the castle and there commanded him to carve once more and today, many hundreds of years later, amongst the fallen stone and hollow walls of the place that was called Rascas, only that archway stands and these words may be read above it;

'He who turns to evil will, at the end, find it turned against him.'

16 Bluebeard's Egg

Margaret Atwood

Sally stands at the kitchen window, waiting for the sauce she's reducing to come to a simmer, looking out. Past the garage the lot sweeps downwards, into the ravine; it's a wilderness there, of bushes and branches and what Sally thinks of as vines. It was her idea to have a kind of terrace, built of old railroad ties, with wild flowers growing between them, but Edward says he likes it the way it is. There's a playhouse down at the bottom, near the fence; from here she can just see the roof. It has nothing to do with Edward's kids, in their earlier incarnations, before Sally's time; it's more ancient than that, and falling apart. Sally would like it cleared away. She thinks drunks sleep in it, the men who live under the bridges down there, who occasionally wander over the fence (which is broken down, from where they step on it) and up the hill, to emerge squinting like moles into the light of Sally's well-kept back lawn.

Off to the left is Ed, in his windbreaker; it's officially spring, Sally's blue scylla is in flower, but it's chilly for this time of year. Ed's windbreaker is an old one he won't throw out; it still says WILDCATS, relic of some team he was on in high school, an era so prehistoric Sally can barely imagine it; though picturing Ed at high school is not all that difficult. Girls would have had crushes on him, he would have been unconscious of it; things like that don't change. He's puttering around the rock garden now; some of the rocks stick out too far and are in danger of grazing the side of Sally's Peugeot, on its way to the garage, and he's moving them around. He likes doing things like that, puttering, humming to himself. He won't wear work gloves, though she keeps telling him he could squash his fingers.

Watching his bent back with its frayed, poignant lettering, Sally dissolves; which is not infrequent with her. *My darling Edward,* she thinks. *Edward Bear, of little brain. How I love you.* At times like this she feels very protective of him.

Sally knows for a fact that dumb blondes were loved, not because they were blondes, but because they were dumb. It was their helplessness and confusion that were so sexually attractive, once; not their hair. It wasn't false, the rush of tenderness men must have felt for such women. Sally understands it.

For it must be admitted: Sally is in love with Ed because of his stupidity, his monumental and almost energetic stupidity: energetic, because Ed's stupidity is not passive. He's no mere blockhead; you'd have to be working at it to be that stupid. Does it make Sally feel smug, or smarter than he is, or even smarter than she really is herself? No; on the contrary, it makes her humble. It fills her with wonder that the world can contain such marvels as Ed's colossal and endearing thickness. He is just so *stupid*. Every time he gives her another piece of evidence, another tile that she can glue into place in the vast mosaic of his stupidity she's continually piecing together, she wants to hug him, and often does; and he is so stupid he can never figure out what for.

Because Ed is so stupid he doesn't even know he's stupid. He's a child of luck, a third son who, armed with nothing but a certain feeble-minded amiability, manages to make it through the forest with all its witches and traps and pitfalls and end up with the princess, who is Sally, of course. It helps that he's handsome.

On good days she sees his stupidity as innocence, lamb-like, shining with the light of (for instance) green daisied meadows in the sun. (When Sally starts thinking this way about Ed, in terms of the calendar art from the service-station washrooms of her childhood, dredging up images of a boy with curly golden hair, his arm thrown around the neck of an Irish setter — a notorious brainless beast, she reminds herself — she knows she is sliding over the edge, into a ghastly kind of sentimentality, and that she must stop at once, or Ed will vanish, to be replaced by a stuffed facsimile, useful for little else but an umbrella stand. Ed is a real person, with a lot more to him than these simplistic renditions allow for; which sometimes worries her.) On bad days though, she sees his stupidity as wilfulness, a stubborn determination to shut things out. His obtuseness is a wall, within which he can go about his business, humming to himself, while Sally, locked outside, must hack her way through the brambles with hardly so much as a transparent raincoat between them and her skin.

Why did she choose him (or, to be precise, as she tries to be with herself and sometimes is even out loud, *hunt him down),* when it's clear to everyone she had other options? To Marylynn, who is her best though most recent friend, she's explained it by saying she was spoiled when young by reading too many Agatha Christie murder mysteries, of the kind in which the clever and witty heroine passes over the equally clever and witty first-lead male, who's helped solve the crime, in order to marry the second-lead male, the stupid one, the one who would have been arrested and condemned and executed if it hadn't been for her cleverness. Maybe this is how she sees Ed: if it weren't for her, his blundering too-many thumbs kindness would get him into all sorts of quagmires, all sorts of sink-holes he'd never be able to get himself out of, and then he'd be done for.

'Sink-hole' and 'quagmire' are not flattering ways of speaking about other women, but this is what is at the back of Sally's mind; specifically, Ed's two previous wives. Sally didn't exactly extricate him from their clutches. She's never even met the first one, who moved to the west coast fourteen years ago and sends Christmas cards, and the second one was middle-aged and already in the act of severing herself from Ed before Sally came along. (For Sally, 'middle-aged' means anyone five years older than she is. It has always meant this. She applies it only to women, however. She doesn't think of Ed as middle-aged, although the gap between them is considerably more than five years.)

Ed doesn't know what happened with these marriages, what went wrong. His protestations of ignorance, his refusal to discuss the finer points, is frustrating to Sally, because she would like to hear the whole story. But it's also cause for anxiety: if he doesn't know what happened with the other two, maybe the same thing could be happening with her and he doesn't know about that, either. Stupidity like Ed's can be a health hazard, for other people. What if he wakes up one day and decides that she isn't the true bride after all, but the false one? Then she will be put into a barrel stuck full of nails and rolled downhill, endlessly, while he is sitting in yet another bridal bed, drinking champagne. She remembers the brand name, because she bought it herself. Champagne isn't the sort of finishing touch that would occur to Ed, though he enjoyed it enough at the time.

But outwardly Sally makes a joke of all this. 'He doesn't *know*,' she says to Marylynn, laughing a little, and they shake their heads. If it were them, they'd know, all right. Marylynn is in fact divorced, and she can list every single thing that went wrong, item by item. After doing this, she adds that her divorce was one of the best things that ever happened to her. 'I was just a nothing before,' she says. 'It made me pull myself together.'

Sally, looking across the kitchen table at Marylynn, has to agree that she is far from being a nothing now. She started out re-doing people's closets, and has worked that up into her own interior-design firm. She does the houses of the newly rich, those who lack ancestral furniture and the confidence to be shabby, and who wish their interiors to reflect a personal taste they do not in reality possess. 'What they want are mausoleums,' Marylynn says, 'or hotels', and she cheerfully supplies them. 'Right down to the ash-trays. Imagine having someone else pick out your ash-trays for you.'

By saying this, Marylynn lets Sally know that she's not including her in that category, though Sally did in fact hire her, at the very first, to help with a few details around the house. It was Marylynn who redesigned the wall of closets in the master bedroom and who found Sally's massive Chinese mahogany table, which cost her another seven hundred dollars to have stripped. But it turned out to be perfect, as Marylynn said it would. Now she's dug up a nineteenth-century keyhole desk, which both she and Sally know will be exactly right for the bay-windowed alcove off the living room. 'Why do you need it?' Ed said in his puzzled way. 'I thought you worked in your study.' Sally admitted this, but said they could keep the telephone bills in it, which appeared to satisfy him. She knows exactly what she needs it for: she needs it to sit at, in something flowing, backlit by the morning sunlight, gracefully dashing off notes. She saw a 1940's advertisement for coffee like this once, and the husband was standing behind the chair, leaning over, with a worshipful expression on his face.

Marylynn is the kind of friend Sally does not have to explain any of this to, because it's assumed between them. Her intelligence is the kind Sally respects.

Marylynn is tall and elegant, and makes anything she is wearing seem fashionable. Her hair is prematurely grey and she leaves it that way. She goes in for loose blouses in cream-coloured silk, and eccentric scarves gathered from interesting shops and odd corners of the world, thrown carelessly around her neck and over one shoulder. (Sally has tried this toss in the mirror, but it doesn't work.) Marylynn has a large collection of unusual shoes; she says they're unusual because her feet are so big, but Sally knows better. Sally, who used to think of herself as pretty enough and now thinks of herself as doing quite well for her age, envies Marylynn her bone structure, which will serve her well when the inevitable happens.

Whenever Marylynn is coming to dinner, as she is today — she's bringing the desk, too — Sally takes especial care with her clothes and make-up. Marylynn, she knows, is her real audience for such things, since no changes she effects in herself seem to affect Ed one way or the other, or even to register with him. 'You look fine to me', is all he says, no matter how she really looks. (But does she want him to see her more clearly, or not? Most likely, not. If he did he would notice the incipient wrinkles, the small pouches of flesh that are not quite there yet, the network forming beneath her eyes. It's better as it is.)

Sally has repeated this remark of Ed's to Marylynn, adding that he said it the day the Jacuzzi overflowed because the smoke alarm went off, because an English muffin she was heating to eat in the bathtub got stuck in the toaster, and she had to spend an hour putting down newspaper and mopping up, and only had half an hour to dress for a dinner they were going to. 'Really I looked like the wrath of God,' said Sally. These days she finds herself repeating to Marylynn many of the things Ed says, the stupid things. Marylynn is the only one of Sally's friends she has confided in to this extent.

'Ed is cute as a button,' Marylynn said. 'In fact, he's just like a button: he's so bright and shiny. If he were mine, I'd get him bronzed and keep him on the mantelpiece.'

Marylynn is even better than Sally at concocting formulations for Ed's particular brand of stupidity, which can irritate Sally: coming from herself, this sort of comment appears to her indulgent and loving, but from Marylynn it borders on the patronizing. So then she sticks up for Ed, who is by no means stupid about everything. When you narrow it down, there's only one area of life he's hopeless about. The rest of the time he's intelligent enough, some even say brilliant: otherwise, how could he be so successful?

Ed is a heart man, one of the best, and the irony of this is not lost on Sally: who could possibly know less about the workings of hearts, real hearts, the kind symbolized by red satin surrounded by lace and topped by pink bows, than Ed! Hearts with arrows in them. At the same time, the fact that he's a heart man is a large part of his allure. Women corner him on sofas, trap him in bay-windows at cocktail parties, mutter to him in confidential voices at dinner parties. They behave this way right in front of Sally, under her very nose, as if she's invisible, and Ed lets them do it. This would never happen if he were in banking or construction.

As it is, everywhere he goes he is beset by sirens. They want him to fix their hearts. Each of them seems to have a little something wrong — a murmur, a whisper. Or they faint a lot and want him to tell them why. This is always what the conversations are about, according to Ed, and Sally believes it. Once she'd wanted it herself, that mirage. What had she invented for him, in the beginning? A heavy heart, that beat too hard after meals. And he'd been so sweet, looking at her with those stunned brown eyes of his, as if her heart were the genuine topic, listening to her gravely as if he'd never heard any of this twaddle before, advising her to drink less coffee. And she'd felt such triumph, to have carried off her imposture, pried out of him that miniscule token of concern.

Thinking back on this incident makes her uneasy, now that she's seen her own performance repeated so many times, including the hand placed lightly on the heart, to call attention of course to the breasts. Some of these women have been within inches of getting Ed to put his head down on their chests, right there in Sally's living room. Watching all this out of the corners of her eyes while serving the liqueurs, Sally feels the Aztec rise within her. *Trouble with your heart? Get it removed,* she thinks. *Then you'll have no more problems.*

Sometimes Sally worries that she's a nothing, the way Marylynn was before she got a divorce and a job. But Sally isn't a nothing; therefore, she doesn't need a divorce to stop being one. And she's always had a job of some sort; in fact she has one now. Luckily Ed has no objection; he doesn't have much of an objection to anything she does.

Her job is supposed to be full-time, but in effect it's part-time, because Sally can take a lot of the work away and do it at home, and, as she says, with one arm tied behind her back. When Sally is being ornery, when she's playing the dull wife of a fascinating heart man — she does this with people she can't be bothered with — she says she works in a bank, nothing important. Then she watches their eyes dismiss her. When, on the other hand, she's trying to impress, she says she's in PR. In reality she runs the in-house organ for a trust company, a medium-sized one. This is a thin magazine, nicely printed, which is supposed to make the employees feel that some of the boys are doing worthwhile things out there and are human beings as well. It's still the boys, though the few women in anything resembling key positions are wheeled out regularly, bloused and suited and smiling brightly, with what they hope will come across as confidence rather than aggression.

This is the latest in a string of such jobs Sally has held over the years: comfortable enough jobs that engage only half of her cogs and wheels, and that end up leading nowhere. Technically, she's second-in-command: over her is a man who wasn't working out in management, but who couldn't be fired because his wife was related to the chairman of the board. He goes out for long alcoholic lunches and plays a lot of golf, and Sally runs the show. This man gets the official credit for everything Sally does right, but the senior executives in the company take Sally aside when no one is looking and tell her what a great gal she is and what a whiz she is at holding up her end.

The real pay-off for Sally, though, is that her boss provides her with an endless supply of anecdotes. She dines out on stories about his dim-wittedness and pomposity, his lobotomized suggestions about what the two of them should cook up for the magazine; *the organ,* as she says he always calls it. 'He says we need some fresh blood to perk up the organ,' Sally says, and the heart men grin at her. 'He actually said that?' Talking like this about her boss would be reckless — you never know what might get back to him, with the world as small as it is — if Sally were afraid of losing her job, but she isn't. There's an unspoken agreement between her and this man: they both know that if she goes, he goes, because who else would put up with him? Sally might angle for his job, if she were stupid enough to disregard his family connections, if she coveted the trappings of power. But she's just fine where she is. Jokingly, she says she's reached her level of incompetence. She says she suffers from fear of success.

Her boss is white-haired, slender, and tanned, and looks like an English gin ad. Despite his vapidity he's outwardly distinguished, she allows him that. In truth she pampers him outrageously, indulges him, covers up for him at every turn, though she stops short of behaving like a secretary: she doesn't bring him coffee. They both have a secretary who does that anyway. The one time he made a pass at her, when he came in from lunch visibly reeling, Sally was kind about it.

Occasionally, though not often, Sally has to travel in connection with her job. She's sent off to places like Edmonton, where they have a branch. She interviews the boys at the middle and senior levels; they have lunch, and the boys talk about ups and downs in oil or the slump in the real-estate market. Then she gets taken on tours of shopping plazas under construction. It's always windy, and grit blows into her face. She comes back to home base and writes a piece on the youthfulness and vitality of the West.

She teases Ed, while she packs, saying she's going off for a rendezvous with a dashing financier or two. Ed isn't threatened; he tells her to enjoy herself, and she hugs him and tells him how much she will miss him. He's so dumb it doesn't occur to him she might not be joking. In point of fact, it would have been quite possible for Sally to have had an affair, or at least a one- or two-night stand, on several of these occasions: she knows when those chalk lines are being drawn, when she's being dared to step over them. But she isn't interested in having an affair with anyone but Ed.

She doesn't eat much on the planes; she doesn't like the food. But on the return trip, she invariably saves the pre-packaged parts of the meal, the cheese in its plastic wrap, the miniature chocolate bar, the bag of pretzels. She ferrets them away in her purse. She thinks of them as supplies, that she may need if she gets stuck in a strange airport, if they have to change course because of snow or fog, for instance. All kinds of things could happen, although they never have. When she gets home she takes the things from her purse and throws them out.

Outside the window Ed straightens up and wipes his earth-smeared hands down the sides of his pants. He begins to turn, and Sally moves back from the window so he won't see that she's watching. She doesn't like it to be too obvious. She shifts her attention to the sauce: it's in the second stage of a *sauce suprême,* which will make all the difference to the chicken. When Sally was learning this sauce, her cooking instructor quoted one of the great chefs, to the effect that the chicken was merely a canvas. He meant as in painting, but Sally, in an undertone to the woman next to her, turned it around. 'Mine's canvas anyway, sauce or no sauce,' or words to that effect.

Gourmet cooking was the third night course Sally has taken. At the moment she's on her fifth, which is called *Forms of Narrative Fiction.* It's half reading and half writing assignments — the instructor doesn't believe you can understand an art form without at least trying it yourself — and Sally purports to be enjoying it. She tells her friends she takes night courses to keep her brain from atrophying, and her friends find this amusing: whatever else may become of Sally's brain, they say, they don't see atrophying as an option. Sally knows better, but in any case there's always room for improvement. She may have begun taking the courses in the belief that this would make her more interesting to Ed, but she soon gave up on that idea: she appears to be neither more nor less interesting to Ed now than she was before.

Most of the food for tonight is already made. Sally tries to be well organized: the overflowing Jacuzzi was an aberration. The cold watercress soup with walnuts is chilling in the refrigerator, the chocolate mousse ditto. Ed, being Ed, prefers meatloaf to sweetbreads with pine nuts, butterscotch pudding made from a package to chestnut purée topped with whipped cream. (Sally burnt her fingers peeling the chestnuts. She couldn't do it the easy way and buy it tinned.) Sally says Ed's preference for this type of food comes from being pre-programmed by hospital cafeterias when he was younger: show him a burned sausage and a scoop of instant mashed potatoes and he salivates. So it's only for company that she can unfurl her *boeuf en daube* and her salmon *en papillote,* spread them forth to be savoured and praised.

What she likes best about these dinners though is setting the table, deciding who will sit where and, when she's feeling mischievous, even what they are likely to say. Then she can sit and listen to them say it. Occasionally she prompts a little.

Tonight will not be very challenging, since it's only the heart men and their wives, and Marylynn, whom Sally hopes will dilute them. The heart men are forbidden to talk shop at Sally's dinner table, but they do it anyway. 'Not what you really want to listen to while you're eating,' says Sally. All those tubes and valves.' Privately she thinks they're a conceited lot, all except Ed. She can't resist needling them from time to time.

'I mean,' she said to one of the leading surgeons, 'basically it's just an exalted form of dress-making, don't you think?'

'Come again?' said the surgeon, smiling. The heart men think Sally is one hell of a tease.

'It's really just cutting and sewing, isn't it?' Sally murmured. The surgeon laughed.

'There's more to it than that,' Ed said, unexpectedly, solemnly.

'What more, Ed?' said the surgeon. 'You could say there's a lot of embroidery, but that's in the billing.' He chuckled at himself.

Sally held her breath. She could hear Ed's verbal thought processes lurching into gear. He was delectable.

'Good judgement,' Ed said. His earnestness hit the table like a wet fish. The surgeon hastily downed his wine.

Sally smiled. This was supposed to be a reprimand to her, she knew, for not taking things seriously enough. *Oh, come on, Ed,* she could say. But she knows also, most of the time, when to keep her trap shut. She should have a light-up JOKE sign on her forehead, so Ed would be able to tell the difference.

The heart men do well. Most of them appear to be doing better than Ed, but that's only because they have, on the whole, more expensive tastes and fewer wives. Sally can calculate these things and she figures Ed is about par.

These days there's much talk about advanced technologies, which Sally tries to keep up on, since they interest Ed. A few years ago the heart men got themselves a new facility. Ed was so revved up that he told Sally about it, which was unusual for him. A week later Sally said she would drop by the hospital at the end of the day and pick Ed up and take him out for dinner; she didn't feel like cooking, she said. Really she wanted to check out the facility; she likes to check out anything that causes the line on Ed's excitement chart to move above level.

At first Ed said he was tired, that when the day came to an end he didn't want to prolong it. But Sally wheedled and was respectful, and finally Ed took her to see his new gizmo. It was in a cramped, darkened room with an examining table in it. The thing itself looked like a television screen hooked up to some complicated hardware. Ed said that they could wire a patient up and bounce sound waves off the heart and pick up the echoes, and they would get a picture on the screen, an actual picture, of the heart in motion. It was a thousand times better than an electrocardiogram, he said: they could see the faults, the thickenings and cloggings, much more clearly.

'Colour?' said Sally.

'Black and white,' said Ed.

Then Sally was possessed by a desire to see her own heart, in motion, in black and white, on the screen. At the dentist's she always wants to see the X-rays of her teeth, too, solid and glittering in her cloudy head. 'Do it,' she said, 'I want to see how it works,' and though this was the kind of thing Ed would ordinarily evade or tell her she was being silly about, he didn't need much persuading. He was fascinated by the thing himself, and he wanted to show it off.

He checked to make sure there was nobody real booked for the room. Then he told Sally to slip out of her clothes, the top half, brassière and all. He gave her a paper gown and turned his back modestly while she slipped it on, as if he didn't see her body every night of the week. He attached electrodes to her, the ankles and one wrist, and turned a switch and fiddled with the dials. Really a technician was supposed to do this, he told her, but he knew how to run the machine himself. He was good with small appliances.

Sally lay prone on the table, feeling strangely naked. 'What do I do?' she said.

'Just lie there,' said Ed. He came over to her and tore a hole in the paper gown, above her left breast. Then he started running a probe over her skin. It was wet and slippery and cold, and felt like the roller on a roll-on deodorant.

'There,' he said, and Sally turned her head. On the screen was a large grey object, like a giant fig, paler in the middle, a dark line running down the centre. The sides moved in and out; two wings fluttered in it, like an uncertain moth's.

'That's it?' said Sally dubiously. Her heart looked so insubstantial, like a bag of gelatin, something that would melt, fade, disintegrate, if you squeezed it even a little.

Ed moved the probe, and they looked at the heart from the bottom, then the top. Then he stopped the frame, then changed it from a positive to a negative image. Sally began to shiver.

'That's wonderful,' she said. He seemed so distant, absorbed in his machine, taking the measure of her heart, which was beating over there all by itself, detached from her, exposed and under his control.

Ed unwired her and she put on her clothes again, neutrally, as if he were actually a doctor. Nevertheless this transaction, this whole room, was sexual in a way she didn't quite understand; it was clearly a dangerous place. It was like a massage parlour, only for women. Put a batch of women in there with Ed and they would never want to come out. They'd want to stay in there while he ran his probe over their wet skins and pointed out to them the defects of their beating hearts.

'Thank you,' said Sally.

Sally hears the back door open and close. She feels Ed approaching, coming through the passages of the house towards her, like a small wind or a ball of static electricity. The hair stands up on her arms. Sometimes he makes her so happy she thinks she's about to burst; other times she thinks she's about to burst anyway.

He comes into the kitchen, and she pretends not to notice. He puts his arms around her from behind, kisses her on the neck. She leans back, pressing herself into him. What they should do now is go into the bedroom (or even the living room, even the den) and make love, but it wouldn't occur to Ed to make love in the middle of the day. Sally often comes across articles in magazines about how to improve your sex life, which leave her feeling disappointed, or reminiscent: Ed is not Sally's first and only man. But she knows she shouldn't expect too much of Ed. If Ed were more experimental, more interested in variety, he would be a different kind of man altogether: slyer, more devious, more observant, harder to deal with.

As it is, Ed makes love in the same way, time after time, each movement following the others in an exact order. But it seems to satisfy him. Of course it satisfies him: you can always tell when men are satisfied. It's Sally who lies awake, afterwards, watching the pictures unroll across her closed eyes.

Sally steps away from Ed, smiles at him. 'How did you make out with the women today?' she says.

'What women?' says Ed absently, going towards the sink. He knows what women.

'The ones out there, hiding in the forsythia,' says Sally. 'I counted at least ten. They were just waiting for a chance.'

She teases him frequently about these troops of women, which follow him around everywhere, which are invisible to Ed but which she can see as plain as day.

'I bet they hang around outside the front door of the hospital,' she will say, 'just waiting till you come out. I bet they hide in the linen closets and jump out at you from behind, and then pretend to be lost so you'll take them by the short cut. It's the white coat that does it. None of those women can resist the white coats. They've been conditioned by Young Doctor Kildare.'

'Don't be silly,' says Ed today, with equanimity. Is he blushing, is he embarrassed? Sally examines his face closely, like a geologist with an aerial photograph, looking for telltale signs of mineral treasure: markings, bumps, hollows. Everything about Ed means something, though it's difficult at times to say what.

Now he's washing his hands at the sink, to get the earth off. In a minute he'll wipe them on the dish towel instead of using the hand towel the way he's supposed to. Is that complacency, in the back turned to her? Maybe there really are these hordes of women, even though she's made them up. Maybe they really do behave that way. His shoulders are slightly drawn up: is he shutting her out?

'I know what they want,' she goes on. 'They want to get into that little dark room of yours and climb up onto your table. They think you're delicious. They'll gobble you up. They'll chew you into tiny pieces. There won't be anything left of you at all, only a stethoscope and a couple of shoelaces.'

Once Ed would have laughed at this, but today he doesn't. Maybe she's said it, or something like it, a few times too often. He smiles though, wipes his hands on the dish towel, peers into the fridge. He likes to snack.

'There's some cold roast beef,' Sally says, baffled.

* * *

Sally takes the sauce off the stove and sets it aside for later: she'll do the last steps just before serving. It's only two-thirty. Ed has disappeared into the cellar, where Sally knows he will be safe for a while. She goes into her study, which used to be one of the kids' bedrooms, and sits down at her desk. The room has never been completely redecorated: there's still a bed in it, and a dressing table with a blue flowered flounce Sally helped pick out, long before the kids went off to university: 'flew the coop,' as Ed puts it.

Sally doesn't comment on the expression, though she would like to say that it wasn't the first coop they flew. Her house isn't even the real coop, since neither of the kids is hers. She'd hoped for a baby of her own when she married Ed, but she didn't want to force the issue. Ed didn't object to the idea, exactly, but he was neutral about it, and Sally got the feeling he'd had enough babies already. Anyway, the other two wives had babies, and look what happened to them. Since their actual fates have always been vague to Sally, she's free to imagine all kinds of things, from drug addiction to madness. Whatever it was resulted in Sally having to bring up their kids, at least from puberty onwards. The way it was presented by the first wife was that it was Ed's turn now. The second wife was more oblique: she said that the child wanted to spend some time with her father. Sally was left out of both these equations, as if the house wasn't a place she lived in, not really, so she couldn't be expected to have any opinion.

Considering everything, she hasn't done badly. She likes the kids and tries to be a friend to them, since she can hardly pretend to be a mother. She describes the three of them as having an easy relationship. Ed wasn't around much for the kids, but it's him they want approval from, not Sally; it's him they respect. Sally is more like a confederate, helping them get what they want from Ed.

When the kids were younger, Sally used to play Monopoly with them, up at the summer place in Muskoka Ed owned then but has since sold. Ed would play too, on his vacations and on the weekends when he could make it up. These games would all proceed along the same lines. Sally would have an initial run of luck and would buy up everything she had a chance at. She didn't care whether it was classy real estate, like Boardwalk or Park Place, or those dingy little houses on the other side of the tracks; she would even buy train stations, which the kids would pass over, preferring to save their cash reserves for better investments. Ed, on the other hand, would plod along, getting a little here, a little there. Then, when Sally was feeling flush, she would blow her money on next-to-useless luxuries such as the electric light company; and when the kids started to lose, as they invariably did, Sally would lend them money at cheap rates or trade them things of her own, at a loss. Why not? She could afford it.

Ed meanwhile would be hedging his bets, building up blocks of property, sticking houses and hotels on them. He preferred the middle range, respectable streets but not flashy. Sally would land on his spaces and have to shell out hard cash. Ed never offered deals, and never accepted them. He played a lone game, and won more often than not. Then Sally would feel thwarted. She would say she guessed she lacked the killer instinct; or she would say that for herself she didn't care, because after all it was only a game, but he ought to allow the kids to win, once in a while. Ed couldn't grasp the concept of allowing other people to win. He said it would be condescending towards the children, and anyway you couldn't arrange to have a dice game turn out the way you wanted it to, since it was partly a matter of chance. If it was chance, Sally would think, why were the games so similar to one another? At the end, there would be Ed, counting up his paper cash, sorting it out into piles of bills of varying denominations, and Sally, her vast holdings dwindled to a few shoddy blocks on Baltic Avenue, doomed to foreclosure: extravagant, generous, bankrupt.

On these nights, after the kids were asleep, Sally would have two or three more rye-and-gingers than were good for her. Ed would go to bed early — winning made him satisfied and drowsy — and Sally would ramble about the house or read the ends of murder mysteries she had already read once before, and finally she would slip into bed and wake Ed up and stroke him into arousal, seeking comfort.

Sally has almost forgotten these games. Right now the kids are receding, fading like old ink; Ed on the contrary looms larger and larger, the outlines around him darkening. He's constantly developing, like a Polaroid print, new colours emerging, but the result remains the same: Ed is a surface, one she has trouble getting beneath.

'Explore your inner world,' said Sally's instructor in *Forms of Narrative Fiction,* a middle-aged woman of scant frame who goes in for astrology and the Tarot pack and writes short stories, which are not published in any of the magazines Sally reads. 'Then there's your outer one,' Sally said afterwards, to her friends. 'For instance, she should really get something done about her hair.' She made this trivial and mean remark because she's fed up with her inner world; she doesn't need to explore it. In her inner world is Ed, like a doll within a Russian wooden doll, and in Ed is Ed's inner world, which she can't get at.

She takes a crack at it anyway: Ed's inner world is a forest, which looks something like the bottom part of their ravine lot, but without the fence. He wanders around in there, among the trees, not heading in any special direction. Every once in a while he comes upon a strange-looking plant, a sickly plant choked with weeds and briars. Ed kneels clears a space around it, does some pruning, a little skilful snipping and cutting, props it up. The plant revives, flushes with health, sends out a grateful red blossom. Ed continues on his way. Or it may be a conked-out squirrel, which he restores with a drop from his flask of magic elixir. At set intervals an angel appears, bringing him food. It's always meatloaf. That's fine with Ed, who hardly notices what he eats, but the angel is getting tired of being an angel. Now Sally begins thinking about the angel: why are its wings frayed and dingy grey around the edges, why is it looking so withered and frantic? This is where all Sally's attempts to explore Ed's inner world end up.

She knows she thinks about Ed too much. She knows she should stop. She knows she shouldn't ask, 'Do you still love me?' in the plaintive tone that sets even her own teeth on edge. All it achieves is that Ed shakes his head, as if not understanding why she would ask this, and pats her hand. 'Sally, Sally,' he says, and everything proceeds as usual; except for the dread that seeps into things, the most ordinary things, such as rearranging the chairs and changing the burnt-out lightbulbs. But what is it she's afraid of? She has what they call everything: Ed, their wonderful house on a ravine lot, something she's always wanted. (But the hill is jungly, and the house is made of ice. It's held together only by Sally, who sits in the middle of it, working on a puzzle. The puzzle is Ed. If she should ever solve it, if she should ever fit the last cold splinter into place, the house will melt and flow away down the hill, and then. . . .) It's a bad habit, fooling around with her head this way. It does no good. She knows that if she could quit she'd be happier. She ought to be able to: she's given up smoking.

She needs to concentrate her attention on other things. This is the real reason for the night courses, which she picks almost at random, to coincide with the evenings Ed isn't in. He has meetings, he's on the boards of charities, he has trouble saying no. She runs the courses past herself, mediaeval history, cooking, anthropology, hoping her mind will snag on something; she's even taken a course in geology, which was fascinating, she told her friends, all that magma. That's just it: everything is fascinating, but nothing enters her. She's always a star pupil, she does well on the exams and impresses the teachers, for which she despises them. She is familiar with her brightness, her techniques; she's surprised other people are still taken in by them.

Forms of Narrative Fiction started out the same way. Sally was full of good ideas, brimming with helpful suggestions. The workshop part of it was anyway just like a committee meeting, and Sally knew how to run those, from behind, without seeming to run them: she'd done it lots of times at work. Bertha, the instructor, told Sally she had a vivid imagination and a lot of untapped creative energy. 'No wonder she never gets anywhere, with a name like Bertha,' Sally said, while having coffee afterwards with two of the other night-coursers. 'It goes with her outfits, though.' (Bertha sports the macramé look, with health food sandals and bulky-knit sweaters and hand-weave skirts that don't do a thing for her square figure, and too many Mexican rings on her hands, which she doesn't wash often enough.) Bertha goes in for assignments: she likes things that can be completed and then discarded, and for which she gets marks.

The first thing Bertha assigned was The Epic. They read *The Odyssey* (selected passages, in translation, with a plot summary of the rest; then they poked around in James Joyce's *Ulysses,* to see how Joyce had adapted the epic form to the modern-day novel. Bertha had them keep a Toronto notebook, in which they had to pick out various spots around town as the ports of call in *The Odyssey,* and say why they had chosen them. The notebooks were read out loud in class, and it was a scream to see who had chosen what for Hades. (The Mount Pleasant Cemetery, McDonald's, where, if you eat the forbidden food, you never get back to the land of the living, the University Club with its dead ancestral souls, and so forth.) Sally's was the hospital, of course; she had no difficulty with the trench filled with blood, and she put the ghosts in wheelchairs.

After that they did The Ballad, and read gruesome accounts of murders and betrayed love. Bertha played them tapes of wheezy old men singing traditionally, in the Doric mode, and assigned a newspaper scrapbook, in which you had to clip and paste up-to-the minute equivalents. The *Sun* was the best newspaper for these. The fiction that turned out to go with this kind of plot was the kind Sally liked anyway, and she had no difficulty concocting a five-page murder mystery, complete with revenge.

But now they are on Folk Tales and the Oral Tradition, and Sally is having trouble. This time, Bertha wouldn't let them read anything. Instead she read to them, in a voice, Sally said, that was like a gravel truck and was not conducive to reverie. Since it was the Oral Tradition, they weren't even allowed to take notes; Bertha said the original hearers of these stories couldn't read, so the stories were memorized. 'To recreate the atmosphere,' said Bertha, 'I should turn out the lights. These stories were always told at night.' 'To make them creepier?' someone offered. 'No,' said Bertha. 'In the days, they worked.' She didn't do that, though she did make them sit in a circle.

'You should have seen us,' Sally said afterwards to Ed, 'sitting in a circle, listening to fairy stories. It was just like kindergarten. Some of them even had their mouths open. I kept expecting her to say, "If you need to go, put up your hand." ' She was meaning to be funny, to amuse Ed with this account of Bertha's eccentricity and the foolish appearance of the students, most of them middle-aged, sitting in a circle as if they had never grown up at all. She was also intending to belittle the course, just slightly. She always did this with her night courses, so Ed wouldn't get the idea there was anything in her life that was even remotely as important as he was. But Ed didn't seem to need this amusement or this belittlement. He took her information earnestly, gravely, as if Bertha's behaviour was, after all, only the procedure of a specialist. No one knew better than he did that the procedures of specialists often looked bizarre or incomprehensible to onlookers. 'She probably has her reasons,' was all he would say.

The first stories Bertha read them, for warm-ups ('No memorizing for *her*,' said Sally), were about princes who got amnesia and forgot about their true loves and married girls their mothers had picked out for them. Then they had to be rescued, with the aid of magic. The stories didn't say what happened to the women the princes had already married, though Sally wondered about it. Then Bertha read them another story, and this time they were supposed to remember the features that stood out for them and write a five-page transposition, set in the present and cast in the realistic mode. ('In other words,' said Bertha, 'no real magic.') They couldn't use the Universal Narrator, however: they had done that in their Ballad assignment. This time they had to choose a point of view. It could be the point of view of anyone or anything in the story, but they were limited to one only. The story she was about to read, she said, was a variant of the Bluebeard motif, much earlier than Perrault's sentimental rewriting of it. In Perrault, said Bertha, the girl has to be rescued by her brothers; but in the earlier version things were quite otherwise.

This is what Bertha read, as far as Sally can remember:

There were once three young sisters. One day a beggar with a large basket on his back came to the door and asked for some bread. The eldest sister brought him some, but no sooner had she touched him than she was compelled to jump into his basket, for the beggar was really a wizard in disguise. ('So much for United Appeal,' Sally murmured. 'She should have said, "I gave at the office." ') The wizard carried her away to his house in the forest, which was large and richly furnished. 'Here you will be happy with me, my darling,' said the wizard, 'for you will have everything your heart could desire.'

This lasted for a few days. Then the wizard gave the girl an egg and a bunch of keys. 'I must go away on a journey,' he said, 'and I am leaving the house in your charge. Preserve this egg for me, and carry it about with you everywhere; for a great misfortune will follow from its loss. The keys open every room in the house. You may go into each of them and enjoy what you find there, but do not go into the small room at the top of the house, on pain of death.' The girl promised, and the wizard disappeared.

At first the girl contented herself with exploring the rooms, which contained many treasures. But finally her curiosity would not let her alone. She sought out the smallest key, and, with beating heart, opened the little door at the top of the house. Inside it was a large basin full of blood, within which were the bodies of many women, which had been cut to pieces; nearby were a chopping block and an axe. In her horror, she let go of the egg, which fell into the basin of blood. In vain did she try to wipe away the stain: every time she succeeded in removing it, back it would come.

The wizard returned, and in a stern voice asked for the egg and the keys. When he saw the egg, he knew at once she had disobeyed him and gone into the forbidden room. 'Since you have gone into the room against my will,' he said, 'you shall go back into it against your own.' Despite her pleas he threw her down, dragged her by her hair into the little room, hacked her into pieces and threw her body into the basin with the others.

Then he went for the second girl, who fared no better than her sister. But the third was clever and wily. As soon as the wizard had gone, she set the egg on a shelf, out of harm's way, and then went immediately and opened the forbidden door. Imagine her distress when she saw the cut-up bodies of her two beloved sisters; but she set the parts in order, and they joined together and her sisters stood up and moved, and were living and well. They embraced each other, and the third sister hid the other two in a cupboard.

When the wizard returned he at once asked for the egg. This time it was spotless. 'You have passed the test,' he said to the third sister. 'You shall be my bride.' ('And second prize,' said Sally, to herself this time, 'is *two* weeks in Niagara Falls.') The wizard no longer had any power over her, and had to do whatever she asked. There was more, about how the wizard met his come-uppance and was burned to death, but Sally already knew which features stood out for her.

At first she thought the most important thing in the story was the forbidden room. What would she put in the forbidden room, in her present-day realistic version? Certainly not chopped-up women. It wasn't that they were too unrealistic, but they were certainly too sick, as well as being too obvious. She wanted to do something more clever. She though it might be a good idea to have the curious woman open the door and find nothing there at all, but after mulling it over she set this notion aside. It would leave her with the problem of why the wizard would have a forbidden room in which he kept nothing.

That was the way she was thinking right after she got the assignment, which was a full two weeks ago. So far she's written nothing. The great temptation is to cast herself in the role of the cunning heroine, but again it's too predictable. And Ed certainly isn't the wizard; he's nowhere near sinister enough. If Ed were the wizard, the room would contain a forest, some ailing plants and feeble squirrels, and Ed himself, fixing them up; but then, if it were Ed the room wouldn't even be locked, and there would be no story.

Now, as she sits at her desk, fiddling with her felt-tip pen, it comes to Sally that the intriguing thing about the story, the thing she should fasten on, is the egg. Why an egg? From the night course in Comparative Folklore she took four years ago, she remembers that the egg can be a fertility symbol, or a necessary object in African spells, or something the world hatched out of. Maybe in this story it's a symbol of virginity, and that is why the wizard requires it unbloodied. Women with dirty eggs get murdered, those with clean ones get married.

But this isn't useful either. The concept is so outmoded. Sally doesn't see how she can transpose it into real life without making it ridiculous, unless she sets the story in, for instance, an immigrant Portuguese family, and what would she know about that?

Sally opens the drawer of her desk and hunts around in it for her nail file. As she's doing this, she gets the brilliant idea of writing the story from the point of view of the egg. Other people will do the other things: the clever girl, the wizard, the two blundering sisters, who weren't smart enough to lie, and who will have problems afterwards, because of the thin red lines running all over their bodies, from where their parts joined together. But no one will think of the egg. How does it feel, to be the innocent and passive cause of so much misfortune?

(Ed isn't the Bluebeard: Ed is the egg. Ed Egg, blank and pristine and lovely. Stupid, too. Boiled, probably, Sally smiles fondly.)

But how can there be a story from the egg's point of view, if the egg is so closed and unaware? Sally ponders this, doodling on her pad of lined paper. Then she resumes the search for her nail file. Already it's time to begin getting ready for her dinner party. She can sleep on the problem of the egg and finish the assignment tomorrow, which is Sunday. It's due on Monday, but Sally's mother used to say she was a whiz at getting things done at the last minute.

After painting her nails with *Nuit Magique,* Sally takes a bath, eating her habitual toasted English muffin while she lies in the tub. She begins to dress, dawdling; she has plenty of time. She hears Ed coming up out of the cellar; then she hears him in the bathroom, which he has entered from the hall door. Sally goes in through the other door, still in her slip. Ed is standing at the sink with his shirt off, shaving. On the weekends he leaves it until necessary, or until Sally tells him he's too scratchy.

Sally slides her hands around his waist, nuzzling against his naked back. He has very smooth skin, for a man. Sally smiles to herself: she can't stop thinking of him as an egg.

'Mmm,' says Ed. It could be appreciation, or the answer to a question

Sally hasn't asked and he hasn't heard, or just an acknowledgement that she's there.

'Don't you ever wonder what I think about?' Sally says. She's said this more than once, in bed or at the dinner table, after dessert. She stands behind him, watching the swaths the razor cuts in the white of his face, looking at her own face reflected in the mirror, just the eyes visible above his naked shoulder. Ed, lathered, is Assyrian, sterner than usual; or a frost-covered Arctic explorer; or demi-human, a white-beared forest mutant. He scrapes away at himself, methodically destroying the illusion.

'But I already know what you think about,' says Ed.

'How?' Sally says, taken aback.

'You're always telling me,' Ed says, with what might be resignation or sadness; or maybe this is only a simple statement of fact.

Sally is relieved. If that's all he's going on, she's safe.

Marylynn arrives half an hour early, her pearl-coloured Porsche leading two men in a delivery truck up the driveway. The men install the keyhole desk, while Marylynn supervises: it looks, in the alcove, exactly as Marylynn has said it would, and Sally is delighted. She sits at it to write the cheque. Then she and Marylynn go into the kitchen, where Sally is finishing up her sauce, and Sally pours them each a Kir. She's glad Marylynn is here: it will keep her from dithering, as she tends to do just before people arrive. Though it's only the heart men, she's still a bit nervous. Ed is more likely to notice when things are wrong than when they're exactly right.

Marylynn sits at the kitchen table, one arm draped over the chairback, her chin on the other hand; she's in soft grey, which makes her hair look silver, and Sally feels once again how banal it is to have ordinary dark hair like her own, however well-cut, however shiny. It's the confidence she envies, the negligence. Marylynn doesn't seem to be trying at all, ever.

'Guess what Ed said today?' Sally says.

Marylynn leans further forward. 'What?' she says, with the eagerness of one joining in a familiar game.

'He said, 'Some of these femininists go too far.' Sally reports. ' "Femininists". Isn't that sweet?'

Marylynn holds the pause too long, and Sally has a sudden awful thought: maybe Marylynn thinks she's showing off, about Ed. Marylynn has always said she's not ready for another marriage yet; still, Sally should watch herself, not rub her nose in it. But then Marylynn laughs indulgently, and Sally, relieved, joins in.

'Ed is unbelievable,' says Marylynn. 'You should pin his mittens to his sleeves when he goes out in the morning.'

'He shouldn't be let out alone,' says Sally.

'You should get him a seeing-eye dog,' says Marylynn, 'to bark at women.'

'Why?' says Sally, still laughing but alert now, the cold beginning at the ends of her fingers. Maybe Marylynn knows something she doesn't; maybe the house is beginning to crumble, after all.

'Because he can't see them coming,' says Marylynn. 'That's what you're always telling me.'

She sips her Kir; Sally stirs the sauce. 'I bet he thinks I'm a femininist,' says Marylynn.

'You?' says Sally. 'Never.' She would like to add that Ed has given no indication of thinking anything at all about Marylynn, but she doesn't. She doesn't want to take the risk of hurting her feelings.

The wives of the heart men admire Sally's sauce; the heart men talk shop, all expect Walter Morly, who is good at by-passes. He's sitting beside Marylynn, and paying far too much attention to her for Sally's comfort. Mrs Morly is at the other end of the table, not saying much of anything, which Marylynn appears not to notice. She keeps on talking to Walter about St Lucia, where they've both been.

So after dinner, when Sally has herded them all into the living room for coffee and liqueurs, she takes Marylynn by the elbow. 'Ed hasn't seen our desk yet,' she says, 'not up close. Take him away and give him your lecture on nineteenth-century antiques. Show him all the pigeon-holes. Ed loves pigeon-holes.' Ed appears not to get this.

Marylynn knows exactly what Sally is up to. 'Don't worry,' she says, 'I won't rape Dr Morly; the poor creature would never survive the shock,' but she allows herself to be shunted off to the side with Ed.

Sally moves from guest to guest, smiling, making sure everything is in order. Although she never looks directly, she's always conscious of Ed's presence in the room, any room; she perceives him as a shadow, a shape seen dimly at the edge of her field of vision, recognizable by the outline. She likes to know where he is, that's all. Some people are on their second cup of coffee. She walks towards the alcove: they must have finished with the desk by now.

But they haven't, they're still in there. Marylynn is bending forward, one hand on the veneer. Ed is standing too close to her, and as Sally comes up behind them she sees his left arm, held close to his side, the back of it pressed against Marylynn, her shimmering upper thigh, her ass to be exact. Marylynn does not move away.

It's a split second, and then Ed sees Sally and the hand is gone; there it is, on top of the desk, reaching for a liqueur glass.

'Marylynn needs more Tia Maria,' he says. 'I just told her that people who drink a little now and again live longer.' His voice is even, his face is as level as ever, a flat plain with no signposts.

Marylynn laughs. 'I once had a dentist who I swear drilled tiny holes in my teeth, so he could fix them later,' she says.

Sally sees Ed's hand outstretched towards her, holding the empty glass. She takes it, smiling, and turns away. There's a roaring sound at the back of her head; blackness appears around the edges of the picture she is seeing, like a television screen going dead. She walks into the kitchen and puts her cheek against the refrigerator and her arms around it; as far as they will go. She remains that way, hugging it; it hums steadily, with a sound like comfort. After a while she lets go of it and touches her hair, and walks back into the living room with the filled glass.

Marylynn is over by the french doors, talking with Walter Morly. Ed is standing by himself, in front of the fireplace, one arm on the mantelpiece, his left hand out of sight in his pocket.

Sally goes to Marylynn, hands her the glass. 'Is that enough?' she says.

Marylynn is unchanged. 'Thanks, Sally,' she says, and goes on listening to Walter, who has dragged out his usual piece of mischief: some day, when they've perfected it, he says, all hearts will be plastic, and this will be a vast improvement on the current model. It's an obscure form of flirtation. Marylynn winks at Sally, to show that she knows he's tedious. Sally, after a pause, winks back.

She looks over at Ed, who is staring off into space, like a robot which has been parked and switched off. Now she isn't sure whether she really saw what she thought she saw. Even if she did, what does it mean? Maybe it's just that Ed, in a wayward intoxicated moment, put his hand on the nearest buttock, and Marylynn refrained from a shriek or a flinch out of good breeding or the desire not to offend him. Things like this have happened to Sally.

Or it could mean something more sinister: a familiarity between them, an understanding. If this is it, Sally has been wrong about Ed, for years, forever. Her version of Ed is not something she's perceived but something that's been perpetrated on her, by Ed himself, for reasons of his own. Possibly Ed is not stupid. Possibly he's enormously clever. She thinks of moment after moment when this cleverness, this cunning, would have shown itself if it were there, but didn't. She has watched him so carefully. She remembers playing Pick Up Sticks, with the kids,

Ed's kids, years ago: how if you moved one stick in the tangle, even slightly, everything else moved also.

She won't say anything to him. She can't say anything: she can't afford to be wrong, or to be right either. She goes back into the kitchen and begins to scrape the plates. This is unlike her — usually she sticks right with the party until it's over — and after a while Ed wanders out. He stands silently, watching her. Sally concentrates on the scraping: dollops of *sauce supreme* slide into the plastic bag, shreds of lettuce, rice, congealed and lumpy. What is left of her afternoon.

'What are you doing out here?' Ed asks at last.

'Scraping the plates,' Sally says, cheerful, neutral. 'I just thought I'd get a head start on tidying up.'

'Leave it,' says Ed. 'The woman can do that in the morning.' That's how he refers to Mrs Rudge, although she's been with them for three years now: *the woman*. And Mrs Bird before her, as though they are interchangeable. This has never bothered Sally before. 'Go on out there and have a good time.'

Sally puts down the spatula, wipes her hands on the hand towel, puts her arms around him, holds on tighter than she should. Ed pats her shoulder. 'What's up?' he says; then, 'Sally, Sally.' If she looks up, she will see him shaking his head a little, as if he doesn't know what to do about her. She doesn't look up.

Ed has gone to bed. Sally roams the house, fidgeting with the debris left by the party. She collects empty glasses, picks up peanuts from the rug. After a while she realizes that she's down on her knees, looking under a chair, and she's forgotten what for. She goes upstairs, creams off her make-up, does her teeth, undresses in the darkened bedroom and slides into bed beside Ed, who is breathing deeply as if asleep. *As if.*

Sally lies in bed with her eyes closed. What she sees is her own heart, in black and white, beating with that insubstantial moth-like flutter, a ghostly heart, torn out of her and floating in space, an animated valentine with no colour. It will go on and on forever; she has no control over it. But now she's seeing the egg, which is not small and cold and white and inert but larger than a real egg and golden pink, resting in a nest of brambles, glowing softly as though there's something red and hot inside it. It's almost pulsing; Sally is afraid of it. As she looks it darkens: rose-red, crimson. This is something the story left out, Sally thinks: the egg is alive, and one day it will hatch. But what will come out of it?

III Feminist Literary Criticism

17 'Some Day My Prince Will Come': Female Acculturation through the Fairy Tale

Marcia K. Lieberman

In a review of children's stories for a Christmas issue of the *New York Review of Books,* Alison Lurie praised traditional fairy and folk tales as

> one of the few sorts of classic children's literature of which a radical feminist would approve...These stories suggest a society in which women are as competent and active as men, at every age and in every class. Gretel, not Hansel, defeats the Witch; and for every clever youngest son there is a youngest daughter equally resourceful. The contrast is greatest in maturity, where women are often more powerful than men. Real help for the hero or heroine comes most frequently from a fairy godmother or wise woman, and real trouble from a witch or wicked stepmother...To prepare children for women's liberation, therefore, and to protect them against Future Shock, you had better buy at least one collection of fairy tales...[1]

Radical feminists, apparently, bought neither Ms Lurie's ideas nor the collections of fairy tales. It is hard to see how children could be 'prepared' for women's liberation by reading fairy tales; an analysis of those fairy tales that children actually read indicates instead that they serve to acculturate women to traditional social roles.

Ms Lurie has now repeated her argument in a recent article, in which she objects to the opinion that feminists actually have of such stories as 'Cinderella' and 'Snow White':

> It is true that some of the tales we know best, those that have been popularized by Disney, have this sort of heroine. But from the point of

> view of European folklore they are a very unrepresentative selection. They reflect the taste of the refined literary men who edited the first popular collections of fairy tales for children during the Victorian era. Andrew Lang, for instance, chose the tales in his *Blue Fairy Book* (first published in 1889) from among literally thousands known to him as a folklorist; and he chose them... partly for their moral lesson. Folk tales recorded in the field by scholars are full of everything Lang leaves out: sex, death, low humor, and female initiative.
>
> In the other more recent collections of tales — as well as in Lang's later collections — there are more active heroines... [2]

No one would disagree with Ms Lurie that Andrew Lang was very selective in choosing his tales, but to a feminist who wishes to understand the acculturation of women, this is beside the point. Only the best-known stories, those that everyone has read or heard, indeed, those that Disney has popularized, have affected masses of children in our culture. Cinderella, the Sleeping Beauty, and Snow White are mythic figures who have replaced the old Greek and Norse gods, goddesses, and heroes for most children. The 'folk tales recorded in the field by scholars', to which Ms Lurie refers, or even Andrew Lang's later collections, are so relatively unknown that they cannot seriously be considered in a study of the meaning of fairy tales to women.

In this light, *The Blue Fairy Book* is a very fruitful book to analyze, for it contains many of the most famous stories, and has perhaps been the best-known and hence most influential collection of tales. It was compiled by Andrew Lang and first published by Longman's Green, and Co. in London in 1889. It was followed by *The Red Fairy Book*, and then the *Green*, and then by many others, the *Yellow*, the *Brown*, the *Rose*, the *Violet*, etc. In the preface to *The Green Fairy Book*, in 1892, Lang noted that the stories were made not only to amuse children, but also to teach them. He pointed out that many of the stories have a moral, although, he wrote, 'we think more as we read them of the diversion than of the lesson'. [3] The distinction that Lang drew between diversions and lessons is misleading, for children do not categorize their reading as diverting or instructive, but as interesting or boring. If we are concerned, then, about what our children are being taught, we must pay particular attention to those stories that are so beguiling that children think more as they read them 'of the diversion than of the lesson'; perhaps literature is suggestive in direct proportion to its ability to divert. We know that children are socialized or culturally conditioned by movies, television programs, and the stories they read or hear, and we have begun to wonder at the influence that children's stories and entertainments had upon us, though we cannot now measure the extent of that influence.

Generations of children have read the popular fairy books, and in doing so may have absorbed far more from them than merely the outlines of the various stories. What is the precise effect that the story of 'Snow-White and the Seven Dwarfs' has upon a child? Not only do children find out what happens to the various princes and princesses, wood-cutters, witches, and children of their favorite tales, but they also learn behavioral and associational patterns, value systems, and how to predict the consequences of specific acts or circumstances. Among other things, these tales present a picture of sexual roles, behavior, and psychology, and a way of predicting outcome or fate according to sex, which is important because of the intense interest that children take in 'endings'; they always want to know how things will 'turn out'. A close examination of the treatment of girls and women in fairy tales reveals certain patterns which are keenly interesting not only in themselves, but also as material which has undoubtedly played a major contribution in forming the sexual role concept of children, and in suggesting to them the limitations that are imposed by sex upon a person's chances of success in various endeavors. It is now being questioned whether those traits that have been characterized as feminine have a biological or a cultural basis: discarding the assumptions of the past, we are asking what is inherent in our nature, and what has become ours through the gentle but forcible process of acculturation. Many feminists accept nothing as a 'given' about the nature of female personality; nearly all the work on that vast subject is yet to be done. In considering the possibility that gender has a cultural character and origin we need to examine the primary channels of acculturation. Millions of women must surely have formed their psycho-sexual self-concepts, and their ideas of what they could or could not accomplish, what sort of behavior would be rewarded, and of the nature of reward itself, in part from their favorite fairy tales. These stories have been made the repositories of the dreams, hopes, and fantasies of generations of girls. An analysis of the women in *The Blue Fairy Book* presents a picture that does not accord with Ms Lurie's hypothesis.

Certain premises and patterns emerge at once, of which only the stereotyped figures of the wicked step-mother has received much general notice. The beauty contest is a constant and primary device in many of the stories. Where there are several daughters in a family, or several unrelated girls in a story, the prettiest is invariably singled out and designated for reward, or first for punishment and later for reward. Beautiful girls are never ignored; they may be oppressed at first by wicked figures, as the jealous Queen persecutes Snow White, but ultimately they are chosen for reward. Two fundamental conventions are associated here: the special destiny of the youngest child when there are several children in a family (this holds true for youngest brothers as well as for youngest sisters, as long as the siblings are of the same sex), and the focus on beauty as a girl's most valuable asset, perhaps her only valuable asset. Good-temper and meekness are so regularly associated with beauty, and ill-temper with ugliness, that this in itself must influence children's expectations. The most famous example of this associational pattern occurs in 'Cinderella,' with the opposition of the ugly, cruel, bad-tempered older sisters to the younger, beautiful, sweet Cinderella, but in *The Blue Fairy Book* it also occurs in many other stories, such as 'Beauty and the Beast' and 'Toads and Diamonds'. Even when there is no series of sisters (in 'Snow-White and Rose-Red' both girls are beautiful and sweet) the beautiful single daughter is nearly always noted for her docility, gentleness and good temper.

This pattern, and the concomitant one of reward distribution, probably acts to promote jealousy and divisiveness among girls. The stories reflect an intensely competitive spirit: they are frequently about contests, for which there can be only one winner because there is only one prize. Girls win the prize if they are the fairest of them all; boys win if they are bold, active, and lucky. If a child identifies with the beauty, she may learn to be suspicious of ugly girls, who are portrayed as cruel, sly, and unscrupulous in these stories; if she identifies with the plain girls, she may learn to be suspicious and jealous of pretty girls, beauty being a gift of fate, not something that can be attained. There are no examples of a crossed-pattern, that is, of plain but good-tempered girls. It is a psychological truth that as children, and as women, girls fear homeliness (even attractive girls are frequently convinced that they are plain), and this fear is a major source of anxiety, diffidence, and convictions of inadequacy and inferiority among women. It is probably also a source of envy and discord among them. Girls may be predisposed to imagine that there is a link between the lovable face and the lovable character, and to fear, if plain themselves, that they will also prove to be unpleasant, thus using the patterns to set up self-fulfilling prophecies.

The immediate and predictable result of being beautiful is being chosen, this word having profound importance to a girl. The beautiful girl does not have to *do* anything to merit being chosen; she does not have to show pluck, resourcefulness, or wit; she is chosen because she is beautiful. Prince Hyacinth chooses the Dear Little Princess for his bride from among the portraits of many princesses that are shown to him because she is the prettiest; the bear chooses the beautiful youngest daughter in 'East of the Sun & West of the Moon'; at least twenty kings compete to win Bellissima in 'The Yellow Dwarf'; the prince who penetrates the jungle of thorns and briars to find the Sleeping Beauty does so because he had heard about her loveliness; Cinderella instantly captivates her prince during a ball that amounts to a beauty contest; the old king in 'The White Cat' says he will designate as his heir whichever of his sons brings home the loveliest princess, thereby creating a beauty contest as a hurdle to inheriting his crown; the prince in 'The Water-Lily or The Gold-Spinners' rescues and marries the youngest and fairest of the three enslaved maidens; the King falls in love with Goldilocks because of her beauty; the enchanted sheep dies for love of the beautiful Miranda in 'The Wonderful Sheep'; Prince Darling pursues Celia because she is beautiful; the young king in 'Trusty John' demands the Princess of the Golden Roof for her beauty, and so on. This is a principal factor contributing to the passivity of most of the females in these stories (even those few heroines who are given some sort of active role are usually passive in another part of the story). Since the heroines are chosen for their beauty (*en soi*), not for anything they do (*pour soi*), they seem to exist passively until they are seen by the hero, or described to him. They wait, are chosen, and are rewarded.

Marriage is the fulcrum and major event of nearly every fairy tale; it is the reward for girls, or sometimes their punishment. (This is almost equally true for boys, although the boy who wins the hand of the princess gets power as well as a pretty wife, because the princess is often part of a package deal including half or all of a kingdom). While it would be futile and anachronistic to suppose that these tales could or should have depicted alternate options or rewards for heroines or heroes, we must still observe that marriage dominates them, and note what they show as leading to marriage, and as resulting from it. Poor boys play an active role in winning kingdoms and princesses; Espen Cinderlad, the despised and youngest of the three brothers in so many Norwegian folk tales, wins the Princess on the Glass Hill by riding up a veritable hill of glass. Poor girls are chosen by princes because they have been seen by them.

Marriage is associated with getting rich: it will be seen that the reward basis in fairy and folk tales is overwhelmingly mercenary. Good, poor, and pretty girls always win rich and handsome princes, never merely handsome, good, but poor men. (If the heroine or hero is already rich, she or he may marry someone of equal rank and wealth, as in 'The White Cat', 'Trusty John', 'The Sleeping Beauty', etc'; if poor, she or he marries someone richer.) Since girls are chosen for their beauty, it is easy for a child to infer that beauty leads to wealth, that being chosen means getting rich. Beauty has an obviously commercial advantage even in stories in which marriage appears to be a punishment rather than a reward: 'Bluebeard', in which the suitor is wealthy though ugly, and the stories in which a girl is wooed by a beast, such as 'Beauty and the Beast', 'East of the Sun & West of the Moon', and 'The Black Bull of Norroway'.

The bear in 'East of the Sun & West of the Moon' promises to enrich the whole family of a poor husbandman if they will give him the beautiful youngest daughter. Although the girl at first refuses to go, her beauty is seen as the family's sole asset, and she is sold, like a commodity, to the bear (the family does not know that he is a prince under an enchantment). 'Beauty and the Beast' is similar to this part of 'East of the Sun', and the Snow-White of 'Snow-White and Rose-Red' also becomes rich upon marrying an enchanted prince who had been a bear.[4] Cinderella may be the best-known story of this type.

Apart from the princesses who are served out as prizes in competitions (to the lad who can ride up a glass hill, or slay a giant, or answer three riddles, or bring back some rarity), won by lucky fellows like Espen Cinderlad, a few girls in *The Blue Fairy Book* find themselves chosen as brides for mercantile reasons, such as the girl in 'Toads and Diamonds' who was rewarded by a fairy so that flowers and jewels dropped from her mouth whenever she spoke. In 'Rumpelstiltzkin', the little dwarf helps the poor miller's daughter to spin straw into gold for three successive nights, so that the King thinks to himself, ' "She's only a miller's daughter, it's true. . . but I couldn't find a richer wife if I were to search the whole world over" ', consequently making her his queen.[5] The system of rewards in fairy tales, then, equates these three factors: being beautiful, being chosen, and getting rich.

Alison Lurie suggests that perhaps fairy tales are the first real women's literature, that they are literally old wives' tales: 'throughout Europe. . . the story-tellers from whom the Grimm Brothers and their followers heard them were most often women; in some areas they were all women.'[6] She wonders if the stories do not reflect a matriarchal society in which women held power, and she mentions Gretel as an example of an active, resourceful young heroine (I will set aside the problem of the power of older women for the moment). An examination of the best-known stories shows that active resourceful girls are in fact rare; most of the heroines are passive, submissive, and helpless. In the story of 'Hansel and Gretel' it is true that Gretel pushes the witch into the oven; Hansel is locked up in the stable, where the witch has been fattening him. At the beginning of the story, however, when the children overhear their parents' plan to lose them in the forest, we read that 'Gretel wept bitterly and spoke to Hansel: "Now it's all up with us." "No, no, Gretel," said Hansel, "don't fret yourself, I'll be able to find a way of escape, no fear." ' (p.251) It is Hansel who devises the plan of gathering pebbles and dropping them on the path as they are led into the forest. 'Later in the dark forest, Gretel began to cry, and said: "How are we ever to get out of the wood?" But Hansel comforted her. "Wait a bit," he said, "till the moon is up, and then we'll find our way sure enough." And when the full moon had risen he took his sister by the hand and followed the pebbles, which shone like new threepenny bits, and showed them the path.' (p.252)

After they get home, they overhear their parents scheming to lose them again. Gretel weeps again, and again Hansel consoles her. Gretel does perform the decisive action at the end, but for the first half of the story she is the frightened little sister, looking to her brother for comfort and help.

Even so, Gretel is one of the most active of the girls, but her company is small. The heroines of the very similar 'East of the Sun' and 'The Black Bull of Norroway' are initially passive, but then undertake difficult quests when they lose their men. The heroine of 'East of the Sun' succumbs to curiosity (the common trap for women: this story is derived from the myth of Cupid and Psyche), and attempts to look at her bear-lover during the night, and the second heroine forgets to remain motionless while her bull-lover fights with the devil (good girls sit still). The lovers disappear when their commands are broken. The girls travel to the ends of the earth seeking them, but they cannot make themselves seen or recognized by their men until the last moment. The Master-maid, in a story whose conclusion resembles these other two, is concealed in a backroom of a giant's house. A prince, looking for adventure, comes to serve the giant, who gives him tasks that are impossible to accomplish. The Master-maid knows the giant's secrets and tells the prince how to do the impossible chores. She knows what to do, but does not act herself. When the giant tells her to kill the prince, she helps the prince to run away, escaping with him. Without her advice the escape would be impossible, yet apparently she had never attempted to run away herself, but had been waiting in the back room for a prince-escort to show up.

Most of the heroines in *The Blue Fairy Book*, however, are entirely passive, submissive, and helpless. This is most obviously true of the Sleeping Beauty, who lies asleep, in the ultimate state of passivity, waiting for a brave prince to awaken and save her. (She is like the Snow-White of 'Snow-White and the Seven Dwarfs,' who lies in a death-like sleep, her beauty being visible through her glass coffin, until a prince comes along and falls in love with her.) When the prince does penetrate the tangle of thorns and brambles, enters the castle, finds her chamber, and awakens her, the princess opens her eyes and says,' "Is it you, my Prince? You have waited a long while." ' (p.59) This is not the end of the story, although it is the most famous part. The Sleeping Beauty, who was, while enchanted, the archetype of the passive, waiting beauty, retains this character in the second part, when she is awake. She marries the prince, and has two children who look savory to her mother-in-law, an Ogress with a taste for human flesh. While her son is away on a hunting trip the Ogress Queen orders the cook to kill and serve for dinner first one child and then the other. The cook hides the children, serving first a roast lamb and then a kid, instead. When the Ogress demands that her daughter-in-law be killed next, the cook tells her the Queen-mother's orders. The young Queen folds up at once: ' "Do it; do it" (said she, stretching out her neck). "Execute your orders, and then I shall go and see my children ... whom I so much and so tenderly loved." ' (p.62) The compassionate cook, however, decides to hide her too, and the young King returns in time to save them all from the Ogress' wrath and impending disaster.

Cinderella plays as passive a role in her story. After leaving her slipper at the ball she has nothing more to do but stay home and wait. The prince has commanded that the slipper be carried to every house in the kingdom, and that it be tried on the foot of every woman. Cinderella can remain quietly at home; the prince's servant will come to her house and will discover her identity. Cinderella's male counterpart, Espen Cinderlad, the hero of a great many Norwegian folk tales, plays a very different role. Although he is the youngest of the three brothers, as Cinderella is the youngest sister, he is a Cinderlad by choice. His brothers may ridicule and despise him, but no one forces him to sit by the fire and poke in the ashes all day; he elects to do so. All the while, he knows that he is the cleverest of the three, and eventually he leaves the fireside and wins a princess and half a kingdom by undertaking some adventure or winning a contest.

The Princess on the Glass Hill is the prototype of female passivity. The whole story is in the title; the Princess has been perched somehow on top of a glass hill, and thus made virtually inaccessible. There she sits, a waiting prize for whatever man can ride a horse up the glassy slope. So many of the heroines of fairy stories, including the well-known Rapunzel, are locked up in towers, locked into a magic sleep, imprisoned by giants, or otherwise enslaved, and waiting to be rescued by a passing prince, that the helpless, imprisoned maiden is the quintessential heroine of the fairy tale.

In the interesting story of 'The Goose-Girl,' an old Queen sends off her beautiful daughter, accompanied by a maid, to be married to a distant prince. The Queen gives her daughter a rag stained with three drops of her own blood. During the journey the maid brusquely refuses to bring the Princess a drink of water, saying ' "I don't mean to be your servant any longer." ' The intimidated Princess only murmurs, ' "Oh! heaven, what am I to do?" ' (p.266) This continues, the maid growing ruder, the Princess meeker, until she loses the rag, whereupon the maid rejoices, knowing that she now has full power over the girl, 'for in losing the drops of blood the Princess had become weak and powerless.' (p.268) The maid commands the Princess to change clothes and horses with her, and never to speak to anyone about what has happened. The possession of the rag had assured the Princess' social status; without it she becomes *déclassée*, and while her behavior was no less meek and docile before losing the rag than afterwards, there is no formal role reversal until she loses it. Upon their arrival the maid presents herself as the Prince's bride, while the Princess is given the job of goose-girl. At length, due solely to the intervention of others, the secret is discovered, the maid killed, and the goose-girl married to the Prince.

The heroine of 'Felicia and the Pot of Pinks' is equally submissive to ill-treatment. After their father's death, her brother forbids her to sit on his chairs:

> Felicia, who was very gentle, said nothing, but stood up crying quietly; while Bruno, for that was her brother's name, sat comfortably by the fire. Presently, when suppertime came, Bruno had a delicious egg, and he threw the shell to Felicia, saying: 'There, that is all I can give you; if you don't like it, go out and catch frogs; there are plenty of them in the marsh close by.' Felicia did not answer but she cried more bitterly than ever, and went away to her own little room. (p.148)

The underlying associational pattern of these stories links the figures of the victimized girl and the interesting girl; it is always the interesting girl, the special girl, who is in trouble. It needs to be asked whether a child's absorption of the associational patterns found in these myths and legends may not sensitize the personality, rendering it susceptible to melodramatic self-conceptions and expectations. Because victimized girls like Felicia, the Goose-girl, and Cinderella are invariably rescued and rewarded, indeed glorified, children learn that suffering goodness can afford to remain meek, and need not and perhaps should not strive to defend itself, for if it did so perhaps the fairy godmother would not turn up for once, to set things right at the end. Moreover, the special thrill of persecution, bordering at once upon self-pity and self-righteousness, would have to be surrendered. Submissive, meek, passive female behavior is suggested and rewarded by the action of these stories.

Many of the girls are not merely passive, however; they are frequently victims and even martyrs as well. The Cinderella story is not simply a rags-to-riches tale. Cinderella is no Horatio Alger; her name is partly synonymous with female martyrdom. Her ugly older sisters, who are jealous of her beauty, keep her dressed in rags and hidden at home. They order her to do all the meanest housework. Cinderella bears this ill-treatment meekly: she is the patient sufferer, an object of pity. When the older sisters go off to the ball she bursts into tears; it is only the sound of her weeping that arouses her fairy godmother. Ultimately, her loneliness and her suffering are sentimentalized and become an integral part of the glamor. 'Cinderella' and the other stories of this type show children that the girl who is singled out for rejection and bad treatment, and who submits to her lot, weeping but never running away, has a special compensatory destiny awaiting her. One of the pleasures provided by these stories is that the child-reader is free to indulge in pity, to be sorry for the heroine. The girl in tears is invariably the heroine; that is one of the ways the child can identify the heroine, for no one mistakenly feels sorry for the ugly older sisters, or for any of the villains or villainesses. When these characters suffer, they are only receiving their 'just deserts'. The child who dreams of being a Cinderella dreams perforce not only of being chosen and elevated by a prince, but also of being a glamorous sufferer or victim. What these stories convey is that women in distress are interesting. Fairy stories provide children with a concentrated early introduction to the archetype of the suffering heroine, who is currently alive (though not so well) under the name of Jenny Cavilleri.

The girl who marries Blue Beard is a prime example of the helpless damsel-victim, desperately waiting for a rescuer. She knows that her husband will not hesitate to murder her, because she has seen the corpses of his other murdered wives in the forbidden closet. The enraged Blue Beard announces that he will cut off her head; he gives her fifteen minutes to say her prayers, after which he bellows for her so loudly that the house trembles:

> The distressed wife came down, and threw herself at his feet, all in tears, with her hair about her shoulders.
>   'This signifies nothing,' said Blue Beard: 'you must die': then, taking hold of her hair with one hand, and lifting up the sword with the other,

he was going to take off her head. The poor lady, turning about to him, and looking at him with dying eyes, desired him to afford her one little moment to recollect herself. 'No, no,' said he, 'recommend thyself to God,' and was just about to strike. ... (p.295)

'At this very instant,' as the story continues, her brothers rush in and save her.

It is worth noticing that the one Greek legend that Lang included in *The Blue Fairy Book* is the Perseus story, which Lang entitled 'The Terrible Head'. It features two utterly helpless women, the first being Danae, who is put into a chest with her infant son, Perseus, and thrown out to sea, to drown or starve or drift away. Fortunately the chest comes to land, and Danae and her baby are saved. At the conclusion of the story, as the grown-up Perseus is flying home with the Gorgon's head, he looks down and sees 'a beautiful girl chained to a stake at the high-water mark of the sea. The girl was so frightened or so tired that she was only prevented from falling by the iron chain about her waist, and there she hung, as if she were dead'. (p.190) Perseus learns that she has been left there as a sacrifice to a sea-monster, he cuts her free, kills the monster, and carries her off as his bride.

Few other rescues are as dramatic as that of Blue Beard's wife or of Andromeda, but the device of the rescue itself is constantly used. The sexes of the rescuer and the person in danger are almost as constantly predictable, men come along to rescue women who are in danger of death, or are enslaved, imprisoned, abused, or plunged into an enchanted sleep which resembles death. Two well-known stories that were not included in *The Blue Fairy Book,* 'Snow-White and the Seven Dwarfs' and 'Rapunzel', are notable examples of this type: Snow-White is saved from a sleep which everyone assumes is death by the arrival of a handsome prince; Rapunzel, locked up in a tower by a cruel witch, is found and initially rescued by her prince.

Whatever the condition of younger women in fairy tales, Alison Lurie claims that the older women in the tales are often more active and powerful than men. It is true that some older women in fairy tales have power, but of what kind? In order to understand the meaning of women's power in fairy tales, we must examine the nature, the value, and the use of their power.

There are only a few powerful good women in *The Blue Fairy Book,* and they are nearly all fairies: the tiny, jolly, ugly old fairy in 'Prince Hyacinth', the stately fairies in 'Prince Darling', 'Toads and Diamonds', and 'Felicia', and of course Cinderella's fairy godmother.

They are rarely on the scene; they only appear in order to save young people in distress, and then they're off again. These good fairies have gender only in a technical sense; to children, they probably appear as women only in the sense that dwarfs and wizards appear as men. They are not human beings, they are asexual, and many of them are old. They are not examples of powerful women with whom children can identify as role models; they do not provide meaningful alternatives to the stereotype of the younger, passive heroine. A girl may hope to become a princess, but can she ever become a fairy?

Powerful, bad, older women appear to outnumber powerful, good ones. A certain number of these are also not fully human; they are fairies, witches, trolls, or Ogresses. It is generally implied that such females are wicked because of their race: thus the young king in 'The Sleeping Beauty' fears his mother while he loves her, 'for she was of the race of the Ogres, and the King (his father) would never have married her had it not been for her vast riches; it was even whispered about the Court that she had Ogreish inclinations, and that, whenever she saw little children passing by, she had all the difficulty in the world to avoid falling upon them'. (p. 60) Either extra-human race or extreme ugliness is often associated with female wickedness, and in such a way as to suggest that they explain the wickedness. The evil Fairy of the Desert in 'The Yellow Dwarf' is described as a 'tall old woman, whose ugliness was even more surprising than her extreme old age'. (p. 39) The sheep-king in 'The Wonderful Sheep' tells Miranda that he was transformed into a sheep by a fairy ' "whom I had known as long as I could remember, and whose ugliness had always horrified me." ' (p. 223) The bear-prince in 'East of the Sun' is under a spell cast by a troll-hag, and the fairy who considers herself slighted by the Sleeping Beauty's parents is described as being old: the original illustration for Lang's book shows her to be an ugly old crone, whereas the other fairies are young and lovely.

In the case of wicked but human women, it is also implied that being ill-favored is corollary to being ill-natured, as with Cinderella's step-mother and step-sisters. Cinderella is pretty and sweet, like her dead mother. The step-mother is proud and haughty, and her two daughters by her former husband are like her, so that their ill-temper appears to be genetic, or at least transmitted by the mother. The circumstances in 'Toads and Diamonds' are similar: the old widow has two daughters, of whom the eldest resembles her mother 'in face and humour. ... They were both so disagreeable and so proud that there was no living with them. The youngest, who was the very picture of her father for courtesy and sweetness of temper, was withal one of the most beautiful girls ever seen'. (p. 274)

Powerful good women are nearly always fairies, and they are remote: they come only when desperately needed. Whether human or extra-human, those women who are either partially or thoroughly evil are generally shown as active, ambitious, strong-willed and, most often, ugly. They are jealous of any woman more beautiful than they, which is not surprising in view of the power deriving from beauty in fairy tales. In 'Cinderella' the domineering step-mother and step-sisters contrast with the passive heroine. The odious step-mother wants power, and successfully makes her will prevail in the house; we are told that Cinderella bore her ill-treatment patiently, 'and dared not tell her father, who would have rattled her off; for his wife governed him entirely'. The wicked maid in 'The Goose-Girl' is not described as being either fair or ugly (except that the Princess appears to be fairer than the maid at the end), but like the other female villains she is jealous of beauty and greedy for wealth. She decides to usurp the Princess' place, and being evil she is also strong and determined, and initially successful. Being powerful is mainly associated with being unwomanly.

The moral value of activity thus beomes sex-linked.[7] The boy who sets out to seek his fortune, like Dick Whittington, Jack the Giant-Killer, or Espen Cinderlad, is a stock figure and, provided that he has a kind heart, is assured of success. What is praiseworthy in males, however, is rejected in females; the counterpart of the energetic, aspiring boy is the scheming, ambitious woman. Some heroines show a kind of strength in their ability to endure, but they do not actively seek to change their lot. (The only exceptions to this rule are in the stories that appear to derive from the myth of Cupid and Psyche: 'East of the Sun' and 'The Black Bull of Norroway', in which the heroines seek their lost lovers. We may speculate whether the pre-Christian origin of these stories diminishes the stress placed on female passivity and acceptance, but this is purely conjectural.) We can remark that these stories reflect a bias against the active, ambitious, 'pushy' woman, and have probably also served to instil this bias in young readers. They establish a dichotomy between those women who are gentle, passive, and fair, and those who are active, wicked, and ugly. Women who are powerful and good are never human; those women who are human, and who have power or seek it, are nearly always portrayed as repulsive.

While character depiction in fairy tales is, to be sure, meagre, and we can usually group characters according to temperamental type (beautiful and sweet, or ugly and evil), there are a couple of girls who are not portrayed as being either perfectly admirable or as wicked. The princesses in 'The Yellow Dwarf', 'Goldilocks', and 'Trusty John' are described as being spoiled, vain, and wilful: the problem is that they refuse to marry anyone. The Queen in 'The Yellow Dwarf' expostulates with her daughter:

> 'Bellissima,' she said, 'I do wish you would not be so proud. What makes you despise all these nice kings? I wish you to marry one of them, and you do not try to please me.'
> 'I am so happy,' Bellissima answered: 'do leave me in peace, madam. I don't want to care for anyone.'
> 'But you would be very happy with any of these princes,' said the Queen, 'and I shall be very angry if you fall in love with anyone who is not worthy of you.'
> But the Princess thought so much of herself that she did not consider any one of her lovers clever or handsome enough for her; and her mother, who was getting really angry at her determination not to be married, began to wish that she had not allowed her to have her own way so much.
> (p. 31)

Princess Goldilocks similarly refuses to consider marriage, although she is not as adamant as Bellissima. The princess in the Grimms' story, 'King Thrushbeard,' which is not included in this collection, behaves like Bellissima; her angry father declares that he will give her to the very next comer, whatever his rank: the next man to enter the castle being a beggar, the king marries his daughter to him. This princess suffers poverty with her beggar-husband, until he reveals himself as one of the suitor kings she had rejected. Bellissima is punished more severely; indeed, her story is remarkable because it is one of the rare examples outside of H. C. Andersen of a story with a sad ending. Because Bellissima had refused to marry, she is forced by a train of circumstances to promise to marry the ugly Yellow Dwarf. She tries to avoid this fate by consenting to wed one of her suitors at last, but the dwarf intervenes at the wedding. Ultimately the dwarf kills the suitor, whom Bellissima had come to love, and she dies of a broken heart. A kind mermaid transforms the ill-fated lovers into two palm trees.

These princesses are portrayed as reprehensible because they refuse to marry; hence, they are considered 'stuck-up,' as children would say. The alternate construction, that they wished to preserve their freedom and their identity, is denied or disallowed (although Bellissima had said to her mother, ' "I am so happy, do leave me in peace, madam." ') There is a sense of triumph when a wilful princess submits or is forced to submit to a husband.

The Blue Fairy Book is filled with weddings, but it shows little of married life. It contains thirty stories in which marriage is a component, but eighteen of these stories literally end with the wedding. Most of the other twelve show so little of the marital life of the hero or heroine that technically they too may be said to end with marriage. Only a few of the stories show any part of the married life of young people, or even of old ones. The Sleeping Beauty is a totally passive wife and mother, and Blue Beard's wife, like the Sleeping Beauty, depends on a man to rescue her. Whereas the Sleeping Beauty is menaced by her mother-in-law who, being an Ogress, is only half-human, Blue Beard's wife is endangered by *being* the wife of her ferocious husband. (Her error may be ascribed to her having an independent sense of curiosity, or to rash disobedience.) This widely-known story established a potent myth in which a helpless woman violates her husband's arbitrary command and then is subject to his savage, implacable fury. It is fully the counterpoise of the other stock marital situation containing a scheming, overbearing wife and a timid, hen-pecked husband, as in 'Cinderella'; moreover, whereas the domineering wife is always implicitly regarded as abhorrent, the helpless, threatened, passive wife is uncritically viewed and thus implicitly approved of. As Andromeda, Blue Beard's wife, or the imperiled Pauline, her function is to provide us with a couple of thrills of a more or less sadistic tincture.

The other peculiar aspect of the depiction of marriage in these stories is that nearly all the young heroes and heroines are the children of widows or widowers; only five of the thirty-seven stories in the book contain a set of parents: these include 'The Sleeping Beauty', in which the parents leave the castle when the hundred-year enchantment begins, and the two similar tales of 'Little Thumb' and 'Hansel and Gretel', in both of which the parents decide to get rid of their children because they are too poor to feed them. (In 'Little Thumb' the husband persuades his reluctant wife, and in 'Hansel and Gretel' the wife persuades her reluctant husband.) Cinderella has two parents, but the only one who plays a part in the story is her step-mother. In general, the young people of these stories are described as having only one parent, or none. Although marriage is such a constant event in the stories, and is central to their reward system, few marriages are indeed shown in fairy tales. Like the White Queen's rule, there's jam tomorrow and jam yesterday, but never jam today. The stories can be described as being preoccupied with marriage without portraying it; as a real condition, it's nearly always off-stage.

In effect, these stories focus upon courtship, which is magnified into the most important and exciting part of a girl's life, brief though courtship is, because it is the part of her life in which she most counts as a person herself. After marriage she ceases to be wooed, her consent is no longer sought, she derives her status from her husband, and her personal identity is thus snuffed out. When fairy tales show courtship as exciting, and conclude with marriage, and the vague statement that 'they lived happily ever after,' children may develop a deep-seated desire always to be courted, since marriage is literally the end of the story.

The controversy about what is biologically determined and what is learned has just begun. These are the questions now being asked, and not yet answered: to what extent is passivity a biological attribute of females; to what extent is it culturally determined; Perhaps it will be argued that these stories show archetypal female behavior, but one may wonder to what extent they reflect female attributes, or to what extent they serve as training manuals for girls? If one argued that the characteristically passive behavior of female characters in fairy stories is a reflection of an attribute inherent in female personality, would one also argue, as consistency would require, that the mercantile reward system of fairy stories reflects values that are inherent in human nature? We must consider the possibility that the classical attributes of 'femininity' found in these stories are in fact imprinted in children and reinforced by the stories themselves. Analyses of the influence of the most popular children's literature may give us an insight into some of the origins of psycho-sexual identity.

Notes

1   Alison Lurie, 'Fairy Tale Liberation', *The New York Review of Books,* December 17, 1970, p. 42.
2   Lurie, 'Witches and Fairies: Fitzgerald to Updike', *The New York Review of Books,* 2 December, 1971, p. 6.
3   Andrew Lang, ed., *The Green Fairy Book* (New York: McGraw-Hill, 1966), pp. ix-xi.
4   In these stories, the girl who marries a beast must agree to accept and love a beast as a husband; the girl must give herself to a beast in order to get a man. When she is willing to do this, he can shed his frightening, rough appearance and show his gentler form, demonstrating the softening agency of women (as in the story of Jane Eyre and Mr. Rochester). These heroines have an agentive role, insofar as they are responsible for the literal reformation of the male.
5   Lang, ed., *The Blue Fairy Book* (New York: McGraw-Hill, 1966) p. 98. All quotations are from this edition.
6   Lurie, 'Fairy Tale Liberation,' *loc. cit.*
7   Ruth Kelso's *Doctrine for the Lady of the Renaissance* (Urbana: University of Illinois Press. 1956) demonstrates that 'the moral ideal for the lady is essentially Christian . . . as that for the gentleman is essentially pagan. For him the ideal is self-expansion and realization. . . . For the lady the direct opposite is prescribed. The eminently Christian virtues of chastity, humility, piety, and patience under suffering and wrong, are the necessary virtues.' (p. 36)

18 The Queen's Looking Glass

Sandra M. Gilbert and *Susan Gubar*

As the legend of Lilith shows, and as psychoanalysts from Freud and Jung onward have observed, myths and fairy tales often both state and enforce culture's sentences with greater accuracy than more sophisticated literary texts. If Lilith's story summarizes the genesis of the female monster in a single useful parable, the Grimm tale of 'Little Snow White' dramatizes the essential but equivocal relationship between the angel-woman and the monster-woman, a relationship that is also implicit in Aurora Leigh's bewildered speculations about her dead mother. 'Little Snow White', which Walt Disney entitled 'Snow White and the Seven Dwarves', should really be called Snow White and Her Wicked Stepmother, for the central action of the tale — indeed, its only real action — arises from the relationship between these two women: the one fair, young, pale, the other just as fair, but older, fiercer; the one a daughter, the other a mother; the one sweet, ignorant, passive, the other both artful and active: the one a sort of angel, the other an undeniable witch.

Significantly, the conflict between these two women is fought out largely in the transparent enclosures into which, like all the other images of women we have been discussing here, both have been locked: a magic looking glass, an enchanted and enchanting glass coffin. Here, wielding as weapons the tools patriarchy suggests that women use to kill themselves into art, the two women literally try to kill each other with art. Shadow fights shadow, image destroys image in the crystal prison, as if the 'fiend' of Aurora's mother's portrait should plot to destroy the 'angel' who is another one of her selves.

The story begins in midwinter, with a Queen sitting and sewing, framed by a window. As in so many fairy tales, she pricks her finger, bleeds, and is thereby assumed into the cycle of sexuality William Blake called the realm of 'generation', giving birth 'soon after' to a daughter 'as white as snow, as red as blood, and as black as the wood of the window frame'.[1] All the motifs introduced in this prefatory first paragraph — sewing, snow, blood, enclosure — are associated with key themes in female lives (hence in female writing), and they are thus themes we shall be studying throughout this book. But for our purposes here the tale's opening *is* merely prefatory. The real story begins when the Queen, having become a mother, metamorphoses also into a witch — that is, into a wicked 'step' mother: '. . . when the child was born, the Queen died,' and 'After a year had passed the King took to himself another wife.'

When we first encounter this 'new' wife, she is framed in a magic looking glass, just as her predecessor — that is, her earlier self — had been framed in a window. To be caught and trapped in a mirror rather than a window, however, is to be driven inward, obsessively studying self-images as if seeking a viable self. The first Queen seems still to have had prospects; not yet fallen into sexuality, she looked outward, if only upon the snow. The second Queen is doomed to the inward search that psychoanalysts like Bruno Bettelheim censoriously define as 'narcissism,'[2] but which (as Mary Elizabeth Coleridge's 'The Other Side of the Mirror' suggested) is necessitated by a state from which all outward prospects have been removed.

That outward prospects *have* been removed — or lost or dissolved away — is suggested not only by the Queen's mirror obsession but by the absence of the King from the story as it is related in the Grimm version. The Queen's husband and Snow White's father (for whose attentions, according to Bettelheim, the two women are battling in a feminized Oedipal struggle) never actually appears in this story at all, a fact that emphasizes the almost stifling intensity with which the tale concentrates on the conflict in the mirror between mother and daughter, woman and woman, self and self. At the same time, though, there is clearly at least one way in which the King *is* present. His, surely, is the voice of the looking glass, the patriarchal voice of judgment that rules the Queen's — and every woman's — self-evaluation. He it is who decides, first, that his consort is 'the fairest of all,' and then, as she becomes maddened, rebellious, witchlike, that she must be replaced by his angelically innocent and dutiful daughter, a girl who is therefore defined as 'more beautiful still' than the Queen. To the extent, then, that the King, and only the King, constituted the first Queen's prospects, he need no longer appear in the story because, having assimilated the meaning of her own sexuality (and having, thus, become the second Queen) the woman has internalized the King's rules: his voice resides now in her own mirror, her own mind.

But if Snow White is 'really' the daughter of the second as well as of the first Queen (i.e., if the two Queens are identical), why does the Queen hate her so much? The traditional explanation — that the mother is as threatened by her daughter's 'budding sexuality' as the daughter is by the mother's 'possession' of the father is helpful but does not seem entirely adequate, considering the depth and ferocity of the Queen's rage.

It is true, of course, that in the patriarchal Kingdom of the text these women inhabit, the Queen's life can be literally imperilled by her daughter's beauty, and true (as we shall see throughout this study) that, given the female vulnerability such perils imply, female bonding is extraordinarily difficult in patriarchy: women almost inevitably turn against women because the voice of the looking glass sets them against each other. But, beyond all this, it seems as if there is a sense in which the intense desperation with which the Queen enacts her rituals of self-absorption causes (or is caused by) her hatred of Snow White. Innocent, passive, and self-lessly free of the mirror madness that consumes the Queen, Snow White represents the ideal of renunciation that the Queen has already renounced at the beginning of the story. Thus Snow White is destined to replace the Queen *because* the Queen hates her, rather than vice versa. The Queen's hatred of Snow White, in other words, exists before the looking glass has provided an obvious reason for hatred.

For the Queen, as we come to see more clearly in the course of the story, is a plotter, a plot-maker, a schemer, a witch, an artist, an impersonator, a woman of almost infinite creative energy, witty, wily, and self-absorbed as all artists traditionally are. On the other hand, in her absolute chastity, her frozen innocence, her sweet nullity, Snow White represents precisely the ideal of 'contemplative purity' we have already discussed, an ideal that could quite literally kill the Queen. An angel in the house of myth, Snow White is not only a child but (as female angels always are) childlike, docile, submissive, the heroine of a life that *has no story*. But the Queen, adult and demonic, plainly wants a life of 'significant action,' by definition an 'unfeminine' life of stories and story-telling. And therefore, to the extent that Snow White, as her daughter, is a part of herself, she wants to kill the Snow White *in herself,* the angel who would keep deeds and dramas out of her own house.

The first death plot the Queen invents is a naïvely straightforward murder story: she commands one of her huntsmen to kill Snow White. But, as Bruno Bettelheim has shown, the huntsman is really a surrogate for the King, a parental — or, more specifically, patriarchal — figure 'who dominates, controls, and subdues wild ferocious beasts' and who thus 'represents the subjugation of the animal, asocial, violent tendencies in man'.[3] In a sense, then, the Queen has foolishly asked her patriarchal master to act for her in doing the subversive deed she wants to do in part to retain power over him and in part to steal his power from him. Obviously, he will not do this. As patriarchy's angelic daughter, Snow White is, after all, *his* child, and he must save her, not kill her. Hence he kills a wild boar in her stead, and brings its lung and liver to the Queen as proof that he has murdered the child. Thinking that she is devouring her ice-pure enemy, therefore, the Queen consumes, instead, the wild boar's organs; that is, symbolically speaking, she devours her own beastly rage, and becomes (of course) even more enraged.

When she learns that her first plot has failed, then, the Queen's story-telling becomes angrier as well as more inventive, more sophisticated, more subversive. Significantly, each of the three 'tales' she tells — that is, each of the three plots she invents — depends on a poisonous or parodic use of a distinctively female device as a murder weapon, and in each case she reinforces the sardonic commentary on 'femininity' that such weaponry makes by impersonating a 'wise' woman, a 'good' mother, or, as Ellen Moers would put it, an 'educating heroine'.[4] As a 'kind' old pedlar woman, she offers to lace Snow White 'properly' for once — then suffocates her with a very Victorian set of tight laces. As another wise old expert in female beauty, she promises to comb Snow White's hair 'properly,' then assaults her with a poisonous comb. Finally, as a wholesome farmer's wife, she gives Snow White a 'very poisonous apple', which she has made in 'a quite secret, lonely room, where no one ever came'. The girl finally falls, killed, so it seems, by the female arts of cosmetology and cookery. Paradoxically, however, even though the Queen has been using such feminine wiles as the sirens' comb and Eve's apple subversively, to destroy angelic Snow White so that she (the Queen) can assert and aggrandize herself, these arts have had on her daughter an opposite effect from those she intended. Strengthening the chaste maiden in her passivity, they have made her into precisely the eternally beautiful, inanimate *objet d'art* patriarchal aesthetics want a girl to be. From the point of view of the mad, self-assertive Queen, conventional female arts *kill*. But from the point of view of the docile and selfless princess, such arts, even while they kill, confer the only measure of power available to a woman in a patriarchal culture.

Certainly, when the kindly huntsman-father saved her life by abandoning her in the forest at the edge of his kingdom, Snow White discovered her own powerlessness. Though she had been allowed to live because she was a 'good' girl, she had to find her own devious way of resisting the onslaughts of the maddened Queen, both inside and outside her self. In this connection, the seven dwarves probably represent her own dwarfed powers, her stunted selfhood, for, as Bettelheim points out, they can do little to help save the girl from the Queen. At the same time, however, her life with them is an important part of her education in submissive femininity, for in serving them she learns essential lessons of service, of selflessness, of domesticity. Finally, that at this point Snow White is a housekeeping angel in a *tiny* house conveys the story's attitude toward 'woman's world and woman's work': the realm of domesticity is a miniaturized kingdom in which the best of women is not only like a dwarf but like a dwarf's servant.

Does the irony and bitterness consequent upon such a perception lead to Snow White's few small acts of disobedience? Or would Snow White ultimately have rebelled anyway, precisely because she *is* the Queen's true daughter? The story does not, of course, answer such questions, but it does seem to imply them, since its turning point comes from Snow White's significant willingness to be tempted by the Queen's 'gifts', despite the dwarves' admonitions. Indeed, the only hint of self-interest that Snow White displays throughout the whole story comes in her 'narcissistic' desire for the stay-laces, the comb, and the apple that the disguised murderess offers. As Bettelheim remarks, this 'suggests how close the stepmother's temptations are to Snow White's inner desires'.[5] Indeed, it suggests that, as we have already noted, the Queen and Snow White are in some sense one: while the Queen struggles to free herself from the passive Snow White in herself, Snow White must struggle to repress the assertive Queen in herself. That both women eat from the same deadly apple in the third temptation episode merely clarifies and dramatizes this point. The Queen's lonely art has enabled her to contrive a two-faced fruit — one white and one red 'cheek' — that represents her ambiguous relationship to this angelic girl who is both her daughter and her enemy, her self and her opposite. Her intention is that the girl will die of the apple's poisoned red half — red with her sexual energy, her assertive desire for deeds of blood and triumph — while she herself will be unharmed by the passivity of the white half.

But though at first this seems to have happened, the apple's effect is, finally, of course, quite different. After the Queen's artfulness has killed Snow White into art, the girl becomes if anything even more dangerous to her 'step' mother's autonomy than she was before, because even more opposed to it in both mind and body. For, dead and self-less in her glass coffin, she is an object, to be displayed and desired, patriarchy's marble 'opus', the decorative and decorous Galatea with whom every ruler would like to grace his parlor. Thus, when the Prince first sees Snow White in her coffin, he begs the dwarves to give 'it' to him as a gift, 'for I cannot live without seeing Snow White. I will honour and prize her as my dearest possession'. An 'it,' a possession, Snow White has become an idealized image of herself, a woman in a portrait like Aurora Leigh's mother, and as such she has definitely proven herself to be patriarchy's ideal woman, the perfect candidate for Queen. At this point, therefore, she regurgitates the poison apple (whose madness had stuck in her throat) and rises from her coffin. The fairest in the land, she will marry the most powerful in the land; bidden to their wedding, the egotistically assertive, plotting Queen will become a former Queen, dancing herself to death in red-hot iron shoes.

What does the future hold for Snow White, however? When her Prince becomes a King and she becomes a Queen, what will her life be like? Trained to domesticity by her dwarf instructors, will she sit in the window, gazing out on the wild forest of her past, and sigh, and sew, and prick her finger, and conceive a child white as snow, red as blood, black as ebony wood? Surely, fairest of them all, Snow White has exchanged one glass coffin for another, delivered from the prison where the Queen put her only to be imprisoned in the looking glass from which the King's voice speaks daily. There is, after all, no female model for her in this tale except the 'good' (dead) mother and her living avatar the 'bad' mother. And if Snow White escaped her first glass coffin by her goodness, her passivity and docility, her only escape from her second glass coffin, the imprisoning mirror, must evidently be through 'badness,' through plots and stories, duplicitous schemes, wild dreams, fierce fictions, mad impersonations. The cycle of her fate seems inexorable. Renouncing 'contemplative purity,' she must now embark on that life of 'significant action' which, for a woman, is defined as a witch's life because it is so monstrous, so unnatural. Grotesque as Errour, Duessa, Lucifera, she will practise false arts in her secret, lonely room. Suicidal as Lilith and Medea, she will become a murderess bent on the self-slaughter implicit in her murderous attempts against her life of her own child. Finally, in fiery shoes that parody the costumes of femininity as surely as the comb and stays she herself contrived, she will do a silent terrible death-dance out of the story, the looking glass, the transparent coffin of her own image. Her only deed, this death will imply, can be a deed of death, her only action the pernicious action of self-destruction.

In this connection, it seems especially significant that the Queen's dance of death is a silent one. In 'The Juniper Tree', a version of 'Little Snow White' in which a *boy's* mother tries to kill him (for different reasons, of course) the dead boy is transformed not into a silent art object but into a furious golden bird who sings a song of vengeance against his murderess and finally crushes her to death with a millstone. [6] The male child's progress toward adulthood is a growth toward both self-assertion and self-articulation, 'The Juniper Tree' implies, a development of the *powers* of speech. But the girl child must learn the arts of silence either as herself a silent image invented and defined by the magic looking glass of the male-authored text, or as a silent dancer of her own woes, a dancer who enacts rather than articulates. From the abused Procne to the reclusive Lady of Shallott, therefore, women have been told that their art, like the witch's dance in 'Little Snow White', is an art of silence. Procne must record her sufferings with what Geoffrey Hartman calls 'the voice of the shuttle' because when she was raped her tongue was cut out. [7] The Lady of Shallott must weave her story because she is imprisoned in a tower as adamantine as any glass coffin, doomed to escape only through the self-annihilating madness of romantic love (just as the Queen is doomed to escape only through the self-annihilating madness of her death dance), and her last work of art is her own dead body floating downstream in a boat. And even when such maddened or grotesque female artists make sounds, they are for the most part, say patriarchal theorists, absurd or grotesque or pitiful. Procne's sister Philomel, for instance, speaks with an unintelligible bird's voice (unlike the voice of the hero of 'The Juniper Tree'). And when Gerard Manley Hopkins, with whom we began this meditation on pens and penises and kings and queens, wrote of her in an epigram 'On a Poetess,' he wrote as follows:

> Miss M.'s a nightingale. 'Tis well
>   Your simile I keep.
> It is the way with Philomel
>   To sing while others sleep. [8]

Even Matthew Arnold's more sympathetically conceived Philomel speaks 'a wild, unquenched, deep-sunken, old-world pain' that arises from the stirrings of a 'bewildered brain'. [9]

Yet, as Mary Elizabeth Coleridge's yearning toward that sane and serious self concealed on the other side of the mirror suggested — and as Anne Finch's complaint and Anne Elliot's protest told us too — women writers, longing to attempt the pen, have longed to escape from the many-faceted glass coffins of the patriarchal texts whose properties male authors insisted that they are. Reaching a hand to the stern, self-determining self behind the looking-glass portrait of her mother, reaching past those grotesque and obstructive images of 'Ghost, fiend, and angel, fairy, witch, and sprite', Aurora Leigh, like all the women artists whose careers we will trace in this book, tries to excavate the real self buried beneath the 'copy' selves. Similarly, Mary Elizabeth Coleridge, staring into a mirror where her own mouth appears as a 'hideous wound' bleeding 'in silence and in secret,' strives for a 'voice to speak her dread'.

In their attempts at the escape that the female pen offers from the prison of the male text, women like Aurora Leigh and Mary Elizabeth Coleridge begin, as we shall see, by alternately defining themselves as angel-women or as monster-women. Like Snow White and the wicked Queen, their earliest impulses, as we shall also see, are ambivalent. Either they are inclined to immobilize themselves with suffocating tight-laces in the glass coffins of patriarchy, or they are tempted to destroy themselves by doing fiery and suicidal tarantellas out of the looking glass. Yet, despite the obstacles presented by those twin images of angel and monster, despite the fears of sterility and the anxieties of authorship from which women have suffered, generations of texts *have* been possible for female writers. By the end of the eighteenth century — and here is the most important phenomenon we will see throughout this volume — women were not only writing, they were conceiving fictional worlds in which patriarchal images and conventions were severely, radically revised. And as self-conceiving women from Anne Finch and Anne Elliot to Emily Brontë and Emily Dickinson rose from the glass coffin of the male-authored text, as they exploded out of the Queen's looking glass, the old silent dance of death became a dance of triumph, a dance into speech, a dance of authority.

Notes

1 'Little Snow White'. All references are to the text as given in *The Complete Grimm's Fairy Tales* (New York: Random House, 1972).
2 Bruno Bettelheim, *The Uses of Enchantment: The Meaning and Importance of Fairy Tales* (New York: Knopf, 1976), pp. 202—3.
3 *Ibid.*, p. 205.
4 See Ellen Moers, *Literary Women* (New York: Doubleday, 1976), pp. 211—42.
5 Bettelheim, p. 211.
6 See 'The Juniper Tree', in *The Complete Grimm's Fairy Tales*.
7 Geoffrey Hartman, 'The Voice of the Shuttle', in *Beyond Formalism* (New Haven: Yale University Press, 1970), pp. 337—55.
8 *The Poems of Gerard Manley Hopkins*, ed. W. H. Gardner and N. H. MacKenzie (Oxford: Oxford University Press, 1970), p. 133.
9 See Matthew Arnold, 'Philomela', in *Poetry and Criticism of Matthew Arnold,* ed. A. Dwight Culler (Boston: Houghton Mifflin, 1961), p. 144, 1.7.

19 Feminism and Fairy Tales

Karen E. Rowe

To examine selected popular folktales from the perspective of modern feminism is to revisualize those paradigms which shape our romantic expectations and to illuminate psychic ambiguities which often confound contemporary women. Portrayals of adolescent waiting and dreaming, patterns of double enchantment, and romanticizations of marriage contribute to the potency of fairy tales. Yet, such alluring fantasies gloss the heroine's inability to act self-assertively, total reliance on external rescues, willing bondage to father and prince, and her restriction to hearth and nursery. Although many readers discount obvious fantasy elements, they may still fall prey to more subtle paradigms through identification with the heroine. Thus, subconsciously women may transfer from fairy tales into real life cultural norms which exalt passivity, dependency, and self-sacrifice as a female's cardinal virtues. In short, fairy tales perpetuate the patriarchal *status quo* by making female subordination seem a romantically desirable, indeed an inescapable fate.

Some day my prince will come.[1] With mingled adolescent assurance and anxiety, young girls for many centuries have paid homage to the romantic visions aroused by this article of faith in fairy tale. Even in modern society where romance co-habits uncomfortably with women's liberation, barely disguised forms of fairy tales transmit romantic conventions through the medium of popular literature. Degenerate offspring of fairy tales, such as *Real Romances, Secret Romances, Intimate Romances,* and *Daring Romances,* capitalize on the allure of romance, but sell instead a grotesque composite of pornography and melodrama ('He Brought My Body to Peaks of Ecstasy on His Water-Bed ... Yet I Knew I Had to Leave Him for Another Lover').[2] Traditional fairy tales fuse morality with romantic fantasy in order to portray cultural ideals for human relationships. In contrast, pulp romances strip the fantastic machinery and social sanctions to expose, then graphically exploit the implicit sexuality.

Chaster descendants of fairy tales, the 'ladies fictions' of *Good Housekeeping, Redbook,* and *McCalls,* pass on homogenized redactions of romantic conventions. A 1974 version, 'The Garlands of Fortune' proffers the predictable narrative, only a shadow away from folklore fantasies of princes: 'She was a girl who didn't believe in luck, let alone miracles, or at least she didn't until that fabulous man came along.'³ These 'domestic fictions' reduce fairy tales to sentimental clichés, while they continue to glamorize a heroine's traditional yearning for romantic love which culminates in marriage. Distinguished from the pulp magazines' blatant degradation of romance into sexual titillation, women's magazines preserve moral strictures from fairy tales, even as they rationalize the fantastic events. They render diminished counterfeits of Victorian novels of sensibility and manners. More conscious imitators of commonplace nineteenth-century fictions and, thereby, of fairy tales, Victoria Holt, Mary Stewart, and Phyllis Whitney popularize the modern gothic romance. Tell-tale captions from Holt's *Legend of the Seventh Virgin* (1975) highlight the inherited elements: 'It was the most exciting night of my life! Mellyora had wangled an invitation to the masked ball at the Abbas for me, Kerensa Carlee the servant girl!' and 'Johnny St. Larnston danced with me out onto the terrace'.⁴ Virginal dreams of elegant balls, adored princes, and romantic deliverance become captivatingly mysterious when complicated by concealed identities, hints of incest, hidden treasures, ancient curses, supernatural apparitions, and looming mansions. Unlike either sexually exploitative or domesticated romances, these tales of horror maintain historical distance, suppress sexuality, and adhere to rigid social hierarchies. They perpetuate, virtually intact, earlier gothic adaptations of fairy tale motifs.

The mass popularity of these fictions — erotic, ladies, and gothic — testifies to a pervasive fascination with fairy tale romance in literature not merely for children but for twentieth-century adults. Moreover, folklorists counter any casual dismissal of folktales as mere entertainment by arguing that they have always been one of culture's primary mechanisms for inculcating roles and behaviors.⁵ The ostensibly innocuous fantasies symbolically portray basic human problems and appropriate social prescriptions. These tales which glorify passivity, dependency, and self-sacrifice as a heroine's cardinal virtues suggest that culture's very survival depends upon a woman's acceptance of roles which relegate her to motherhood and domesticity. Just how potently folklore contributes to cultural stability may be measured by the pressure exerted upon women to emulate fairy tale prototypes. Few women expect a literally 'royal' marriage with Prince Charming; but, subconsciously at least, female readers assimilate more subtle cultural imperatives. They transfer from fairy tales into real life those fantasies which exalt acquiescence to male power and make marriage not simply one ideal, but the only estate toward which women should aspire. The idealizations, which reflect culture's approval, make the female's choice of marriage and maternity seem commendable, indeed predestined. In short, fairy tales are not just entertaining fantasies, but powerful transmitters of romantic myths which encourage women to internalize only aspirations deemed appropriate to our 'real' sexual functions within a patriarchy.

As long as fairy tale paradigms accord closely with cultural norms, women can and have found in romantic fictions satisfying justifications for their conformity. But recent studies, such as Beauvoir's *The Second Sex,* Greer's *The Female Eunuch,* and Friedan's *The Feminine Mystique,* to mention only the forerunners, have exposed the historical conditions which subordinate women in all areas from the procreative to the political. With progressive suffrage and liberation movements of the twentieth century and radical redefinitions of sexual and social roles, women are challenging both previous mores and those fairy tales which inculcate romantic ideals. Although lingeringly attracted to fantasies (like Eve to the garden after the Fall), many modern women can no longer blindly accept the promise of connubial bliss with the prince. Indeed, fairy tale fantasies come to seem more deluding than problem-solving. 'Romance' glosses over the heroine's impotence: she is unable to act independently or self-assertively; she relies on external agents for rescue; she binds herself first to the father and then the prince; she restricts her ambitions to hearth and nursery. Fairy tales, therefore, no longer provide mythic validations of desirable female behavior; instead, they seem more purely escapist or nostalgic, having lost their potency because of the widening gap between social practice and romantic idealization.

It is a sign of our conflicted modern times that popular romances nevertheless continue to imitate fairy tale prototypes, while concurrently novels, such as Doris Lessing's *Martha Quest* and *A Proper Marriage,* Erica Jong's *Fear of Flying,* or Alix Kates Shulman's *Memoirs of an Ex-Prom Queen* portray disillusionments, if not forthright defiances of romantic conventions. An examination of a few popular folktales from the perspective of modern feminism not only reveals why romantic fantasy exerts such a powerful imaginative allure, but also illuminates how contemporary ambiguities cloud women's attitudes toward men and marriage.

I

Among the classic English tales of romance, 'Cinderella', 'Sleeping Beauty in the Wood', 'Snow-Drop', 'The Tale of the Kind and the Unkind Girls', 'Beauty and the Beast', and 'The Frog-Prince' focus on the crucial period of adolescence, dramatizing archetypal female dilemmas and socially acceptable resolutions.[6] Confronted by the trauma of blossoming sexuality, for instance, the young girl subliminally responds to fairy tale projections of adolescent conflicts.[7] She often achieves comforting release from anxieties by subconsciously perceiving in symbolic tales the commonness of her existential dilemma. Moreover, the equal-handed justice and optimistic endings instill confidence that obstacles can be conquered as she progresses from childhood to maturity. More than alleviating psychic fears associated with the rite of passage, however, tales also prescribe approved cultural paradigms which ease the female's assimilation into the adult community.[8]

The stepmother and bad fairy, who invariably appear odious, embody the major obstacles against this passage to womanhood. Not simply dramatic and moral antagonists to the youthful heroine, they personify predatory female sexuality and the adolescent's negative feelings toward her mother. In Perrault's version of 'Cinderella' (AT 510), persecution of the adolescent stems directly from the father's remarriage and the new stepmother's sexual jealousies.[9] Because 'she could not bear the good qualities of this pretty girl; and the less, because they made her own daughters so much the more hated and despised', Cinderella's stepmother displays her 'ill humour' by employing the child 'in the meanest work of the house' (p.123). Similarly proud and vain, Snow-Drop's stepmother in Grimm's recounting plots against the seven-year-old child who 'was as bright as the day, and fairer than the queen herself' (p.177).[10] Although fairy tales carefully displace animosities onto a substitute figure, they in part recreate the fears of a menopausal mother. For the aging stepmother, the young girl's maturation signals her own waning sexual attractiveness and control. In retaliation they jealously torment the more beautiful virginal adolescent who captures the father's affections and threatens the declining queens. Recurrent narrative features make clear this generational conflict, as the stepmothers habitually devise stratagems to retard the heroine's progress. Remanded to the hearth, cursed with one hundred years of sleep, or cast into a death-like trance by a poisoned apple, heroines suffer beneath onslaughts of maternal fear and vengeance. Ironically, both in life and fairy tale, time triumphs, delivering the daughter to inescapable womanhood and the stepmother to aged oblivion or death.

In contrast to persecuting stepmothers, natural mothers provide a counter-pattern of female protection. The christening celebration in Perrault's 'Sleeping Beauty' (AT 410) is a jubilant occasion for the 'King and a Queen, who were so sorry that they had no children, so sorry that it was beyond expression', and so sorry that they tried 'all the waters in the world, vows, pilgrimages, every thing' before successfully conceiving this babe (p.85).[11] Since the King and Queen do not survive the spell, the 'young Fairy' assumes the role of tutelary spirit and promises that the princess 'shall only fall into a profound sleep which shall last a hundred years, at the expiration of which a King's son shall come and awake her' (p.86). Similarly, Cinderella's deceased mother is lauded only briefly as 'the best creature in the world' and the source for the daughter's 'un-parallelled goodness and sweetness of temper' (p.123); in her place the fairy godmother acts as guardian. This prominence of contrasting maternal figures offers a paradigm for traumatic ambivalences.[12] As the child matures, she becomes increasingly conscious of conflicting needs for both infantile nurturing and independence and suffers as a result severe ambivalences toward the mother. By splitting the maternal role to envision, however briefly, a protective mother who blesses the heroine with beauty and virtue, romantic tales assuage fears of total separation. Conversely, the stepmother embodies the adolescent's awesome intimations of female rivalry, predatory sexuality, and constrictive authority. As Bruno Bettelheim argues, romantic tales often recreate oedipal tensions, when a mother's early death is followed by the father's rapid remarriage to a cruel stepmother, as in 'Cinderella'. Kept a child rather than acknowledged as a developing woman and potential recipient of the father's love, a young girl, like Cinderella or Snow-Drop, feels thwarted by her mother's persistent, overpowering intervention. The authoritarian mother becomes the obstacle which seems to stifle natural desires for men, marriage, and hence the achievement of female maturity. Neither heroines nor children rationally explore such deep-rooted feelings; rather, the tales' split depiction of mothers provides a guilt-free enactment of the young female's ambivalences and a means through fantasy for coping with paradoxical impulses of love and hate.

Such traumatic rivalries between young girls and the mother (or heroine and stepmother) comprise, however, only another stage in a progressive cultural as well as psychological pageant. Frequently a good fairy, old woman, or comforting godmother (second substitution for the original mother) releases the heroine from the stepmother's bondage and enables her to adopt appropriate adult roles. Godmothers or wise women may seem merely fortuitous magical agents who promise transformations to make external circumstances responsive to the heroine's inner virtue. Emancipated from enslavement as a cinderlass, Cinderella, for example, blossoms fully into a marriageable young princess at the ball. Functioning more subtly to exemplify cultural expectations, however, the 'dream' figure allows the heroine not only to recall the pattern embedded by the original mother, but also to claim that paradigm of femininity as her own. Aptly, in many versions of 'Cinderella' the supernatural helper is not a random apparition, but the natural mother reincarnated into a friendly creature, such as a red calf in the Scottish 'Rashin Coatie,' or memorialized by a hazel tree and a white bird to grant wishes, as in Grimm's 'Aschenputtel'. [13] When the heroine gains sexual freedom by repudiating the stepmother, she immediately channels that liberty into social goals epitomized by the primary mother. Fairy tales, therefore, do acknowledge traumatic ambivalences during a female's rite of passage; they respond to the need for both detachment from childish symbioses and a subsequent embracing of adult independence. Yet, this evolution dooms female protagonists (and readers) to pursue adult potentials in one way only: the heroine dreamily anticipates conformity to those predestined roles of wife and mother. As Adrienne Rich so persuasively theorizes in *Of Woman Born,* the unheralded tragedy within western patriarchies is found in this mother/daughter relationship. [14] If she imitates domestic martyrdom, the daughter may experience a hostile dependency, forever blaming the mother for trapping her within a constricting role. If a daughter rebels, then she risks social denunciations of her femininity, nagging internal doubts about her gender identity, and rejection by a mother who covertly envying the daughter's courage must yet overtly defend her own choices. Furthermore, romantic tales point to the complicity of women within a patriarchal culture, since as primary transmitters and models for female attitudes, mothers enforce their daughters' conformity.

By accentuating the young female's struggle with a menacing stepmother, many romantic tales only vaguely suggest the father's role in the complex oedipal and cultural dramas. But in other tales, such as 'Beauty and the Beast' the attraction to the father, prohibitions against incest, and the transference of devotion to the prince round out the saga of maturation. In the throes of oedipal ambiguities, a young girl who still desires dependency seizes upon her father's indulgent affection, because it guarantees respite from maternal persecutions and offers a compensating masculine adoration. Many tales implicitly acknowledge the potent attraction between females and the father; but, as purveyors of cultural norms, they often mask latent incest as filial love and displace blatant sexual desires onto a substitute, such as a beast in 'The Frog-Prince' (AT 440) or 'Snow-White and Rose-Red' (AT 426). Madame de Beaumont's telling of 'Beauty and the Beast' (AT 425), for example, focuses on the intimate bonds between father and daughter which impede the heroine's rite of passage.[15] Pursued by suitors, the fifteen-year-old Beauty 'civilly thanked them that courted her, and told them she was too young yet to marry, but chose to stay with her father for a few years longer' (p.139). For a heroine Beauty acts with unusual decisiveness in consigning herself to a passive waiting and in prolonging her allegiance to the father. The abrupt loss of the merchant's wealth casts the family into genteel poverty, which again elicits Beauty's determination: 'Nay, several gentlemen would have married her, tho' they knew she had not a penny; but she told them she could not think of leaving her poor father in his misfortunes, but was determined to go along with him into the country to comfort and attend him' (p.139). She sacrifices individual happiness yet a third time by volunteering to die in her father's stead to satisfy the offended Beast: 'Since the monster will accept of one of his daughters, I will deliver myself up to all his fury, and I am very happy in thinking that my death will save my father's life, and be a proof of my tender love for him' (p.143). Lacking a jealous stepmother to prevent this excessive attachment and to force her into a rebellious search for adult sexuality, Beauty clings childishly to her father. The tale suppresses intimations of incest; nevertheless, it symbolizes the potent, sometimes problematic oedipal dependency of young girls. Well before her encounter with Beast then, Beauty's three decisions — to stay, to serve, finally to sacrifice her life — establish her willing subservience to paternal needs. Complementary to the natural mother's role as model for appropriate female adaptions the natural father's example of desirable masculine behavior likewise shapes her dreams of a saviour and encourages the heroine's later commitment to the prince.

Beauty's apprenticeship in her father's house reveals an early conformity to domestic roles; but, her subsequent palatial captivity by Beast symbolizes a further stage in her maturation. Relinquishing filial duties, she must confront male sexuality and transmute initial aversion into romantic commitment.[16] Comparable to the substitution of a stepmother, replacement of Beast for the merchant exemplifies the adolescent's ambivalent yearning for continued paternal protection, yet newly awakened anxieties about masculine desires. Initially horrified by Beast's proposal of marriage, Beauty first ignores his overt ugliness, an act which signifies her repression of sexual fears. When she then discovers his spiritual goodness, her repugnance gradually gives way to compassion, then romantic adoration, and finally marital bliss. Having schooled herself to seek virtue beneath a physically repulsive countenance, she commits herself totally: 'No dear Beast, said Beauty, you must not die; live to be my husband; from this moment I give you my hand, and swear to be none but yours. Alas! I thought I had only a friendship for you, but the grief I now feel convinces me that I cannot live without you' (p.149). The magical transformation of Beast into a dazzling prince makes possible a consummation of this love affair which is no longer grotesque. Not just literally, but psychologically, the beast in the bedroom becomes transmuted into the prince in the palace. Just as Cinderella's prince charming arrives with a glass slipper, or Sleeping Beauty's prince awakens her with a kiss to reward these heroines for patient servitude or dreamy waiting, so too Beast's transformation rewards Beauty for embracing traditional female virtues. She has obligingly reformed sexual reluctance into self-sacrifice to redeem Beast from death. She trades her independent selfhood for subordination. She garners social and moral plaudits by acquiescing to this marriage. While realignment of her passions from father to prince avoids incest and psychologically allays her separation anxieties, still the female remains childlike — subjected to masculine supervision and denied any true independence.

Romantic tales require that the heroine's transference of dependency be not only sexual, but also material. Beneath romantic justifications of 'love' lurk actual historical practices which reduce women to marketable commodities. In Perrault's 'Diamonds and Toads' (AT 480) the King's son hardly restrains his pecuniary impulses:

> The King's son, who was returning from hunting, met her, and seeing her so very pretty, asked her what she did there alone, and why she cry'd! *Alack-a-day! Sir, my mamma has turned me out of doors.* The King's son, who saw five or six pearls and as many diamonds come out of her mouth, desired her to tell him whence this happen'd. She accordingly told him the whole story; upon which the King's son fell in love with her; and considering with himself that such a gift as this was worth more than any marriage portion whatsoever in another, conducted her to the palace of the King, his father, and there married her' (p. 102).

Despite this gallant's empathy for a pathetic story, he computes the monetary profit from such an inexhaustible dowry. Heroines do not so crassly calculate the fortune to be obtained through advantageous marriages, bound as they are by virtue to value love as superior.

However, the tales implicitly yoke sexual awakening and surrender to the prince with social elevation and materialistic gain. Originally of regal birth, both Sleeping Beauty and Snow-Drop only regain wealth and a queen's position by marrying a prince. Although Cinderella and little Beauty experience temporary reversals of fortune which lead to servitude or genteel poverty, these heroines also miraculously receive fortunes from their marriages. A strict moral reading would attribute these rewards solely to the heroine's virtue; but, the fictional linkage of sexual awakening with the receipt of great wealth implies a more subtle causality. *Because* the heroine adopts conventional female virtues, that is patience, sacrifice, and dependency, and *because* she submits to patriarchal needs, she consequently receives both the prince and a guarantee of social and financial security through marriage. Status and fortune never result from the female's self-exertion but from passive assimilation into her husband's sphere. Allowed no opportunity for discriminating selection, the princess makes a blind commitment to the first prince who happens down the highway, penetrates the thorny barriers, and arrives *deus ex machina* to release her from the charmed captivity of adolescence. Paradoxically this 'liberation' symbolizes her absolute capitulation, as she now fulfils the roles of wife and mother imprinted in her memory by the natural mother and re-enters a comfortable world of masculine protection shared earlier with her father.

Not designed to stimulate unilateral actions by aggressive, self-motivated women, romantic tales provide few alternative models for female behavior without criticizing their power. The unfortunate heroines of 'The Twelve Dancing Princesses' (AT 306) initially elude marriage by drugging suitors and magically retreating at night to dance with dream princes in an underground kingdom.[17] Apparently unwilling to forgo romantic fantasies for realistic marriages, the twelve princesses are eventually foiled by a clever soldier, who promptly claims the eldest as reward. Not alone among heroines in this aversion to marriage, nonetheless, most reluctant maidens, including little Beauty, a proud daughter in Grimm's 'King Thrushbeard' (AT 900), haughty All-Fair in d'Aulnoy's 'The Yellow Dwarf', and the squeamish princess who disdains the frog-prince, ultimately succumb. Romantic tales thus transmit clear warnings to rebellious females: resistance to the cultural imperative to wed constitutes so severe a threat to the social fabric that they will be compelled to submit. Likewise, tales morally censure bad fairies and vain, villainous stepmothers who exhibit manipulative power or cleverness. Allowed momentary triumph over the seemingly dead Snow-White or comatose Beauty, eventually these diabolic stepmothers are thwarted by the prince's greater powers. Facing punishment through death, banishment, or disintegration, the most self-disciplined and courageous villainesses execute justice upon themselves, thereby leaving the sterling morality of the prince and princess untarnished. Thus, in Perrault's 'Sleeping Beauty' the ogrish mother-in-law voluntarily casts 'her self head foremost into the tub' which she had 'filled with toads, vipers, snakes, and all kinds of serpents' and where she is now 'devoured in an instant by the ugly creatures she had ordered to be thrown into it for others' (p.92).[18] In condign punishment for jealousy, Snow-White's stepmother dances herself to death on iron-hot shoes, while the witch of 'Hansel and Gretel' (AT 327) roasts in her own oven. Because cleverness, will-power, and manipulative skill are allied with vanity, shrewishness, and ugliness, and because of their gruesome fates, odious females hardly recommend themselves as models for young readers. And because they surround alternative roles as life-long maidens or fiendish stepmothers with opprobrium, romantic tales effectively sabotage female assertive-ness. By punishing exhibitions of feminine force, tales admonish, moreover, that any disruptive non-conformity will result in annihilation or social ostracism. While readers dissociate from these portraitures of feminine power, defiance, and/or self-expression, they readily identify with the prettily passive heroine whose submission to commendable roles insures her triumphant happiness.

II

Romantic tales exert an awesome imaginative power over the female psyche — a power intensified by formal structures which we perhaps take too much for granted. The pattern of enchantment and disenchantment, the formulaic closing with nuptial rites, and the plot's comic structure seem so conventional that we do not question the implications. Yet, traditional patterns, no less than fantasy characterizations and actions, contribute to the fairy tale's potency as a purveyor of romantic archetypes and, thereby, of cultural precepts for young women. Heroines, for example, habitually spend their adolescence in servitude to an evil stepmother, father, or beast, or in an enchanted sleep, either embalmed in a glass coffin or imprisoned in a castle tower. On one level an 'enchantment' serves as a convenient metaphor to characterize the pubertal period during which young women resolve perplexing ambivalences toward both parents, longingly wish and wait for the rescuing prince, and cultivate beauty as well as moral and domestic virtues. Perrault's sixteen-year-old Beauty slumbers blissfully for a hundred years, but retains her capacity to dream, even to plot gambits for her opening conversation with the prince: 'He was more at a loss than she, and we need not wonder at it; she had time to think on what to say to him; for it is very probable (tho' history mentions nothing of it) that the good fairy, during so long a sleep, had given her very agreeable dreams' (p.88). By dramatizing adolescence as an enchanted interlude between childhood and maturity, romantic tales can, however, aggravate the female's psychic helplessness. Led to believe in fairy godmothers, miraculous awakenings, and magical transformations of beasts into lovers, that is, in external powers rather than internal self-initiative as the key which brings release, the reader may feel that maturational traumas will disappear with the wave of a wand or prince's fortuitous arrival. This symbolic use of enchantment can subtly undermine feminine self-confidence. By portraying dream-drenched inactivity and magical redemptions, enchantment makes vulnerability, avoidance, sublimation, and dependency alluringly virtuous.

On another level, tales of romance frequently employ a structure of double enchantment, the stepmother's malevolent spell and the seemingly beneficent counter-charm instituted by a guardian spirit. In 'Sleeping Beauty', for instance, the double enchantment occurs early: two different fairies bewitch the young princess. The narrator reports that 'the old Fairy fancied she was slighted and mutter'd some threats between her teeth. One of the young Fairies, who sat by her, heard her, and judging that she might give the little Princess some unhappy gift, went as soon as they rose from table and hid herself behind the hangings, that she might speak last, and repair as much as possibly she could the evil that the old Fairy might do her' (p. 85). Though the narrative centers on the fulfilment of the old fairy's dire curse, the promises of the young fairy linger in the background, finally to emerge for the denouément. Both the pernicious and felicitous enchantments receive fulfilment: 'The princess shall indeed pierce her hand with a spindle; but instead of dying, she shall only fall into a profound sleep which shall last a hundred years, at the expiration of which a King's son shall come and awake her' (p. 86). Likewise, in 'Beauty and the Beast' the disenchanted prince attributes his monstrous disguise to the wiles of 'a wicked fairy who had condemned me to remain under that shape till a beautiful virgin should consent to marry me' (p. 150). Appropriately enough, it is a 'beautiful lady, that appeared to her in her dream' (p. 150) who reunites Beauty with her family, transforms the envious sisters into statues, rewards Beauty's judicious choice of Beast, and transports everyone to the prince's kingdom. This supernatural lady stage-manages the finale with a 'stroke with her wand' (p. 150), counteracting the wicked fairy's earlier enchantment. Double enchantment thus reinforces cultural myths about *both* female adolescence *and* maturity. It suggests that marriage, like the adolescent sleep or servitude, is also an 'enchanted' state with the prince or a fairy godmother rather than evil stepmother or bad fairy as charmer. Not really disenchanted into reality or self-reliance, the heroine simply trades one enchanted condition for another; she is subjected in adolescence to anticipatory dreams of rescue and in womanhood to expectations of continuing masculine protection. Romantic tales thus transmit to young women an alarming prophecy that marriage is an *enchantment* which will shield her against harsh realities outside the domestic realm and guarantee everlasting happiness.

Nuptial rites conventionally climax trials through which the heroine passes: separation from the original mother, a stepmother's persecutions, the father's desertion, adolescent waiting and dreaming, and a final awakening by the prince. But marriage stands for more than a single individual's triumph over psychic tribulations. Festive nuptials signify the heroine's conformity to the socially dictated roles of wife and mother and signal her assimilation into the community. Although usually absent from central portions in which the heroine endures her trials *en famille* or alone, a royal court frequently appears at the tale's beginning and end to emphasize the communal context for the individual's passage. For instance in 'Sleeping Beauty' the kingdom gathers at the christening, a ritual which auspiciously celebrates the heroine's birth. Then as part of her benevolent charm, the good fairy who thinks that 'when the princess should awake she might not know what to do with herself, being all alone in this old palace' (pp. 86—87) enchants the household staff. Decorously they remain aloof from the actual bedchamber in which the princess receives the prince's revivifying kiss. Nevertheless, the palace household comes awake in time to prepare a festive ball in honour of the rebirth and subsequent wedding, when 'after supper, without losing any time, the Lord Almoner married them in the chapel of the castle, and the chief lady of honour drew the curtains' (p. 89). Comparable to the christening which acknowledges the birth, the ceremonial wedding here expresses the community's approval of sexuality within marriage. Typically in romantic tales, births, parental remarriages, and the prevalent 'debutante' balls mark the preliminary stages in the heroine's progress toward maturity. But as the culminating event in most folktales and in life, marriage more importantly displays the victory of patriarchal culture itself, since the female receives her reward for tailoring personal behavior to communal norms.

Because it is a major social institution, marriage functions not merely as a comic ending, but also as a bridge between the worlds of fantasy and reality. Whereas 'once upon a time' draws the reader into a timeless fantasy realm of ogresses, fairies, animistic nature, metamorphoses, and wish-fulfilment, the wedding ceremony catapults her back into contemporary reality. Precisely this close association of romantic fiction with the actuality of marriage as a social institution proves the most influential factor in shaping female expectations. Delivered from the inherent improbability of extreme fantasies, the impressionable young girl falls prey to more subtle fancies, seemingly more real because thought possible. For example, one rarely expects fairy godmothers to transform rags into ball gowns, beasts into men, and the spoken word into diamonds and pearls. Even wealth, beauty, and position may be viewed skeptically as magical accoutrements suitable for princesses, yet hardly accessible to most social classes. But marriage is an estate long sanctioned by culture and theoretically attainable by all women; thus, the female may well expect it to provide a protected existence of happy domesticity, complete with an ever hovering male to rescue her from further dangers. As irrational as this translation of fantasies into ideals for real life may seem, it is often true that romantic myth rather than actual experience governs many women's expectations of men and marriage. If she cannot be a literal princess, she can still hope to become the sheltered mistress of a domestic realm, admired by a 'prince of a man' and by children for her self-sacrifices to keep the home fires burning. Certainly marriage need not be a totally unacceptable or self-abnegating goal. Nonetheless, fairy tale portrayals of matrimony as a woman's *only* option limit female visions to the arena of hearth and cradle, thereby perpetuating a patriarchal *status quo*. Whatever the daily reality of women's wedded or professional life, fairy tales require her *imaginative* assent to the proposition that marriage is the best of all possible worlds. Hence, the comic endings call upon young females to value communal stability over individual needs, because their conformity is the cornerstone for all higher social unities — as moral plaudits and festive celebrations testify. As long as women acquiesce to cultural dicta set forth so mythically in romantic *Märchen,* then the harmonious continuity of civilization will be assured. We cannot ask fairy tales to metamorphosize into Greek tragedies. But we should recognize that the conventional patterns of double enchantment, communal rituals, and nuptial climaxes have serious implications for women's role in society.

III

It is perhaps too easy to ignore the significance of romantic tales in forming female attitudes toward the self, men, marriage, and society by relegating them to the nursery. Or one can dispute their impact by asserting that worldly education enables women to distinguish fantasy promises of bliss from conjugal actualities. Either dismissal of fairy tale implies that adult wisdom is entirely rational, thus negating the potency of cultural myths and personal fantasies in shaping one's experience. Precisely this close relationship between fantasy and reality, art and life, explains why romantic tales have in the past and continue in the present to influence so significantly female expectations of their role in patriarchal cultures. Even in the 'liberated' twentieth century, many women internalize romantic patterns from ancient tales. They genuinely hope that their maturation will adhere to traditional prototypes and culminate with predicted felicity — they desperately fear that it won't. Although conscious that all men are not princes and some are unconvertible beasts and that she isn't a princess, even in disguise, still the female dreams of that 'fabulous man'. But as long as modern women continue to tailor their aspirations and capabilities to conform with romantic paradigms, they will live with deceptions, disillusionments, and/or ambivalences. Dedicated romanticists will reconstruct their reality into tenuous, self-deluding fantasies by suppressing any recognition of a secondary status and defending more vehemently the glories of matrimony and the patriarchy — witness the popularity of Marabel Morgan's *The Total Women,* Phyllis Schafly, and the anti-ERA forces and corporate profits from sales of historical, gothic, and Harlequin romances. Grown skeptical by the constant discrepancy between romantic expectations and actual relationships, other women will feel disillusioned. Consider Anne Sexton's acerbic irony as she dissects fairy tales in *Transformations* or those fictional characters who radically renounce all romance and all men, as in Marge Piercy's *Small Changes.* Between these two extremes, other women wallow in confusion, some blaming themselves for failing to actualize their potential as human beings, some assuming a personal guilt for their inability to adapt fully to widespread cultural norms. Think of Edna Pontellier in Chopin's *The Awakening,* Martha Quest in Lessing's *Children of Violence,* or Isadora Wing in Jong's *Fear of Flying.*

While feminist political movements of the last century may seem to signal women's liberation from traditional roles, too often the underlying truth is far more complicated: the liberation of the female psyche has not matured with sufficient strength to sustain a radical assault on the patriarchal culture. Despite an apparent susceptibility to change, modern culture remains itself stubbornly antithetical to ideals of female and male equality. Politically and existentially, women still constitute, to adopt Simone de Beauvoir's classic terms, the Other for the male Subject. Whether expressed in pornographic, domestic, and gothic fictions or enacted in the daily relations of men and women, fairy tale visions of romance also continue to perpetuate cultural ideals which subordinate women. As a major form of communal or 'folk' lore, they preserve rather than challenge the patriarchy. Today women are caught in a dialectic between the cultural *status quo* and the evolving feminist movement, between a need to preserve values and yet to accommodate changing mores, between romantic fantasies and contemporary realities. The capacity of women to achieve equality and of culture to rejuvenate itself depends, I would suggest, upon the metamorphosis of these tensions into balances, of antagonisms into viable cooperations. But one question remains unresolved: do we have the courageous vision and energy to cultivate a newly fertile ground of psychic and cultural experience from which will grow fairy tales for human beings in the future?

Notes

1 See Marcia R. Lieberman, ' "Some Day My Prince Will Come": Female Acculturation Through the Fairy Tale', *College English,* 34 (December 1972), 383 —95; Kay Stone, 'Things Walt Disney Never Told Us', *Journal of American Folklore,* 88 (1975), 42–9; Alison Lurie, 'Fairy Tale Liberation', *The New York Review of Books,* 17 December 1970, pp. 42–4; and Alison Lurie, 'Witches and Fairies: Fitzgerald to Updike', *The New York Review of Books,* 2 December 1971, pp. 6–11.

2 'He Brought My Body to Peaks of Ecstasy on His Water-Bed', *Real Story,* May 1975, pp. 17–19. 66–8.

3 Leonhard Dowty, 'The Garlands of Fortune', *Good Housekeeping,* December 1974, pp. 75, 175–83.

4 Victoria Holt, 'Legend of the Seventh Virgin', in *Gothic Tales of Love,* April 1975, pp. 13–33.

5 See William Bascom, 'Four Functions of Folklore', *Journal of American Folklore* 67 (1954) rpt. in *The Study of Folklore,* ed. Alan Dundes (Englewood Cliffs. N.J.: Prentice-Hall, 1965), pp. 279–98. Inheriting his assumptions from anthropologists and folklorists, such as Franz Boas, Ruth Benedict, Melville J. Herskovits, and Bronislaw Malinowski, Bascom succinctly articulates the functional approach to folklore: 'Viewed in this light, folklore is an important mechanism for maintaining the stability of culture. It is used to inculcate the customs and ethical standards of the young, and as an adult to reward him with praise when he conforms, to punish him with ridicule or criticism when he deviates, to provide him with rationalizations

when the institutions and conventions are challenged or questioned, to suggest that he be content with things as they are, and to provide him with a compensatory escape from "the hardships, the inequalities, the injustices" of everyday life. Here, indeed, is the basic paradox of folklore, that while it plays a vital role in transmitting and maintaining the institutions of a culture and in forcing the individual to conform to them, at the same time it provides socially approved outlets for the repressions which these same institutions impose upon him' (p. 298). See also Bascom's 'Folklore and Anthropology', *Journal of American Folklore*, 66 (1953), rpt. in *The Study of Folklore*, pp. 25–33.

6   Iona and Peter Opie, *The Classic Fairy Tales* (London: Oxford University Press, 1974). All further references to the tales will be to this edition which gives the texts of the 'best-known fairy tales as they were first printed in English, or in their earliest surviving or prepotent text' (p. 5) and will be cited parenthetically in the text. The most significant European literary collections appear first in Renaissance Italy (Gianfrancesco Straparola, *Le piacevoli Notti*, 1550–53, and Giambattista Basile, *Lo Cunto de li Cunti*, often called the *Pentamerone*, 5 vols., 1634–36), then in France (Charles Perrault, *Histoires ou Contes du temps passé. Avec des Moralitez*, 1697), and eventually in England with Robert Samber's translation of Perrault *(Histories or Tales of Past Times*, 1729). Comtesse d'Aulnoy contributes the now familiar term by titling her tales *Contes des fées* (1697–98), establishes fairy tales as a literary genre through imaginative retellings of older stories in *A Collection of Novels and Tales, Written by that Celebrated Wit of France, The Countess D'Anois* (1721); and introduces 'The Story of Finetta the Cinder-Girl' into English (1721). Another French woman, Madame Marie Le Prince de Beaumont, clearly perceives the value of tales for the engagement and instruction of the young when she publishes her *Magasin des enfans, ou dialogues entre une sage Gouvernante et plusieurs de ses Elèves* (1756), translated as *The Young Misses Magazine* (1759). The eighteenth century tolerates this new vogue of fairy tales, popularly attributed to Mother Goose and Mother Bunch, by relegating them to the nursery. However, such folktales gain a new and lasting respectability with Edgar Taylor's publication of *German Popular Stories* (1823–26), translated from the three volume *Kinder- und Hausmärchen* (1812–22) of the Brothers Grimm. Illustrated by George Cruikshank, this volume provides permissible fantasies for the young, a learned account of the antique origins and diffusions of tales, an inspiration for romantic poets and novelists, and the basis for all future studies of folklore in English. Consult Opie and Opie, 'Introduction', pp. 11–23; and Michael Kotzin, *Dickens and the Fairy Tale* (Bowling Green, Ohio: Bowling Green University Popular Press, 1972) for more complete histories of the fairy tale in English literary tradition.

7   See Bruno Bettelheim, *The Uses of Enchantment: The Meaning and Importance of Fairy Tales* (New York: Knopf, 1976) for a thorough-going Freudian analysis of fairy tales; Marie-Louise Von Franz, *Problems of the Feminine in Fairy Tales*, ed. James Hillman (New York: Spring Publications, 1972) and Hedwig Von Beit, *Das Märchen: Sein Ort in der geistigen Entwicklung* (Bern: A. Francke, 1965) for Jungian analyses; and Max Lüthi, *Once Upon a Time: On the Nature of Fairy Tales*, trans. Lee Chadeayne and Paul Gottwald (1962; reprint, ed., New York: Ungar, 1970). Lüthi reads 'Sleeping Beauty', 'Cinderella', and particularly 'Rapunzel' as representations of maturation processes and acknowledges that 'behind many features in our fairy tales there are old customs and beliefs; but in the context of the tale, they have lost their original character. Fairy tales are experienced by their hearers and readers, not as realistic, but as symbolic poetry' (p. 66).

8   See J. L. Fischer, 'The Sociopsychological Analysis of Folktales', *Current Anthropology*, 4 (1963), 235–95. In this rigorous survey of recent trends Fischer argues cogently for the complex interaction of psychological, sociological, and

structuralist interpretations of tales and formulates a functionalized approach: 'For a tale to persist, therefore, some sort of balance must be achieved between two sets of demands: one, the demands of the individual for personal pleasure and the reduction of his anxiety, and the other, the demands of the other members of the society that the individual pursue his personal goals only in ways which will also contribute to, or at least not greatly harm, the welfare of the society' (p. 259).

9   Tale type numbers are taken from Antti A. Aarne, *The Types of the Folktale: A Classification and Bibliography,* trans. and enl. Stith Thompson, 2nd rev., Folklore Fellows Communications, no. 184 (Helsinki: Suomalainen Tiedeakatemia, 1961). See Marrian Roalfe Cox, *Cinderella,* Publications of the Folk-Lore Society, vol. 31 (London: D. Nutt, 1893) and Anna Birgitta Rooth, *The Cinderella Cycle* (Lund: C. W. K. Gleerup, 1951). Although this tale dates back 2,500 years, the earliest recorded version occurs in a Chinese book written about 850 A.D. See Arthur Waley, 'The Chinese Cinderella Story', *Folk-Lore: Being the Quarterly Transactions of the Folk-Lore Society,* 58 (1947), 226–38.

10   Grimm's 'Snow-Drop' is the most well-known modern version, popularized in America by Walt Disney's film adaptation, although Basile's variation in the *Pentamerone* makes clearer the oedipal entanglements which give rise to the stepmother's jealousy. See also Stith Thompson, *The Folktale* (New York: Holt, 1946), pp. 123–4; and Ernst Böklen, *Sneewittchenstudien,* Mythologische Bibliothek, vols. 3 and 7 (Leipzig: Hinrichs, 1910 and 1915).

11   Thompson in *The Folktale* notes that stories only slightly variant from the familiar Perrault version of 'Sleeping Beauty' appear in Basile's *Pentamerone,* Grimm's *Kinder- und Hausmärchen,* and in outline in the French prose romance of *Perceforest* from the 15th century (p. 97). Lüthi uses the three versions by Grimm, Basile, and Perrault for an analysis of differences in literary content and style (pp. 21–46), while Bettelheim notes significant psychoanalytic variations (pp. 225–36). Consult also Hedwig von Beit, *Symbolik des Märchens; Versuch einer Deutung,* 2 vols. (Bern: A. Francke, 1952–56); Johannes Bolte and George Polívka, *Anmerkungen zu den Kinder- und Hausmärchen der Brüder Grimm,* 5 vols (Leipzig: Dieterich, 1913–32); Fritz Ernst, ed. *Dornröschen. In drei Sprachen* (Bern: H. Huber, 1949); Karl J. Obenauer, *Das Märchen: Dichtung und Deutung* (Frankfurt: Klostermann, 1959); Jan de Vries, 'Dornröschen', *Fabula: Journal of Folktale Studies,* 2 (1958), 110–21, for further commentary.

12   Bettelheim, pp. 236–77, focuses upon the sibling rivalry in 'Cinderella', but also examines variants of this tale, the 'basic trust' between mother and child which asserts itself later with the godmother, the displacements of anger to the stepmother, and the oedipal tensions which the tale dramatizes. Although heavy-handed in his Freudian reading, Bettelheim argues convincingly that 'in order to achieve personal identity and gain self-realization on the highest level, the story tells us, both are needed: the original good parents, and later the 'step'-parents who seemed to demand 'cruelly' and 'insensitively'. The two together make up the 'Cinderella' story. If the good mother did not for a time turn into the evil stepmother, there would be no impetus to develop a separate self' (p. 274).

13   Opie and Opie, pp. 117–21; Rooth, pp. 153–6.

14   Adrienne Rich, *Of Woman Born: Motherhood as Experience and Institution* (New York: Norton, 1973). Defining 'matrophobia' as the fear of *'becoming one's mother,'* Rich articulates the tension between mothers and daughters: 'Thousands of daughters see their mothers as having taught a compromise and self-hatred they are struggling to win free of, the one through whom the restrictions and degradations of a female existence were perforce transmitted ... Matrophobia can be seen as a womanly splitting of the self in the desire to become purged once and for all of our mothers' bondage, to become individuated and free. The mother

226 *Don't Bet on the Prince*

stands for the victim in ourselves, the unfree woman, the martyr. Our personalities seem dangerously to blur and overlap with our mothers'; and, in a desperate attempt to know where mother ends and daughter begins, we perform radical surgery' (pp. 235–6).

15 Thompson, *The Folktale*, pp. 97–102, discusses the variant tale types of the monstrous bridegroom, a theme given its classical form in the story of Cupid and Psyche, recorded in Apuleius' narrative *The Golden Ass* (2nd c, A.D.) Consult also Erich Neumann, *Amor and Psyche; The Psychic Development of the Feminine: A Commentary on the Tale by Apuleius,* trans. Ralph Manheim, Bollingen Series, no. 54 (1952; reprint ed., Princeton, N.J.: Princeton University Press, 1956); W. R. S. Ralston, 'Beauty and the Beast', *The Nineteenth Century,* 4 (1878), 990–1012; Jan Öjvind Swahn, *'The Tale of Cupid and Psyche* (Lund: C. W. K. Gleerup, 1955); and Ernst Tegethoff, *Studien zum Märchentypus von Amor und Psyche,* Rhein: Beiträge und Hilfsbücher zur Germ. Philologie und Volkskunde, no. 4 (Bonn: K. Shroëder, 1922).

16 See Bettelheim, pp. 277–310, for a strict Freudian reading of the animal-groom cycle of fairy tales.

17 Opie and Opie, pp. 188–89, report that in its current form, 'The Twelve Dancing Princesses' is 'unlikely to be earlier than the seventeenth century'. Recorded first by the Brothers Grimm, it appears in English translation in Edgar Taylor's *German Popular Stories* (1823–26).

18 In Perrault's version of 'Sleeping Beauty', the prince discourteously rapes and deserts the slumbering princess, unknowingly engendering twins who remove the offending splinter while sucking, and then returns to discover the awakened woman. The prince keeps his marriage secret for two years, but makes regular hunting trips into the forest to visit his wife and children. After the King's death, the prince proclaims his marriage and departs to the wars. During his absence, the queen-mother, who is descended from the race of ogres, plots to kill and eat the princess and her children. Although they escape through the compassion of the clerk of the kitchen, the queen discovers the deception and is about to execute them when the prince providentially returns. The second portion of Perrault's version closely resembles Basile's original, although Basile makes the hero an already married King, whose wife discovers his adulterous relationship with Sleeping Beauty.

20 A Second Gaze at Little Red Riding Hood's Trials and Tribulations

Jack Zipes

In my book *The Trials and Tribulations of Little Red Riding Hood,*[1] I demonstrated that the origins of the literary fairy tale can be traced to male phantasies about women and sexuality. In particular, I showed how Charles Perrault and the Grimm Brothers transformed an oral folk tale about the social initiation of a young woman into a narrative about rape in which the heroine is obliged to bear the responsibility for sexual violation. Such a radical literary transformation is highly significant because the male-cultivated literary versions became dominant in both the oral and literary traditions of nations such as Germany, France, Great Britain, and the United States, nations which exercise cultural hegemony in the West. Indeed, the Perrault and Grimm versions became so crucial in the socialisation process of these countries that they generated a literary discourse about sexual roles and behaviour, a discourse whose fascinating antagonistic perspectives shed light on different phases of social change. In discussing this development, however, I did not devote sufficient time to an examination of the illustrations which in many cases are as important or even more important for conveying notions of sexuality and violence than the texts themselves. Since a complete re-examination of the illustrations would require another book, I should like to limit my study here to one particular scene, the traditional depiction of the young girl encountering the wolf in the woods, with the intention of exploring further socio-psychological ramifications of the Perrault and Grimm versions. Before re-examining the key illustrations of the standard Red Riding Hood texts, however, I should like once more to summarise my arguments about the socio-psychological implications of the changes made by Perrault and the Grimm Brothers. Here it is important to refamiliarise ourselves with a rendition of the oral tale as it was probably disseminated in the French countryside during the late Middle Ages before Charles Perrault refined and polished it according to his own taste and the conventions of French high society in King Louis XIV's time.²

The Story of Grandmother

There was a woman who had made some bread. She said to her daughter:
    'Go carry this hot loaf and bottle of milk to your granny.'
    So the little girl departed. At the crossway she met *bzou,* the werewolf, who said to her:
    'Where are you going?'
    'I'm taking this hot loaf and a bottle of milk to my granny.'
    'What path are you taking,' said the werewolf, 'the path of needles or the path of pins?
    'The path of needles,' the little girl said.
    'All right, then I'll take the path of pins.'
    The little girl entertained herself by gathering needles. Meanwhile the werewolf arrived at the grandmother's house, killed her, put some of her meat in the cupboard and a bottle of her blood on the shelf. The little girl arrived and knocked at the door.
    'Push the door,' said the werewolf, 'It's barred by a piece of wet straw.'
    'Good day, Granny. I've brought you a hot loaf of bread and a bottle of milk.'
    'Put it in the cupboard, my child. Take some of the meat which is inside and the bottle of wine on the shelf.'
    After she had eaten, there was a little cat which said: 'Phooey! ... A slut is she who eats the flesh and drinks the blood of her granny.'
    'Undress yourself, my child,' the werewolf said, 'and come lie down beside me.'
    'Where should I put my apron?'
    'Throw it into the fire, my child, you won't be needing it anymore.'
    And each time she asked where she should put all her other clothes, the bodice, the dress, the petticoat, and the long stockings, the wolf responded:
    'Throw them into the fire, my child, you won't be needing them anymore.'

When she laid herself down in the bed, the little girl said:
'Oh, Granny, how hairy you are!'
'The better to keep myself warm, my child!'
'Oh, Granny, what big nails you have!'
'The better to scratch me with, my child!'
'Oh, Granny, what big shoulders you have!'
'The better to carry the firewood, my child!'
'Oh, Granny, what big ears you have!'
'The better to hear you with, my child!'
'Oh, Granny, what big nostrils you have!'
'The better to snuff my tobacco with, my child!'
'Oh, Granny, what a big mouth you have!'
'The better to eat you with, my child!'
'Oh, Granny, I've got to go badly. Let me go outside.'
'Do it in bed, my child!'
'Oh, no, Granny, I want to go outside.'
'All right, but make it quick.'
The werewolf attached a woollen rope to her foot and let her go outside.

When the little girl was outside, she tied the end of the rope to a plum tree in the courtyard. The werewolf became impatient and said: 'Are you making a load out there? Are you making a load?'

When he realised that nobody was answering him, he jumped out of bed and saw that the little girl had escaped. He followed her but arrived at her house just at the moment she entered.[3]

It is obvious from this oral tale that the narrative perspective is sympathetic to a young peasant girl (age uncertain) who learns to cope with the world around her. She is shrewd, brave, tough, and independent. Evidence indicates she was probably undergoing a social ritual connected to sewing communities:[4] the maturing young woman proves she can handle needles, replace an older woman, and contend with the opposite sex. In 1697 Charles Perrault revised the oral tale to make it the literary standardbearer for good Christian upbringing. Moreover, his fear of women and his own sexual drives are incorporated in his *new* literary version, which also reflects general male attitudes about women portrayed as eager to be seduced or raped. In this regard, Perrault began a series of literary transformations which have caused nothing but trouble for the female object of male desire and have also reflected the crippling aspect of male desire itself.

What are the significant changes he made? First, she is donned with a *red* hat, a *chaperon*,[5] making her into a type of bourgeois girl tainted with sin since red, like the scarlet letter A, recalls the devil and heresy. Second, she is spoiled, negligent, and naïve. Third, she speaks to a wolf in the woods — rather dumb on her part — and makes a type of contract with him: she accepts a wager which, it is implied, she wants to lose. Fourth, she plays right into the wolf's hands and is too stupid to trick him. Fifth, she is swallowed or raped like her grandmother. Sixth, there is no salvation, simply an ironic moral in verse which warns little girls to beware of strangers, otherwise they will deservedly suffer the consequences. Sex is obviously sinful. Playful intercourse outside of marriage is likened to rape, which is primarily the result of the little girl's irresponsible acts.

In 1812, the Grimm Brothers delivered the second classic version of *Little Red Riding Hood,* based on Perrault's narrative, which had already become widely known through printed editions and oral transmission by people from different social classes. The Grimms made further alterations worth noting. Here the mother plays a more significant role by warning Little Red Riding Hood not to stray from the straight path through the woods. Little Red Riding Hood is more or less incited by the wolf to enjoy nature and to pick flowers. Her choice symbolises her agreement with a devilish creature whom she has already directed to her grandmother. Instead of being raped to death, both grandma and granddaughter are saved by a male hunter or gamekeeper, who polices the woods. Only a strong male figure can rescue a girl from herself and her lustful desires.

The Perrault and the Grimm versions became *the* classical stories of Little Red Riding Hood and have served as the models for numerous writers of both sexes throughout the world who have either amplified, distorted, or disputed the facts about the little girl's rape. Obviously, one need not interpret the fairy tale as one of rape, though I suspect that the sexual motif has been dominant in the minds of most writers. Of course, lest eyebrows be raised too high, most literary critics have tended to shun the thought of rape and the manner in which the girl is made to feel responsible for an atrocious act. However, there have been numerous psychologically oriented critics — mainly German, of course — 'brave' enough to discuss the sexual nature of the story.

For instance, commenting on the Grimm version, Erich Fromm maintains: 'This fairy tale, in which the main figures are three generations of women (the huntsman at the end is the conventional father figure without real weight), speaks of the male – female conflict; it is a story of triumph by man-hating women, ending with their victory, exactly the opposite of the Oedipus myth, which lets the male emerge victorious from this battle.'[6]

Bruno Bettelheim views the tale differently:

> Deviating from the straight path in defiance of mother and superego was temporarily necessary for the young girl, to gain a higher state of personality organization. Her experience convinced her of the dangers of giving into her oedipal desires. It is much better, she learns, not to rebel against the mother, nor to try to seduce or permit herself to be seduced by the as yet dangerous aspects of the male. Much better, despite one's ambivalent desires, to settle for a while longer for the protection the father provides when he is not seen in his seductive aspects. She has learned that it is better to build father and mother, and their values, deeper and in more adult ways into one's superego, to become able to deal with life's dangers. [7]

My difficulty with such 'enlightening' interpretations by two of the foremost German psychoanalysts of the twentieth century is that they fail to take into account that the tale which they treat is *not* an ancient and anonymous folk tale reflecting 'universal' psychic operations of men and women, but rather it is the product of gifted male European writers, who projected their needs and values onto the actions of fictitious characters within a socially conventionalised genre. Certainly the psychic condition of the creators of these tales needs some explanation before one deals with the psychological implications of their creations, not to mention the social and historical background of the creators. Moreover, Fromm and Bettelheim are totally unconscious of their own male biases. They feel more compelled to prove their theoretical assumptions about the oedipal or non-oedipal features of the story than to comprehend the historical derivation of the text and the possible psychological designation in terms of the changing sociogenetic civilising process. Their response to the text can be contrasted with Susan Brownmiller's reaction in her book *Against Our Will*.

> Rape seeps into our childhood consciousness by imperceptible degrees. Even before we learn to read we have become indoctrinated into a victim mentality. Fairy tales are full of a vague dread, a catastrophe that seems to befall only little girls. Sweet, feminine Little Red Riding Hood is off to visit her dear old grandmother in the woods. The wolf lurks in the shadows, contemplating a tender morsel. Red Riding Hood and her grandmother, we learn, are equally defenseless before the male wolf's strength and cunning. His big blue eyes, his big hands, his big teeth — 'The better to see you, the better to catch you, to eat you, my dear.' The wolf swallows both females with no sign of a struggle. But enter the huntsman — he will right this egregious wrong. The kindly huntsman's

strength and cunning are superior to the wolf's. With the twist of a knife Red Riding Hood and her grandmother are rescued from inside the wolf's stomach. 'Oh, it was so dark in there,' Red Riding Hood whimpers. 'I will never again wander off into the forest as long as I live...'

Red Riding Hood is a parable of rape. There are frightening male figures abroad in the woods — we call them wolves, among other names — and females are helpless before them. Better stick close to the path, better not be adventurous. If you are lucky, a good *friendly* male may be able to save you from certain disaster.[8]

After commenting on her own youthful fantasies of rape which recall poster images relating to World War I (Belgium's rape by the Hun) and concentration camp victims of fascism, Brownmiller makes the following points about male myths of rape, and she implies that *Little Red Riding Hood* can be considered under this aspect: (1) they tend to make women willing participants in their own defeat; (2) they obscure the true nature of rape by implying that women *want* to be raped; (3) they assert the supreme rightness of male power either as offender or protector.

In my opinion Brownmiller's comments on male attitudes toward women and rape shed more light on the historical development of the Little Red Riding Hood story and the debate concerning its essence than the male psychoanalytic point of view which has either repressed the notion of imposed rape — that is, the rape which Perrault imposed on the folk version — or redressed it in a seemingly positive guise. The history of Little Red Riding Hood's textual development has already revealed to what extent Fromm, Bettelheim and other critics have twisted the sexual signs to reaffirm conventional male attitudes toward women: the girl is guilty because of her natural inclinations and disobedience. However, by re-examining the major illustrations of the tale and their signs, we may be able to see other features of the tale noted by Brownmiller — features obscured by a male screening process. I want to work from the texts and illustrations themselves to understand their referential systems. What do the signs refer to within the illustrations? How do they reinforce particular aspects of the literary text? Which text? What is the reference point or signified which the components or signifiers of an image are addressing?

My comments about the illustrations to the Perrault and Grimm versions of *Little Red Riding Hood* are not about an isolated case. All the most popular, classical fairy tales from *Cinderella* to *Snow White* have been illustrated basically in a sexist manner, whether the pictures have been drawn by a male or female hand. By sexist I mean that the signs centre around male power and rationalise male domination as a norm. Thus the history of standard *Little Red Riding Hood* illustrations shares a great deal in common with that of other illustrated fairy tales, and there are several generalisations about fairy-tale illustrations which must be made before dealing exclusively with the intriguing scenes of the little girl and the wolf.

The earliest illustrations of fairy tales, dating back to the eighteenth century, were largely black and white woodcuts.[9] Since the market for such illustrations in Europe did not really develop until the nineteenth century, when fairy tales for children became more acceptable in middle-class homes, the real beginning of fairy-tale illustrations in the Western world — and I am dealing mainly with France, Germany, Great Britain and the United States — is approximately 1800, and it is not really until the 1820s, 1830s, and 1840s that prominent illustrators such as Thomas Bewick, Ludwig Grimm, George Cruikshank, Ludwig Richter, and Gustave Doré turned their hand to illustrating fairy tales. Here again it is important to note that all the pioneers of fairy-tale pictures were men. The industry of design and engraving was controlled by men. Or, in other words, male illustrators were the interpreters or mediators of the fairy-tale texts, and they projected their sexual phantasies through the images they composed.

Throughout the nineteenth century the primary audience for illustrated fairy-tale books was constituted by the middle class and the aristocracy. No illustrator drew a picture without first taking adult censors and conventions of socialisation and the Christian religion into account. In short, the lines laid down by the pen had already been laid down in mind and society before the image came to be printed. Only the subtle variation of the lines leave tell-tale marks of rebellion and subversion by individual needs and dreams. Though the illustrators offered their images primarily to the wealthy because the cost of picture books made them prohibitive for the masses, there were broadsides, penny books, and chapbooks which were mass produced by the mid-nineteenth century. Thus, the advances in technology enabled the fairy-tale illustrations to reach all social classes. And, the early black and white wood cuts with their sharply drawn simple lines yielded gradually to colourful print with subtly drawn characters and scenes. For each one of the classical fairy tales, there are thousands of illustrated books. And yet, despite this number, there are an astonishing number of repetitions, slightly varied images of *standardised* characters and scenes which have prevailed over the years. This is no accident.

In the case of *Little Red Riding Hood* one could almost talk about a

Figure 1. *Le Petit Chaperon Rouge*, Conte d'après Ch. Perrault, Paris: Editions Ruyant, 1979. Illustrator: M. Fauron. This edition is a reprint of a book published by Emile Guérin at the beginning of the twentieth century. The mother is quoted underneath the picture as saying, 'above all, don't amuse yourself along the way!' The image of the temperate mother trying to temper the potentially rebellious or free-spirited daughter is standard fare in the picture books of the last two centuries.

Figure 2. *Little Red Riding Hood.* New York: J.B. Jansen, 1824. Illustrator: unknown. Typical of the early woodblock illustrations, the wolf is as large as the girl, who is in her puberty, and who expresses interest in the wolf instead of fear.

'conspiracy'. There are three major scenes which almost invariably accompany the text, whether it be the Perrault or Grimm version: (1) the mother with a raised finger addressing her daughter (see Figure 1). Generally speaking, the pictures of both the Perrault and Grimm versions have the mother instruct and warn the girl, even though the warning is not explicitly stated in the Perrault text. However, in the minds of the illustrators the girl is already guilty before a crime is committed. She is made responsible for whatever may happen. (2) Little Red Riding Hood's encounter with the wolf as a type of pact or seduction scene (See Figures 2 and 3). The girl is rarely afraid of the wolf, despite his large size and animal appearance. The viewer must ask him/herself on some level whether she is stupid. Does she want to be violated? Is she asking for something? Is she leading him on? We shall return to these questions. (3) The wolf violating Little Red Riding Hood

Figure 3. *The Sleeping Beauty in the Wood and Little Red Riding Hood.*
London: Dean and Munday and A.K. Newman, c. 1830. Illustrator:
unknown. Here the girl appears to smile seductively and to be willing to
help or accompany the wolf. Again, the wolf is almost as tall as she is,
and they are apparently absorbed in their conversation.

---

as punishment according to the strict Perrault version (see Figure 5) or
the stalwart hunter/father saving Little Red Riding Hood according to
the more lenient Grimms' version (see Figure 6). The dreadful
punishment scene generally represents the consequence of Little Red
Riding Hood's illicit desires and designs. Generally speaking it is
preceded by Little Red Riding Hood in bed smiling at the wolf (see
Figure 4). The more prudish version of the Brothers Grimm does not
call for Little Red Riding Hood to strip—and there are striptease
scenes—and get into bed. She is simply gobbled up by the wolf. And,
as in Figure 7, she owes her salvation and life to a male who is likened
to a father figure. Explicit in these illustrations is that a girl receives her
identity through a man, and that without male protection she will
destroy herself and reap chaos in the world outside.

During the course of the past two centuries, these illustrations have
been varied extensively, and there have been some radical changes such

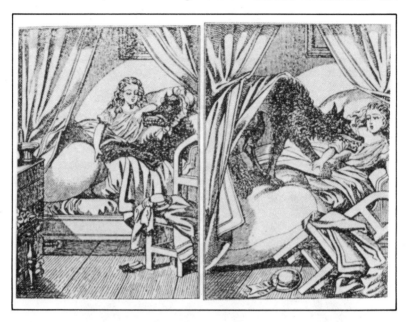

Figures 4 and 5. Jean Boullet, *La Belle et la Bette.* Paris: La Terrain Vague, 1958. Illustrator: unknown. These illustrations date most likely from the late 19th century. They are characteristic of all the standard Perrault versions in which the girl gets into bed with the wolf. Again, the most famous bed scene is that of Gustave Doré. Since she is most often on the far side of the wolf and viewer, she must have had to have climbed over the wolf or have crossed over him. Thus, she would have noticed that the wolf was not a grandmother or a man but a wolf. Yet, she appears to want to get into bed with the wolf and often smiles flirtatiously at him. Such sinful desire is then punished severely by society in the form of brutal retribution. There is no rescue in Perrault's narrative, just rape as punishment.

---

as in Thurber's illustration of the girl who shoots the wolf with a pistol or in the Liverpool feminist group's depiction of the girl and her grandmother slaying the wolf.[10] But, for the most part the traditional images have prevailed and continue to be circulated by a culture industry primarily interested in making profits by gambling with our subliminal sexual phantasies and reinforcing male notions of rape. The underlying question in the images depicting the male/female encounter, whether it be in magazines, books, films, advertisements, or cartoons, concerns women's use of their sexual powers to attain

Figure 6. *The Gingerbread Boy, Little Red Riding Hood, and the House that Jack Built,* Racine, Wisconsin: Whitman, 1945. Illustrators: Hilda Miloche and Wilma Kane. The final scene of salvation and rebirth varies. Often the father/woodsman helps the girl and grandmother step out of the wolf's belly. Sometimes he sits and drinks tea with the two females while the wolf lays slain at their feet. Or, as in this typical illustration, the industrious and fearless woodcutter has no time for pleasure. He is off to work while the two grateful females celebrate their rebirth in orderly fashion. They have time now to re-domesticate themselves.

Figure 7. *Little Red Riding Hood,* New York: Platt & Munk, 1934. Illustrator: Eulalie. Notice how father and daughter resemble each other also to the point that the father's face could be the mother's face as well. She has become his little doll, and the series of illustrations leading to this scene reveals her growing smaller so he can carry her on his broad shoulders. It is through the father that she receives her identity, and she clings to him because she is unable to stand on her own two feet.

---

supreme gratification through male sexual prowess. As every reader/viewer subconsciously knows, Little Red Riding Hood is not really sent into the woods to visit grandma but to meet the wolf and to explore her own sexual cravings and social rules of conduct. Therefore, the most significant enounter is with the wolf because it is here that *she acts* upon her desire to indulge in sexual intercourse with the wolf, and most illustrations imply that she willingly makes a bargain with the wolf, or, in male terms, 'she asks to be raped'.

The wiles of Red Riding Hood are many, or to be more exact, the iconic projections of illustrators reveal a great deal about the semiotic means of fairy-tale illustrations which serve to corroborate male notions about sexuality and rape. Here I should like to focus on several illustrations selected from well over 500 that recurred with significant regularity in similar shape. Not only do they suggest that Little Red Riding Hood is guilty for her own rape, but they reveal a curious *ambivalence* about male phantasies which needs more explanation.

Perhaps the most famous engravings of *Little Red Riding Hood* are those by Gustave Doré (1832–1883), who illustrated Perrault's fairy tales in 1862. His images or imaginings were so striking that they were used in other editions soon after. For example, they appeared in Tom Hood's *A Fairy Realm* (1864) and Morris Hartmann's *Märchen nach Perrault* (1869). By the end of the nineteenth century, they were known throughout the Western world, and Doré's portrayal of Red Riding Hood meeting the wolf (see Figure 8) has undoubtedly influenced numerous other illustrators and continues to frame the manner in which we see Red Riding Hood's encounter with the wolf.

To explore the ideological connotations of Doré's illustration and others, a semiotic approach can be useful. Here the image or sign needs to be broken down into signifiers (the striking features of the major figures) and signifieds (the concepts to which the signifiers allude). By doing this we can move toward a comprehension of the whole sign or image. In the case of a fairy-tale illustration it is important to bear in mind that the signifiers in the image refer to each other and to the text in order to create a sensory impression. It is up to us as viewers/readers to convey ultimate meaning upon the patterns, and we do this in a conscious and unconscious manner but always within a socio-historical context which has already framed the way we receive signals about sex and sexuality. As Bill Nichols has remarked in *Ideology and the Image:* 'Images are always particularized representations, a way of seeing is built in (since a way of seeing built them) and hence connotation is built in.'[11]

In Doré's illustration it seems to me that the more expressive aspects of the image are: the longing if not seductive look of Little Red Riding Hood as she peers into the eyes of the wolf and her faint smile; the enormous size of the powerful wolf who looks down into the eyes of the girl in a non-threatening manner; the proximity of wolf and girl who appear to be touching and to be totally absorbed in an intimate *tête-à-tête*. It is almost as if the viewer were an intruder who chances to come upon an assignation of two lovers in the woods. Certainly the viewer is invited to gaze voyeuristically upon a familiar world and to confirm meaning that seems always to have been there. What then is this meaning?

Figure 8. *Les Contes de Perrault.* Paris: J. Hetzel, 1862. Illustrator: Gustave Doré.

The signifiers point to seduction, intimacy and power. Doré stresses the desire of the girl and wolf for one another. But, by revealing the full face of the girl and her apparent seductive glance, Doré also suggests that it is primarily she who is asking for it. And, what is *it?* In this case it is an immense wolf or phallus, a male creature, who in his animal state represents both the girl's own libidinal drives *and* the voracious appetite of males, whose desire is allegedly to dominate and violate women, to lead them off the straight path — and naturally it is all women's secret desire to be misled. The erotic display in Doré's illustration indicates a transgression of society's rules of sexual behaviour and sexuality while at the same time it confirms what we suppose to be true about both women *and* men: women want men to rape them; men are powerful but weak beasts who cannot help themselves when tempted by alluring female creatures. Since the sexes prey upon one another and cause their own destruction in nature as opposed to society, then another implicit message is that there can be no 'true' love, certainly no Christian love, in sexual intercourse practised outside of the institution of marriage. Only when sexual behaviour is domestically ordered as in the person of the mother and the father at the beginning and end of the fairy tale can sex assume its 'proper' reproductive function in society.

The central scene of the girl/wolf encounter in the chain of signification is the crucial one in all illustrated Red Riding Hood books, for it is the scene of transgression. As we have seen, the first standard image always indicates domestic order and tranquillity in the person of the stern but caring mother. The last scene either represents the punishment as a result of the transgression underlined by Perrault's *moralité*, which we should not forget:

> From this story one learns that children,
> Especially young lasses,
> Pretty, courteous and well-bred,
> Do very wrong to listen to strangers,
> And it is not an unheard thing
> If the Wolf is thereby provided with his dinner.
> I say Wolf, for all wolves
> Are not of the same sort;
> There is one kind with an amenable disposition
> Neither noisy, nor hateful, nor angry,
> But tame, obliging and gentle,
> Following the young maids
> In the streets, even into their homes.
> Alas! who does not know that these gentle wolves
> Are of all such creatures the most dangerous![12]

Or, the last scene represents the restoration of domestic order by a strong male figure as in the Grimm version or a Grimm variant. In Doré's illustration it is obvious that the girl will become completely tainted by sin since she has stopped to talk to this strange creature. Given the enormous size of the wolf, the viewer must ask why the little girl is not afraid of the beast? Certainly any smart peasant girl would have run from this gigantic wolf. Any self-respecting bourgeois girl would have avoided the company of such a hairy monster. But here, Little Red Riding Hood apparently seeks his acquaintance, and the shadow of the wolf begins to cover her.

It is within this shadow that we may be able to locate the ambivalence of male desire. That is, it is possible to interpret Little Red Riding Hood's desire for the wolf as a desire for the other, or a general quest for self-identification. She seeks to know herself in a social context, gazes into the wolf's eyes to see a mirror reflection of who she might be, a confirmation of her feelings. She wants to establish contact with her unconscious and discover what she is lacking. By recognising the wolf outside of her as part of herself, just as the wolf seeks the female in himself, she can become at one with herself. The woods are the natural setting for the fulfilment of desire. The conventions of society are no longer present. The self can explore its possibilities and undergo symbolic exchanges with nature inside and outside the self. If we follow this line of thought, the formation of this scene (girl meeting wolf) by Doré demonstrates *his* unconscious desire to free himself of social restraints in a symbolic exchange with the other, and he also recognises the mutual desire of the other. Yet, as much as Doré *desired* to depict the pleasure of recognition through a sexual symbolic exchange, he probably identified more with the wolf, and thus there is an indication in his illustration that the wolf seeks to *dominate* with his gaze which would cancel out mutuality. The text of the tale dictated the wolf's gaze as phallic domination — a point which I shall discuss later in reference to Jacques Lacan — and the conventions of society reinforced such male desire during Doré's time. In addition, the look or gaze of Little Red Riding Hood appears to invite the wolf's gaze/desire, and therefore, she incriminates herself in his act. Implicit in her gaze is that she may be leading him on — to granny's house, to a bed, to be dominated. She tells him the way, the path to the house. But where is she actually leading him? Why?

Already influenced by other illustrations and the text, Doré's own illustration stamped many of the configurations of the late nineteenth-century images of the girl/wolf encounter.[13] In England there were numerous illustrated books of fairy tales which reflected and embellished Doré's work. For instance, Raphael Tuck and Sons had a studio of artists who pursued Doré's lines and helped Tuck become one of the main distributors of fairy tales in England, France, Germany, the United States and Canada. The illustrators are unknown, but they all maintained a particular style as if one hand drew each scene so that everyone could be attributed to Father Tuck, the name under which most of the fairy-tale books were distributed. One scene (see Figure 9), reminiscent of the Doré illustration, reveals Red Riding Hood on the right smiling and looking down at the wolf. She is intended to be doll-like corresponding to the Victorian image of children, especially young girls, [14] and the colours are bright pastels. But the girl is more than just sweet and virginal. Again she glances seductively at the wolf, ready to accommodate him. Of course, some changes have been made. The wolf comes from the right and is much smaller than the girl. In fact, he looks more like a friendly dog with his left paw raised, almost begging to have a bone. His head is tilted, and his tongue forms a smile with his open jaws. The diminution of dog and girl was typical of Victorian illustrations, for upper-class children were considered fragile and sensitive. [15] Their sexuality had to be adorned in a way which might not disturb them. Nevertheless, the innuendoes in this scene are clear.

In the history of *Little Red Riding Hood* illustrations each nation has cultivated particular characteristics which can be traced in the signifiers of the girl/wolf encounter. Obviously the Doré influence can be found more often in France, where illustrators have expressed a tendency to be more erotic and playful than the German, British, and American artists, who are more restrained and puritanical. For example, another French book which appeared in 1905 (see Figure 10) reveals Little Red Riding Hood and the wolf as if they were going on a picnic together. The intimacy is clear: it is almost as if they were one. The girl's flirtatious smile is matched by the friendly gaze of the wolf, who is more like a companion than a stranger. Unlike the doll-like portrayals in America and England, the French illustrations tend to show a more fully-developed young girl, one approaching puberty. Both the girl and the wolf are oblivious of the woods around them. They only have eyes for each other. In my study of the literary texts, I demonstrated that the wolf and the girl were essentially one and the same figure in the minds of the writers, for the little girl is a potential witch with her red hat — witches, evil fairies, and Jews wore red hats in the oral stories which circulated in the late Middle Ages up through the nineteenth century — and the wolf, whose ancestor was the werewolf, was an accomplice of the devil. The encounter in the woods, a meeting place of witches and the haunting place of werewolves, is an asocial act.

Figure 9. *Friends from Fairyland,* London: Raphael Tuck & Sons, c. 1880. Illustrator: unknown. This book, part of Father Tuck's 'Ever Welcome' Series, was designed in England and printed in Germany. Tuck had offices of distribution in London, Paris, Berlin, New York, and Montreal. The above is typical of Victorian illustrations which often portrayed the girl as seductive innocence.

Figure 10. *Le petit Chaperon Rouge,* Paris: Emile Guérin, c. 1905. Illustrator: unknown. Here, as in many illustrations, the girl and dog are more like companions who exchange knowing looks about the game they are about to play.

The meeting of the eyes (the 'I's), the touching bodies and linked shadows form an apparent oneness, an agreement. Here the anonymous illustrator softens the erotic nature of the scene which is more striking in Doré's illustration. Nevertheless, the smile of Little Red Riding Hood is more than just friendly.

Eye contact and knowing smiles are extremely important in the girl/wolf encounter. The gifted illustrated Walter Crane (1845 – 1915), who, like Doré, left his imprint on future illustrators, raised the wolf on his hind legs and dressed him in peasant clothes (see Figure 11). Crane was by no means the first to elevate and to anthropomorphise the wolf. There were Dutch, French, and German broadsheets which depicted the wolf as soldier or farmer by the mid-nineteenth century. Crane was, however, one of the first to present this scene in a toy book with colour and strong ink lines emphasising the intimate nature of the encounter. Here Little Red Riding Hood is in her teens, and with her raised eyebrows and stiff upper lip she is not as seductive as some of her 'sisters'. Nevertheless, she gazes into his eyes which are practically on the same plane as his while he leans on his cane and addresses her in a friendly way. It is as though he were standing on a corner waiting for her to come by. Here there is a clear separation of the figures emphasised by the straight stick which keeps them apart. Also, in the background we see some woodcutters, the social guardians of morality, who guarantee that the girl and wolf will behave themselves. This is why the eye contact is important, for they must exchange signals. The wolf must know where to go to meet her. He seeks to absorb her in his gaze.

An American version of the Grimms' tale published in 1939 reflects the continued influence of Crane (see Figure 12). The eyes of the young girl and wolf are on the same plane. The figures are separated, but the wolf leans in an intimate way while the girl gazes straight into his eyes. Dressed in overalls, the wolf is obviously an American farmer, and the apple-pie complexion of the girl suggests the sweetness of innocent American girls, who use their innocence as a means of seduction.

Innocence and *naïveté* are generally associated with coyness and stupidity by male illustrators. For instance, another Father Tuck illustration (see Figure 13) reflects a characteristic male attitude toward women. Although the wolf is only saying 'good morning' to the girl, she acts as if she were being propositioned. With her index finger in her mouth and her eyes rolled to the right, she gives the impression of a coquette playing hard to get. Unlike most depictions of this scene, this one shows her facing the viewers while cocking her head toward the wolf. Though she is apparently avoiding eye contact with the wolf, she is also enticing him. The wolf is a debonair gentleman with top hat and

Figure 11. Walter Crane Toy Books, *Little Red Riding Hood*, London: George Routledge, 1870. Illustrator: Walter Crane. Here Crane had the Grimm story adapted to verse, and the caption to this illustration reads:

> *Out set Riding Hood, so obliging and sweet,*
> *And she met a great Wolf in the wood,*
> *Who began most politely the maiden to greet,*
> *as tender a voice as he could.*
> *He asked to what house she was going and why;*
> *Red Riding Hood answered him all:*
> *He said, "Give my love to your Gran; I will try*
> *At my earliest to call."*

Figure 12. *Little Red Riding Hood,* New York: Sam'l Gabriel Sons. Illustrator: unknown.

Figure 13. Father Tuck's Fairy Tale Series, *Little Red Riding Hood*, London: Raphael Tuck & Sons, c. 1880. Illustrator: unknown. Designed at the studios in England, the narrative was written by Grace C. Floyd.

cane, and there is something comical about his appearance in the woods. His courteous and stately manner is in contrast to the *naïveté* of the little girl. One is compelled to ask who is pretending more, the wolf or the girl? Who is leading whom on?

Johnny Gruelle's depiction of the same type of naïve lass is somewhat different (see Figure 14), but not much. Famous as the creator of Raggedy Ann and Raggedy Andy, Gruelle illustrated the complete Grimms' fairy tales in a most unusual manner. Here Little Red Riding Hood plays again at being dumb, while the chevalier wolf makes his intentions obvious by licking his chops. Characteristic of American illustrations in the twentieth century, and to a certain extent of most traditional ones in Europe after World War I (see Figure 15) there is a tendency to make Little Red Riding Hood more babylike and infantile and to suggest the comical side of the encounter, as though it were all in good clean fun because we know how it will turn out in the end, that is, if we believe the Brothers Grimm, whose version is the most prevalent in the world.

More typical than Gruelle's illustration which still has a strong hint of the erotic in the meeting of girl/wolf is the prudish illustration by Hilda Miloche and Wilma Kane (see Figure 16). The girl appears to be impressed by the polite manners of the wolf, whose top hat recalls the Father Tuck illustration. The girl and wolf have been 'desexed' in true Walt Disney fashion. As usual, the wolf is without genitals, and the apple-cheeked girl is more like a cupie doll than a real living person. The eye contact remains, and the girl is apparently interested in what the wolf has to say. But, as in all the illustrations, it is what is unsaid that is best understood by the viewer/reader. The words and images stimulate the imagination, refer to notions and concepts, rules and conventions, preconditioned thoughts about sexual behaviour and sex roles.

The history of the pictures which illustrate the traditional versions of *Little Red Riding Hood* by Perrault and the Brothers Grimm reveal a kind of cleansing process, a gradual censorisation, which is geared to eliminate the sexual connotations of the tales. Whereas the experimental storytellers and illustrators have consciously highlighted the notion of rape to parody and criticise it from different points of view, the conservative re-tellers and illustrators of the Perrault and Grimm narratives want to avoid the issue. Intimacy, seduction, and violation are made comical so as not to upset the delicate sensitivity of young readers and the keen sense of propriety of their watchdog parents. For the most part the wolf will be fully dressed (see Figure 15)

Figure 14. *Grimm's Fairy Tales*, translated by Margaret Hunt, New York: Cupples & Leon, 1914. Illustration: John B. Gruelle.

and caricatured, even to the point of appearing as naïve and stupid as the little girl. He is not allowed to eat the grandmother who either hides in a closet or runs into town. Nor is he allowed to put his paws on Little Red Riding Hood, who is invariably saved by a father/hunter. Nevertheless, the implications of the signals remain. It is the dumb girl who causes a 'near rape'. Men are natural victims of temptation, as the

Figure 15. *The Story ov Littl Red Rieding Hood.* Chicago: Encyclopedia Britannica Education Corporation, 1968. Illustrations from *Classic Fairy Tales,* a series of films produced by Encyclopedia Britannica Films, Inc. Large corporations such as Walt Disney generally package their fairy-tale productions to obtain maximum profit. Thus the narrative will be simultaneously made into a film, record, picture book, coloring book, poster, and toy.

Figure 16. *The Gingerbread Boy, Little Red Riding Hood, and the House that Jack Built,* Racine, Wisconsin: Whitman, 1945. Illustrators: Hilda Miloche and Wilma Kane.

Adam and Eve myth suggested long ago, and generally will behave if fed and clothed properly. Only the domesticated models of mother and father are worth emulating — those strongly structured, well-composed, self-confident figures of law and order.

Ironically, the portrayals of the wolf and the girl were more erotic and sensual in the nineteenth century and early part of the twentieth century than they are today. Michel Foucault has suggested that the Victorians were more obsessed and interested in sex than we believe. [16] That is, given the proliferation of discourses around sexuality which began in the nineteenth century, Foucault calls into question the very notion of repression. Certainly, in the case of *Little Red Riding Hood,* writers and illustrators were not afraid to make sex the major subject of their discourses. Historically speaking the traditional nineteenth century depictions of the girl/wolf encounter bear out Foucault's assertions: they reveal a deep longing for sexual satisfaction, a pursuit of natural inclinations against conformity to a social code. The bodies of girl and wolf are closer, more intimate, more lifelike than images which originate after World War II. In fact, twentieth-century images are marked by a growing alienation: the girl and wolf keep more distance; they are afraid of sex and their bodies; they are clean and sterile, more like wooden cartoon figures or advertising props for good housekeeping.

All this is not to say that nineteenth-century Europeans and Americans were more emancipated in their sexual attitudes than contemporary Europeans and Americans. Rather, it seems to me that the growing rationalisation of society and increased division of labour and more subtle forms of discipline and punishment first generated an intensified discussion about the body and sexuality in the nineteenth century. The question concerned control and use of the body, the instrumentalisation for greater productivity, domination of inner and outer nature within the prescriptions of capitalist industrialisation and the Protestant ethos. Thus, rules for sexual conduct and the definition of sexual roles had to be established firmly in the minds of children and adults. Since the enjoyment of extramarital sex could interfere with production and schooling in the nineteenth century, the sexual act, which had already been more or less equated with sin by the Church, had to be repeatedly associated with irresponsibility, chaos, and violation. Such a process had already begun in an organised way in the late Middle Ages, and the Perrault text was an outcome of such male rationalisation of Christian thought. In the male imagination it was the woman who was devious, sinful, and subversive; her sexual appetite interfered with male institutionalised relations; she was an instigator, in league with the devil, that is, with wolves or male heretics, who represented sexual play, amusement, gathering flowers in the woods. So, by the nineteenth century Little Red Riding Hood and the wolf had become primarily responsible for the violation of bodies, for chaos, disorder, and sin. At the same time, there is an undercurrent in the images of the nineteenth century of a secret longing by the male illustrators to become part of a union of girl/wolf, to enjoy the bodies, to celebrate the eye contact. Since the encounter is the central scene in the chain of signification illustrating the texts, the illustrator could express his/her contradictory desire.

The illustrators of fairy-tale books in the nineteenth century were also influenced by market conditions. As it became cheaper to produce illustrated books, broadsheets, chapbooks, penny books, and toy books, children became more a target audience — and these were also children who began to have more leisure time and were becoming better educated in all social classes. By the turn of the century, publishers sought mainly profit from this new market, and production for children — which meant production for the adult surveyors of children — demanded that the producers pay respect to decent taste and sexual codes, at least in outward form. If *Little Red Riding Hood* was to be marketed in France, Germany, America, Canada, and England as Raphael Tuck and Sons did, then she had to entice buyers by subscribing to male notions of sexual seduction, rape, punishment, and salvation.

As I have already remarked, the major change during the nineteenth century, if one can call it a real change, has been marked by increased sanitisation and standardisation of the text and pictures. International conglomerates have worked together since 1945 to package *Red Riding Hood* as standard commodity to bring profits and to convey male notions about sexuality, specifically about the violation of the body for which women are deemed responsible. The nationality or sex of the illustrator no longer plays a major role since the deviation from the normal 'desexed' girl and wolf will not be tolerated. For example, the Golden Book publishers, which circulate Red Riding Hood in the thousands throughout the US in supermarkets, drugstores, candy-stores, and bookstores, have transformed Little Red Riding Hood into a sterile tale of chastity.[17] The discourse about the body reflects a greater fear of and alienation from the body than ever before. Unlike the Victorians, we are no longer sexually curious, rather sexually controlled and defensive. The non-violence depicted in the illustrations continues to violate minds with implicit messages about the stupidity and culpability of little girls. For instance, the Walt Disney Corporation and Peter Pan Company have produced a record set with text and pictures for little boys and girls to follow the story with music.[18] Naturally, they have cleaned up the act and reduced the girl's incrimination so that the tale has become insipid, totally devoid of erotic tension. Yet, the girl is made to feel that she has done something wrong. *She* is the one who should not talk to strangers. Better to be catatonic, than to be adventurous. Control is of essence today.

Ultimately, the male phantasies of Perrault and the Brothers Grimm can be traced to their socially induced desire and need for control — control of women, control of their own sexual libido, control of their fear of women and loss of virility. That their controlling interests are still reinforced and influential through variant texts and illustrations of *Little Red Riding Hood* in society today is an indication that we are still witnessing an antagonistic struggle of the sexes in all forms of socialisation, in which men are still trying to dominate women. In one of the major theoretical books to deal with male phantasies in the last 50 years, Klaus Theweleit has remarked:

> The apparent rearing of children to become chaste achieves its opposite by creating a stored-up lecherousness, the installation of an unfulfilled deed as a permanent condition. The boy is sexualized. His need is directed toward woman, it is supposed to be directed right toward the woman. All images, hopes, wishes, plans, which the growing boy has, are supposed to come together, to be concentrated and fixed on the conquest of this one object — the woman, and this object women is represented in codified form by a woman of the family.
>
> The growing boy is trained along these lines and during puberty is trained to structure his whole existence almost insanely according to a fictitious before/after scheme: 'After I have first had a woman for just once, *the* woman, then . . .' Decisive here is this 'then' which appears to stand for everything: then the guilt will disappear, the fears, the insecurities, the feelings of inferiority, then life will begin, I'll be strong, I'll be able to conquer the father or leave him, my talents will unfold; She will belong to me and I'll protect her . . .'
>
> The 'meaning of life' is produced from this longed-for salvation, and, since it does not occur, since salvation stems from a false direction of the wish, the crucial question about the meaning of life (thought of as being able to be accomplished in *one* act) does not stop.[19]

In endeavouring to comprehend how unresolved sexual needs contributed to the development of a fascist mentality and male brutality in Germany, Theweleit touches on fundamental questions regarding male upbringing and male phantasies in Western society as a whole, questions which are connected to the fairy tale about Little Red Riding

Hood and its reception. What is played out in the narrative of Little Red Riding Hood is the deep longing of males to possess their own bodies/mothers/sisters, to touch the wild unformed urges in themselves, to possess them — and then, the frustration which comes from the realisation that the desire cannot be fulfilled. The frustration often leads to an act of violence, an insistence that the desire be fulfilled at all costs. Here the notions of Jacques Lacan about masculine and feminine sexuality[20] can be further helpful in explaining the psychological signification of the girl/wolf constellation. As is well known, Lacan attributed a great deal of importance to the gaze in the development of human sexuality. For him, seeing is desire, and the eye functions as a kind of phallus. However, the eye cannot clearly see its object of desire, and in the case of male desire, the female object of desire is an illusion created by the male unconscious. Or, in other words, the male desire for woman expressed in the gaze is auto-erotic and involves the male's desire to have his own identity reconfirmed in a mirror image. As Larysa Mykyta explains in her essay entitled 'Lacan, Literature and the Look',

> the sexual triumph of the male passes through the eye, through the contemplation of the woman. Seeing the women ensures the satisfaction of wanting to be seen, of having one's desire recognized, and thus comes back to the original aim of the scopic drive. Woman is repressed as subject and desired as object in order to efface the gaze of the Other, the gaze that would destroy the illusion of reciprocity and one-ness that the process of seeing usually supports. The female object does not look, does not have its own point of view; rather it is erected as an image of the phallus sustaining male desires.[21]

In the case of the Red Riding Hood illustrations and the classical texts by Perrault and the Grimms, the girl in the encounter with the wolf gazes but really does not gaze, for she is the image of male desire. She is projected by the authors Perrault and Grimm and generally by male illustrators as an object without a will of her own. The gaze of the wolf will consume her and is intended to dominate and eliminate her. The gaze of the wolf is a phallic mode of interpreting the world and is an attempt to gain what is lacking through imposition and force. Thus, the positioning of the wolf involves a movement toward convincing the girl that he is what she wants, and her role is basically one intended to mirror his desire. In such an inscribed and prescribed male discourse, the feminine other has no choice. Her identity will be violated and fully absorbed by male desire either as wolf or gamekeeper.

If *Little Red Riding Hood,* the text as well as the key illustration, is seen in the light of Lacan's psychoanalytic theories as a conservative male phantasy conditioned by social-cultural conventions, then the fairy tale as a whole does little to reduce the possibility for violence and brutality in our society. If anything, it perpetuates sexual notions which contribute to our frustration and aggressiveness.

As long as we are encouraged to point our finger at Little Red Riding Hood as willing conspirator in her own downfall and assign male guardians of law and order to kill the wolf, our minds and bodies will be prevented from grasping the fundamental issues of sexuality at stake in the story and in our lives.

Notes

1 The subtitle is: *Versions of the Tale in Sociocultural Context* (South Hadley: Bergin & Garvey, 1983 and London: Heinemann, 1983).

2 Cf. Dorothy R. Thelander, 'Mother Goose and Her Goslings: The France of Louis XIV as Seen through the Fairy Tale', *The Journal of Modern History,* **54** (September 1982), 467–96 and the chapter 'Setting Standards for Civilization through Fairy Tales', in my book *Fairy Tales and the Art of Subversion* (New York: Wildman, 1983 and London: Heinemann, 1983), pp. 13–44.

3 *The Trials and Tribulations of Little Red Riding Hood,* pp. 5–6. See also Paul Delarue, 'Les contes merveilleux de Perrault et la tradition populaire', *Bulletin folklorique de l'Ile-de-France* (1951), 221–8, 251–60, 283–91; (1953), 511–71.

4 See Yvonne Verdier, 'Grands-mères, si vous saviez: le Petit Chaperon Rouge dans la tradition orale', *Cahiers de litterature orale,* **4** (1978), 17–55.

5 There are numerous theories about the *chaperon rouge.* One of the more interesting theses is to be found in Hans T. Siepe's article 'Rotkäppchen einmal anders. Ein Märchen für den Französischunterricht', *Der fremdsprachliche Unterricht,* **65** (1983), 1–9. Siepe suggests that the term '*grand chaperon*' designated an older woman who was supposed to escort young girls from the upper classes as chaperon in the English sense of the word. The fact that Little Red Riding Hood only has a 'little chaperon', indicates that she did not have enough protection. Whatever the case may be, the chaperon transforms the peasant girl into a bourgeois type and the colour red, which may indeed suggest menstruation, was a clear symbol of her sin. See also Bernadette Bricout 'L'Aiguille et l'epingle', in *La 'Bibliotheque bleue' nel Seicento o della Letteratura per il popole,* eds. P. A. Jannini, G, Dotoli and P. Carile, 4 (1981) pp. 45–58.

6 *The Forgotten Language* (New York: Grove Press, 1957), p. 241.

7 *The Uses of Enchantment. The Meaning and Importance of Fairy Tales* (New York: Knopf, 1976), p. 181.

8 *Men, Women and Rape* (New York: Bantam, 1976), pp. 343–4.

9 See David Bland, *A History of Book Illustration* (London: Faber & Faber, 1958) and Percy Muir, *Victorian Illustrated Books* (London: Batsford, 1971).

10 Cf. *The Trials and Tribulations of Little Red Riding Hood,* p. 210. This book contains over 70 different types of *Little Red Riding Hood Illustrations.*

11 Bloomington: Indiana University Press, 1981, p. 47. See also John Berger, *Ways of Seeing* (Harmondsworth, 1972).

12 I have purposely taken this quotation from a recent book which has had seven printings since 1961. *Perrault's Complete Fairy Tales,* translated from the French

by A. E. Johnson and others (Harmondsworth: Kestrel/Penguin, 1982), p. 77. Illustrations by W. Heath Robinson.

13   In America they have been reprinted since 1969 in *Perrault's Fairy Tales* (New York: Dover, 1969). Since the Dover books are inexpensive, the illustrations are easily accessible to the public. Also, Dover is not the only publisher to have made use of the Doré illustrations.

14   Cf. Peter Coveney, *The Image of Childhood* (Harmondsworth: Penguin, 1967).

15   Cf. Marion Lochhead, *Their First Ten Years. Victorian Childhood* (London: John Murray, 1956).

16   *The History of Sexuality* (New York: Pantheon, 1978), p. 49. 'We must therefore abandon the hypothesis that modern industrial societies ushered in an age of increased sexual repression. We have not only witnessed a visible explosion of unorthodox sexualities; but — and this is the important point — deployment quite different from the law, even if it is locally dependent on procedures of prohibition, has ensured, through a network of interconnecting mechanisms, the proliferation of specific pleasures and the multiplication of disparate sexualities. It is said that no society has been more prudish [Foucault is referring to Victorian society, J. Z.]; never have the agencies of power taken such care to feign ignorance of the thing they prohibited, as if they were determined to have nothing to do with it. But it is the opposite that has become apparent, at least after a general review of the facts: never have there existed more centers of power; never more attention manifested and verbalized; never more circular contacts and linkages; never more sites where the intensity of pleasures and the persistency of power catch hold, only to spread elsewhere.'

17   The same development can be traced in other Western countries. Cf. the Ladybird Easy Reading Books in England. In particular, see *Little Red Riding Hood,* retold by Vera Southgate with illustrations by Eric Winter (Loughborough: Ladybird Books, 1972).

18   The cassette industry has also had a great impact on the market. See *Little Red Riding Hood*, Six More Favourite Stories Played by the Robin Lucas Children's Theatre, London: BiBi Music, BBM82.

19   *Männer Phantasien* (Frankfurt am Main: Roter Stern, 1977), pp. 478–9.

20   See Jacques Lacan, *Feminine Sexuality,* eds. Juliet Mitchell and Jacqueline Rose (New York: Norton, 1983).

21   *SubStance,* 39 (1983), 54.

Bibliography

1. General

Applebee, Arthur N. *The Child's Concept of Story.* Chicago: University of Chicago Press, 1978.

Barrett, Michele. *Women's Oppression Today.* London: Verso, 1980.

Baruch, Grace K., Rosalind C. Barnett, and Caryl Rivers. *Life Prints: New Patterns of Love and Work for Today's Women.* New York: McGraw-Hill, 1983.

Benjamin, Jessica. 'The Oedipal Riddle; Authority, Autonomy, and the New Narcissism'. In *The Problem of Authority in America,* eds. John P. Diggins and Mark E. Kann. Philadelphia: Temple: University Press, 1981, pp. 195–224.

Benwell, Gwen and Arthur Waugh. *Sea Enchantress: The Tale of the Mermaid and Her Kind.* New York: Citadel, 1966.

Berger, John. *Ways of Seeing.* Harmondsworth: Penguin, 1972.

Berryman, Cynthia L. and Virginia A. Eman, eds. *Communication, Language and Sex.* Rowley, Mass.: Newbury House, 1980.

Bland, David. *A History of Book Illustration.* London: Faber & Faber, 1958.

Bland, David. *The Illustration of Books.* London: Faber & Faber, 1962.

Brenner, Johanna and Maria Ramas. 'Rethinking Women's Oppression'. *New Left Review,* **144** (1984), 33–71.

Brownmiller, Susan. *Against Our Will. Men, Women and Rape.* New York: Simon & Schuster, 1975.

Carter, Angela. *The Sadeian Woman.* London: Virago, 1979.

Chodorow, Nancy. *The Reproduction of Mothering. Psychoanalysis and the Sociology of Gender.* Berkeley: University of California Press, 1978.

Coveney, Peter. *The Image of Childhood.* Harmondsworth: Penguin, 1967.

Darling, Harold and Peter Neumeyer. *Image and Maker.* La Jolla, Cal.: Green Tiger Press, 1984.

De Beauvoir, Simone. *The Second Sex.* New York: Knopf, 1953.

Dinnerstein, Dorothy. *The Mermaid and the Minotaur. Sexual Arrangements and Human Malaise.* New York: Harper & Row, 1976.

Dowling, Colette. *The Cinderella Complex. Women's Hidden Fear of Independence.* New York: Simon & Schuster, 1981.

Dubbert, Joe L. *A Man's Place. Masculinity in Transition.* Englewood Cliffs, New Jersey: Prentice-Hall, 1979.

Ehrenreich, Barbara and Deirdre English. *Witches, Midwives and Nurses: A History of Woman Healers.* Old Westbury, New York: Feminist Press, 1973.

Eisenstein, Hester. *Contemporary Feminist Thought.* Boston: G. K. Hall, 1983.

Eisenstein, Hester and Alice Jardine, eds. *The Future of Difference.* Boston: G. K. Hall, 1980.

Feaver, William. *When We Were Young. Two Centuries of Children's Book Illustration.* New York: Holt, Rinehart & Winston, 1977.

Firestone, Shulamith. *The Dialectic of Sex: The Case for Feminist Revolution.* New York: Morrow, 1972.

Foucault, Michel. *The History of Sexuality.* New York: Pantheon, 1978.

Fox-Genovese, Elizabeth. 'Placing Women's History in History'. *New Left Review,* 133 (May–June, 1982), 5–29.

Friedan, Betty. *The Feminine Mystique.* New York: Dell, 1963.

Fromm, Erich. *The Forgotten Language.* New York: Grove Press, 1957.

Gamarnikow, Eva, David H. J. Morgan, June Purvis, and Daphne Taylorson, eds. *Gender, Class and Work.* London: Heinemann, 1983.

Gamarnikow, Eva, David H. J. Morgan, June Purvis, and Daphne Taylorson, eds. *The Public and the Private.* London: Heinemann, 1983.

Garrett, Clarke. 'Women and Witches: Patterns of Analysis'. *Signs,* 3 (1977), 461–70.

Gersoni-Stavn, Diane. *Sexism and Youth.* New York: Xerox, 1974.

Gilligan, Carol. *In a Different Voice: Psychological Theory and Women's Development.* Cambridge: Harvard University Press, 1982.

Godwin, Jean, Catherine G. Cauthorne and Richard T. Rada. 'Cinderella Syndrome: Children Who Simulate Neglect'. *American Journal of Psychiatry,* 137 (1980), 1223–5.

Göttner-Abendroth, Heide. *Die Göttin und ihr Heros.* Munich: Frauenoffensive, 1980.

Graves, Robert. *The White Goddess: A Historial Grammar of Poetic Myth.* New York: Farrar, Straus & Giroux, 1948.

Griffin, Susan. *Women and Nature: The Roaring Inside Her.* New York: Harper & Row, 1978.

Griffin, Susan. *Rape: The Power of Consciousness.* New York: Harper & Row, 1979.

Griffin, Susan. *Pornography and Silence: Culture's Revenge Against Nature.* New York: Harper & Row, 1981.

Hamilton, Victoria. *Narcissus and Oedipus: The Children of Psychoanalysis.* London: Routledge and Kegan Paul, 1982.

Janeway, Elizabeth. *Man's World, Woman's Place: A Study in Social Mythology.* New York: Dell, 1971.

Keohane, Nannerl O., Michelle Z. Rosaldo, and Barbara C. Gelpi, eds. *Feminist Theory. A Critique of Ideology.* Chicago: University of Chicago Press, 1982.

Lacan, Jacques. *Feminine Sexuality.* Eds. Juliet Mitchell and Jacqueline Rose. New York and London: W. W. Norton, 1983.

Lakoff, Robin. *Language and Woman's Place.* New York: Harper & Row, 1974.

Lewontin, R. C., Steven Rose, and Leon J. Kamin. *Not in Out Genes.* New York: Pantheon, 1984.

Lochhead, Marion. *Their First Ten Years. Victorian Childhood.* London: John Murray, 1956.

McClatchy, J. D., ed. *Anne Sexton: The Artist and Her Critics.* Bloomington: Indiana University Press, 1978.

MacLeod, Anne Scott. *A Moral Tale. Children's Fiction and American Culture 1820–1860.* Hamden, Conn.: Archon Books, 1975.

Miller, Alice. *The Drama of the Gifted Child.* New York: Basic Books, 1981.

Miller, Alice. *Am Anfang war Erziehung.* Frankfurt am Main: Suhrkamp, 1983.

Miller, Jean Baker, ed. *Psychoanalysis and Women.* Harmondsworth: Penguin, 1973.

Miller, Jean Baker. *Toward a New Psychology of Women.* Boston: Beacon, 1976.

Millet, Kate. *Sexual Politics.* Garden City: Doubleday, 1970.

Mitchell, Juliet. *Woman's Estate.* New York: Random House, 1971.

Mitchell, Juliet. *Psychoanalysis and Feminism: Freud, Reich, Laing and Women.* New York: Pantheon, 1974.

Morgan, Robin, ed. *Sisterhood is Powerful: An Anthology of Writings from the Women's Liberation Movement.* New York: Vintage, 1970.

Morgan, Robin. *The Anatomy of Freedom: Feminism, Physics, and Global Politics.* New York: Doubleday, 1982.

Muir, Percy. *Victorian Illustrated Books.* London: Batsford, 1971.

Mykyta, Larysa. 'Lacan, Literature and the Look: Woman in the Eye of Psychoanalysis'. *SubStance,* **39** (1983), 49–57.

Newall, Venetia, ed. *The Witch Figure.* London: Routledge & Kegan Paul, 1973.

Nichols, Bill. *Ideology and the Image.* Bloomington: University of Indiana Press, 1981.

Nodelman, Perry. 'How Picture Books Work'. In *Image and Maker,* eds. Harold Darling and Peter Neumeyer. La Jolla, Cal.: Green Tiger Press, 1984, pp. 1–12.

Philipson, Ilene. 'Heterosexual Antagonisms and the Politics of Mothering'. *Socialist Review,* **12** (1982), 55–77.

Pleck, Elizabeth H. and Joseph H. *The American Man.* Englewood Cliffs, New Jersey: Prentice-Hall, 1980.

Rich, Adrienne. *Of Woman Born: Motherhood as Experience and Institution.* New York: Norton, 1976.

Rivers, Caryl, Rosalind C. Barnett, and Grace K. Baruch. *Beyond Sugar and Spice: How Women Grow, Learn and Thrive.* New York: Putnam, 1979.

Rosaldo, Michelle Z. and Louise Laphere, eds. *Woman, Culture, and Society.*

Stanford: Stanford University Press, 1974.

Rosenberg, Rosalind. *Beyond Separate Spheres: Intellectual Roots of Modern Feminism.* New Haven: Yale University Press, 1982.

Rowbotham, Sheila. *Women, Resistance and Revolution: A History of Women and Revolution in the Modern World.* New York: Random House, 1972.

Rowbotham, Sheila. *Hidden from History: Rediscovering Women in History from the Seventeeth Century to the Present.* New York: Random House, 1973.

Rudman, Masha Kabakow. *Children's Literature. An Issues Approach.* 2nd ed. New York: Longman, 1984.

Shannon, George W. B. *Folk Literature and Children.* Westport, Conn.: Greenwood Press, 1981.

Snitow, Ann, Christine Stansell, and Sharon Thompson, eds. *Powers of Desire. The Politics of Sexuality.* New York: Monthly Review Press, 1983.

Stacey, Judith, Susan Béraud and Joan Daniels, eds. *And Jill Came Tumbling After: Sexism in American Education.* New York: Dell, 1984.

Stacey, Meg and Marion Price. *Women, Power and Politics.* London: Tavistock, 1981.

Stinton, Judith, ed. *Racism and Sexism in Children's Books.* London: Writers and Readers, 1979.

Stone, Merlin. *Where God Was a Woman.* New York: Dial, 1976.

Stone, Merlin. *Ancient Mirrors of Womanhood: Our Goddess and Heroine Heritage.* 2 vols. New York: New Sibylline Books, 1979.

Theweleit, Klaus. *Männer Phantasien.* 2 vols. Frankfurt am Main: Verlag Roter Stern, 1977.

Tolson, Andrew. *The Limits of Masculinity. Male Identity and Women's Liberation.* New York: Harper & Row, 1977.

Verdier, Yvonne. *Façons de dire, façons de faire. La laveuse, la couturière, la cuisinière.* Paris: Gallimard, 1979.

Weigle, Marta. *Spiders and Spinsters: Women and Mythology.* Albuquerque: University of New Mexico Press, 1982.

Willis, Ellen. *Beginning to See the Light: Pieces of a Decade.* New York: Wideview Books, 1981.

2. Fairy Tale and Literary Criticism

Baer, Elizabeth R. 'The Sisterhood of Jane Eyre and Antoinette Cosway'. In *The Voyage In: Fictions of Female Development,* eds. Elizabeth Abel, Marianne Hirsch, and Elizabeth Langland. Hanover: University Press of New England, 1983. pp. 131–48.

Bettelheim, Bruno. *The Uses of Enchantment. The Meaning and Importance of Fairy Tales.* New York: Knopf, 1976.

Bottigheimer, Ruth B. 'Tale Spinners: Submerged Voices in Grimms' Fairy Tales'. *New German Critique,* **27** (1982), 141–50.

Briggs, Katharine. *A Dictionary of Fairies.* London: Allen Lane, 1976.

Canham, Stephen. 'What Manner of Beast? Illustrations of "Beauty and the Beast" '. In *Image and Maker,* eds. Harold Darling and Peter Neumeyer, La Jolla, Cal.: Green Tiger Press, 1984, pp. 13–25.

Chervin, Ronda and Mary Neil. *The Woman's Tale. A Journal of Inner Exploration.* New York: Seabury, 1980.

Coffin, Tristram Potter. *The Female Hero in Folklore and Legend.* New York: Seabury, 1975.

Cooper, Susan. 'Womenfolk and Fairy Tales'. *New York Times Book Review,* 13 (April 1975), 6.

Dan, Ilana. 'The Innocent Persecuted Heroine: An Attempt at a Model for the Surface Level of the Narrative Structure of the Female Fairy Tale'. In *Patterns in Oral Literature.* Eds. Heda Jason and Dimitri Segal. The Hague: Mouton, 1977.

Dégh, Linda. *Folktales and Society.* Bloomington: Indiana University Press, 1969.

Delarue, Paul. 'Les contes merveilleux de Perrault et la tradition populaire'. *Bulletin folklorique de l'Ile-de-France* (1951), 221–8, 251–60, 283–91; (1953), 511–71.

Dixon, Bob. *Catching Them Young: Vol. 1, Sex, Race and Class in Children's Fiction; Vol. 2, Political Ideas in Children's Fiction.* London: Pluto, 1977.

Downing, Christine. *The Goddess: Mythological Images of the Feminine.* New York: Continuum, 1982.

Duffy, Maureen. *The Erotic World of Faery.* London: Hodder & Stoughton, 1972.

Dundes, Alan, ed. *Cinderella. A Casebook.* New York: Wildman Press, 1983.

Dworkin, Andrea. *Woman Hating.* New York: Dutton, 1974.

Farrer, Claire R., ed. *Women and Folklore.* Austin: University of Texas Press, 1975.

Franz, Marie Luise von. *Problems of the Feminine in Fairytales.* New York: Spring, 1972.

Gilbert, Sandra M. and Susan Gubar. *The Mad Woman in the Attic. The Women Writer and the Nineteenth-Century Imagination.* New Haven: Yale University Press, 1979.

Harding, M. Esther. *Woman's Mysteries, Ancient and Modern: A Psychological Interpretation of the Feminine Principle as Portrayed in Myth, Story, and Dreams.* New York: Bantam, 1971.

Kolbenschlag, Madonna. *Kiss Sleeping Beauty Good-Bye: Breaking the Spell of Feminine Myths and Models.* New York: Doubleday, 1979.

Lewis, Susan. 'Exploding the Fairy Princess Myth'. *Scholastic Teacher,* 3 (November 1971), 6–12.

Lieberman, Marcia. ' "Some Day My Prince Will Come": Female Acculturation Through the Fairy Tale'. *College English,* 34 (1972), 383–95.

Lieberman, Marcia. 'The Feminist in Fairy Tales — Two Books from the Jung Institute, Zurich'. *Children's Literature,* 2 (1973), 217–18.

Lurie, Alison. 'Fairy Tale Liberation'. *New York Review of Books,* 11 (December 17, 1970), 42–4.

Lurie, Alison. 'Witches and Fairies: Fitzgerald to Updike'. *New York Review of Books* (December 2, 1971), 6.

Lurie, Alison. 'Fairy Tales for a Liberated Age'. *Horizon* (July 1977), 80−5.

Lüthi, Max. *Once Upon a Time. On the Nature of Fairy Tales*. New York: Ungar, 1970.

Lüthi, Max. *The European Folktale: Form and Nature*. Philadelphia: Institute for the Study of Human Issues, 1982.

Lyons, Heather. 'Some Second Thoughts on Sexism in Fairy Tales'. In *Literature and Learning*. Eds. Elizabeth Grugeon and Peter Walden. London: Open University Press, 1978, pp. 42−58.

McCabe, Jane. ' "A Woman Who Writes": A Feminist Approach to the Early Poetry of Anne Sexton'. In *Anne Sexton: The Artist and Her Critics*. Bloomington: Indiana University Press, 1978. pp. 216−34.

MacDonald, Ruth. 'The Tale Retold: Feminist Fairy Tales'. *Children's Literature Association Quarterly*, 7 (1982), 18−20.

Miller, David L. 'Red Riding Hood and Grand Mother Rhea: Images in a Psychology of Inflation'. In *Facing the Gods*. Ed. James Hilman. Irving, Texas: Spring, 1980, pp. 87−99.

Moore, Robert. 'From Rags to Witches: Stereotypes, Distortions and Antihumanism in Fairy Tales'. *Interracial Books for Children*, 6 (1975), 1−3.

Rose, Ellen Cronan. 'Through the Looking Glass: When Women Tell Fairy Tales'. In *The Voyage In: Fiction of Female Development*. Eds. Elizabeth Abel, Marianne Hirsch, and Elizabeth Langland. Hanover: University Press of New England, 1983, pp. 209−27.

Rose, Karen E. ' "Fairy-born and Human-bred": Jane Eyre's Education in Romance'. In *The Voyage In: Fictions of Female Development*, eds. Elizabeth Abel, Marianne Hirsch, and Elizabeth Langland. Hanover: University Press of New England, 1983, pp. 69−89.

Rowe, Karen E. 'Feminism and Fairy Tales'. *Women's Studies*, 6 (1979), 237−57.

Scherf, Walter. 'Family Conflicts and Emancipation in Fairy Tales'. *Children's Literature*, 3 (1974), 77−93.

Schwartz, Emanuel K. 'A Psychoanalytic Study of the Fairy Tale'. *American Journal of Psychotherapy*, 10 (1956), 740−62.

Segel, Elizabeth. 'Feminists and Fairy Tales'. *School Library Journal* (January 1983), 30−1.

Siepe, Hans T. 'Rotkäppchen einmal anders. Ein Märchen für den Französichunterricht'. *Der fremdsprachliche Unterricht*, 65 (1983), 1−9.

Stone, Kay. 'Things Walt Disney Never Told Us'. In *Women and Folklore*. Ed. Claire R. Farrer. Austin: University of Texas Press, 1975, pp. 42−50.

Sullivan, Paula. 'Fairy Tale Elements in *Jane Eyre*'. *Journal of Popular Culture*, 12 (1978), 61−74.

Thelander, Dorothy R. 'Mother Goose and Her Goslings: The France of Louis XIV as seen through the Fairy Tale'. *The Journal of Modern History*, 54 (1982), 467−96.

Travers, P. L. *About the Sleeping Beauty*. London: Collins, 1977.

Verdier, Yvonne. 'Grands-mères, si vous saviez: le Petit Chaperon Rouge dans la tradition orale'. *Cahiers de littérature orale,* **4** (1978), 17 – 55.

Yolen, Jane. 'America's Cinderella'. *Children's Literature in Education,* **8** (1977), 21 – 9.

Yolen, Jane. *Touch Magic. Fantasy, Faerie and Folklore in the Literature of Childhood.* New York: Philomel, 1981.

Zipes, Jack. *Breaking the Magic Spell: Radical Theories of Folk and Fairy Tales.* Austin: University of Texas Press, 1979 and London: Heinemann, 1979.

Zipes, Jack. *The Trials and Tribulations of Little Red Riding Hood: Versions of the Tale in Sociocultural Context.* South Hadley: Bergin & Garvey, 1983 and London: Heinemann, 1983.

Zipes, Jack. *Fairy Tales and the Art of Subversion: The Classical Genre for Children and the Process of Civilization.* New York: Wildman, 1983 and London: Heinemann, 1983.

3. Feminist Fairy Tales and Fantasy Literature

Asbjornsen, P. C. *The Squire's Bride.* New York: Atheneum, 1975.

Atwood, Margret. *Bluebeard's Egg.* Toronto: McClelland & Stewart, 1983.

Bishop, Michael and Ian Watson, eds. *Changes. Stories of Metamorphosis.* New York: Ace, 1983.

Broumas, Olga. *Beginning with O.* New Haven: Yale University Press, 1977.

Budapest, Zscizsanna. *Selene, The Most Famous Bull-leaper On Earth.* Baltimore: Diana Press, 1976.

Carter, Angela. *The Donkey Prince.* New York: Simon & Schuster, 1970.

Carter, Angela. *The Bloody Chamber.* London: Gollancz, 1979.

Chasin, Helen. *Coming Close and Other Poems.* New Haven: Yale University Press, 1968.

Collins, Meghan B. 'The Green Woman'. In *Fine Lines. The Best of Ms. Fiction.* Ed. Ruth Sullivan. New York: Scribner, 1982, pp. 121 – 39.

Coville, Bruce. *Sarah and the Dragon.* New York: Lippincott, 1984.

Dahl, Roald. *Revolting Rhymes.* London: Jonathan Cape, 1982.

De Paola, Tomie. *Helga's Dowry.* New York: Harcourt Brace Jovanovich, 1977.

De Paola, Tomie. *The Legend of Bluebonnet.* New York: G. P. Putman, 1983.

Desy, Jeane. 'The Princess Who Stood on Her Own Two Feet'. In *Stories for Free Children.* Ed. Letty Progrebin. New York: McGraw-Hill, 1982, pp. 43 – 6.

Foreman, Michael. *All the King's Horses.* Scarsdale, New York: Bradbury Press, 1976.

Forman, Joan. *The Princess in the Tower.* London: Faber & Faber, 1973.

Gardner, John. *Gudgekin the Thistle Girl and Other Tales.* New York: Knopf, 1976.

Gardner, John. *The King of the Hummingbirds and Other Tales*. New York: Knopf, 1974.

Gardner, John. *Dragon, Dragon and Other Tales*. New York: Knopf, 1973.

Gardner, John. *In the Suicide Mountains*. New York: Knopf, 1977.

Gardner, Richard A. Dr. *Gardner's Fairy Tales for Today's Children*. Englewood Cliffs, New Jersey: Prentice-Hall, 1974.

Gauch, Patricia. *Once Upon a Dinkelsbuhl*. New York: Putman, 1977.

Hague, Kathleen and Micheal. *The Man Who Kept House*. New York: Harcourt Brace Jovanovich, 1981.

Harris, Christie. *The Mouse Woman and the Vanished Princesses*. New York: Atheneum, 1976.

Harris, Christie. *Mouse Woman and the Mischief Makers*. New York: Atheneum, 1977.

Hart, Carole, Letty Cottin Pogrebin, Mary Rodgers and Marlo Thomas, eds. *Free To Be . . . You and Me*. New York: McGraw-Hill, 1974.

Hay, Sara Henderson. *Story Hour*. Fayetteville: University of Arkansas Press, 1982.

Hearne, Vicki. 'What It Is About the Frog'. *In the Absence of Horses*. Princeton, Princeton University Press, 1983.

Herman, Harriet. *The Forest Princess*. Berkeley: Over the Rainbow Press, 1974.

Herman, Harriet. *The Return of the Forest Princess*. Berkeley: Over the Rainbow Press, 1975.

Howe, Florence and Ellen Bass, eds. *No More Masks! An Anthology of Poems by Women*. Garden City: Doubleday, 1973.

Hunter, Mollie. *A Furl of Fairy Wind*. New York: Harper & Row, 1977.

Larrabeiti, Michael de. 'Malagan and the Lady of Rascas'. In *Elsewhere 3,* eds. Terri Windling and Mark Arnold. New York: Berkley, 1984, pp. 189–204.

Lee, Tanith. *Princess Hynchatti and Some Other Surprises*. London: Macmillan, 1972.

Lee, Tanith. *Red as Blood, Or Tales from the Sisters Grimmer*. New York: Daw Books, 1983.

Lobel, Anita. *The Straw Maid*. New York: Greenwillow Books, 1983.

Lobel, Arnold. *A Treeful of Pigs*. New York: Greenwillow Books, 1979.

Lurie, Alison, ed. *Clever Gretchen and Other Forgotten Folktales*. New York: Crowell, 1980.

Maguire, Gregory. *The Dream Stealer*. New York: Harper & Row, 1983.

Maitland, Sara. *Telling Tales*. London: Journeyman, 1983.

Mayer, Mercer. *Herbert the Timid Dragon*. New York: Golden Press, 1980.

McGoven, Ann. *Half a Kingdom*. New York: Frederick Warne, 1977.

McKinley, Robin. *Beauty.* New York: Harper & Row, 1978.

McKinley, Robin. *The Door in the Hedge.* New York: Ace, 1981.

Merseyside Fairy Storey Collective. *Red Riding Hood*. Liverpool: Fairy Story Collective, 1972.

Merseyside Fairy Story Collective. *The Prince and the Swinehead*. Liverpool:

Fairy Story Collective, 1972.

Merseyside Fairy Story Collective. *Snow White*. In *Spare Rib*, 51 (1976), 44-6.

Miles, Betty. *Atalanta*. In *Free To Be . . . You and Me,* eds. Carole Hart et al. New York: McGraw-Hill, 1974, pp. 128-35.

Minard, Rosemary, ed. *Womenfold and Fairy Tales*. Boston: Houghton Mifflin, 1975.

Openheim, Shulamith. *The Selchie's Seed*. New York: Bradbury Press, 1975.

Phelps, Ethel Johnston, ed. *Tatterhood and Other Tales*. Old Westbury, New York: Feminist Press, 1978.

Phelps, Ethel Johnston, ed. *The Maid of the North. Feminist Folk Tales from around the world*. New York: Holt, Rinehart & Winston, 1981.

Pogrebin, Letty Cottin, ed. *Stories for Free Children*. New York: McGraw-Hill, 1982.

Pomerantz, Charlotte. *The Downtown Fairy Godmother*. Reading, Mass.: Addison-Wesley, 1982.

Pomerantz, Charlotte. 'The Princess and the Admiral'. In *Stories for Free Children*. Ed. Letty Cotton Pogrebin. New York: McGraw-Hill, 1982, pp. 17-20.

Rechter, Judith. 'Fay Wray to the King'. In *No More Masks! An Anthology of Poems by Women*. eds. Florence Howe and Ellen Bass. Garden City: Doubleday, 1973, pp. 257-8.

Russ, Joanna. *Kittatinny*. New York: Daughters, 1978.

Russ, Joanna. *The Adventures of Alyx*. New York: Pocket Books, 1983.

Sexton, Anne. *Transformations*. Boston: Houghton Mifflin, 1971.

Shwartz, Susan, ed. *Hecate's Cauldron*. New York: Daw Books, 1982.

Spivack, Kathleen. *Flying Inland*. Garden City: Doubleday, 1974.

Stamm, Claus. 'Three Strong Women'. In *Stories for Free Children,* Ed. Letty Cotton Pogrebin. New York: McGraw-Hill, 1982, pp. 49–52.

Stor, Catherine. *Clever Polly and the Stupid Wolf*. London: Faber & Faber, 1955, 1979.[2]

Sullivan, Ruth, ed. *Fine Lines. The Best of Ms. Fiction*. New York: Scribner, 1982.

Tompert, Ann. *The Clever Princess*. Chapel Hill, North Carolina; Lollipop Power, 1977.

Turin, Adela, Francesca Cantarelli, and Wella Bosnia. *The Five Wives of Silverbeard*. London: Writers & Readers Publishing Cooperative, 1977.

Turin, Adela and Sylvie Selig. *Of Cannons and Caterpillars*. London: Writers & Readers Publishing Cooperative, 1977.

Van Woerkom, Dorothy. *The Queen Who Couldn't Bake Gingerbread*. New York: Knopf, 1975.

Viorst, Judith. *If I Were in Charge of the World*. New York: Atheneum, 1982.

Werth, Kurt and Mabel Watts. *Molly and the Giant*. New York: Parents Magazine Press, 1973.

Williams, Jay. *The Practical Princess and other Liberating Fairy Tales*. New York: Parents Magazine Press and London: Chatto & Windus, 1979.

Yolen, Jane. *The Girl Who Cried Flowers and Other Tales.* New York: Crowell, 1974.

Yolen, Jane. *The Moon Ribbon and Other Tales.* New York: Crowell, 1976.

Yolen, Jane. *The Hundredth Dove and Other Tales.* New York: Crowell, 1977.

Yolen, Jane. *Dream Weaver.* New York: Collins, 1979.

Yolen, Jane. *Sleeping Ugly.* New York: Coward, McCann & Georghegan, 1981.

Yolen, Jane. *Tales of Wonder.* New York: Schocken, 1983.

Yolen, Jane. *Dragonfield and Other Stories.* New York: Ace, 1985.

Zones, Jane S., ed. *Taking the Fruit. Modern Women's Tales of the Bible.* San Diego: Women's Institute for Continuing Jewish Education, 1981.